中方工作人员 / Chinese Staff List

展览主办 Sponsored by	湖北省博物馆 / Hubei Provincial Museum 馆长 方勤 / Fang Qin, Director 深圳博物馆 / Shenzhen Museum 馆长 叶杨 / Ye Yang, Director 成都金沙遗址博物馆 / Chengdu Jinsha Site Museum 馆长 王毅 / Wang Yi, Director
项目管理 Project Manager	曾攀 / Zeng Pan 程陶 / Cheng Tao
展览协调 Coordinators	湖北省博物馆 / Hubei Provincial Museum 余文扬　张翔　黄建　李蔚　魏冕　姚嫄　翟扶文　余珮瑶　汤文韵　张明　张小羽　杨辰 Yu Wenyang, Zhang Xiang, Huang Jian, Li Wei, Wei Mian, Yao Yuan, Zhai Fuwen, Yu Peiyao, Tang Wenyun, Zhang Ming, Zhang Xiaoyu and Yang Chen 深圳博物馆 / Shenzhen Museum 李维学　张冬煜　周加胜　张小兰　李飞　唐方圆 Li Weixue, Zhang Dongyu, Zhou Jiasheng, Zhang Xiaolan, Li Fei and Tang Fangyuan 成都金沙遗址博物馆 / Chengdu Jinsha Site Museum 黄玉洁　郑漫丽　蔡经纬　刘珂　余卓然　杨建华　田湘萍　陈丽琴　明文秀　吴超明　任华利 Huang Yujie, Zheng Manli, Cai Jingwei, Liu Ke, Yu Zhuoran, Yang Jianhua, Tian Xiangping, Chen Liqin, Ming Wenxiu, Wu Chaoming and Ren Huali
形式设计 Design	湖北省博物馆 / Hubei Provincial Museum 黄翀宇 / Huang Chongyu　伍莹 / Wu Ying 深圳博物馆 / Shenzhen Museum 周艺璇 / Zhou Yixuan 成都金沙遗址博物馆 / Chengdu Jinsha Site Museum 王越 / Wang Yue
图录编辑 Catalogue Editor	湖北省博物馆 Hubei Provincial Museum
策划 Producer	方勤　叶杨　王毅 Fang Qin, Ye Yang and Wang Yi
监制 Supervisor	万全文　郭学雷　朱章义　王方 Wan Quanwen, Guo Xuelei, Zhu Zhangyi and Wang Fang
执行编辑 Project Editor	曾攀 Zeng Pan

美方工作人员 / LACMA Staff List

Megan E. O'Neil / Associate Curator, Art of the Ancient Americas
Aurora Van Zoelen Cortes / Curatorial Administrator
Zoe Kahr / Deputy Director for Curatorial and Planning
Sabrina Lovett / Senior Exhibition Coordinator
Azzurra Di Marcello / Senior Assistant Registrar, Exhibitions
Tsao Wan Kong / Chinese and Korean Art Department
Diana Magaloni-Kerpel / Deputy Director, Program Director
Virginia Fields / Curator of the Art of the Ancient Americas
Anothony J. Meyer / Research Assistant
Amy Crum / Curatorial Assistant
Julia Burtenshaw / Mellon Postdoctoral Curatorial Fellow
Michelle Rich / Mellon Postdoctoral Curatorial Fellow
Lilia Taboada / Mellon Undergraduate Curatorial Fellow
Lauren Churchwell / Mellon Undergraduate Curatorial Fellow
John Hirx / Senior Objects Conservator
Yosi Pozeilov / Senior Conservation Photographer
Abigail Duckor / Assistant Conservator
Ellie Ohara Anderson / Mellon Fellow, Objects Conservation
David Armendariz / Mount Maker
Carinne Klaristenfeld / Project Senior Conservator
Peter Brenner / Supervising Photographer
Jonathan Urban / Photographer
Steve Oliver / Senior Photographer
Laura Cherry / Imaging Coordinator
Alyssa Morasco / Head of Collections Management, Registration & Collections
Suzan Sengoz / Senior Associate Registrar, Special Projects
Joe Lopez / Senior Collections Management Technician
Emory Marshall / Senior Collections Management Technician
Kristin Strid / Associate Collections Manager
Ben Balken / Collections Management Technician
Lisa Mark / Publisher
Piper Severance / Senior Rights & Reproduction Associate
Margery L. Schwartz / Assisting Editor

自然的力量
洛杉矶郡艺术博物馆藏古代玛雅艺术品

FORCES OF NATURE
Ancient Maya Arts from the Los Angeles County Museum of Art

洛杉矶郡艺术博物馆（LACMA） 湖北省博物馆 编

（美）梅根·奥尼尔（Megan E. O'Neil） 主编

目 录
CONTENT

7	**致 辞** Foreword
17	**专 文** Essays
18	自然的力量：古代玛雅世界的艺术与神灵 Forces of Nature: Art and Divinity in the Ancient Maya World
51	**第一部分　玛雅的宇宙** Part I The Maya Cosmos
73	**第二部分　天空、大地、水中和地下的超自然实体** Part II Supernatural Entities of Sky, Earth, Water, and Underworld
145	**第三部分　玛雅艺术和宗教中的动物** Part III Animals in Maya Art and Religion
179	**第四部分　国王和王后的神圣仪式** Part IV Divine Rites of Kings and Queens
255	**展品目录** Exhibits List
258	**参考文献** References
261	**致 谢** Acknowledgements
263	**后 记** Postscript

奇琴伊察天文台

致辞
FOREWORD

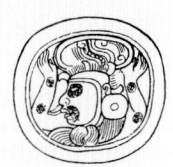

　　玛雅文明是美洲一支重要的古代文明，主要分布在墨西哥南部、危地马拉、伯利兹以及洪都拉斯和萨尔瓦多西部地区。它是哥伦布抵达之前美洲大陆人类成就的杰出代表，在科学（天文历法、工程学、数学）、农业（玉米、可可、烟草的种植）、文化（象形文字、神话）、艺术（雕塑、玉器、陶器）等许多方面做出了巨大贡献。

　　本次展览集中展示了玛雅文明对自然力量的想象和认识。玛雅人对于宇宙有着独特的认识和划分，日、月、雨等自然力量都被人格化为各种神灵，各种奇异的动物也根据习性拥有了神性，具有转化的能力。玛雅统治者通过将自己的名字和神联系在一起，利用舞蹈、球赛、音乐及各种礼仪彰显自己的神力，巩固自己的统治。展览通过200余件精美的艺术品，为中国观众讲述出神秘的玛雅世界观和神话。

　　展览中所有的展品均来自美国洛杉矶郡艺术博物馆，大部分展品是首次展出。本馆与洛杉矶郡艺术博物馆在2014年至2015年的"印度的世界"巡展中已经有过良好的合作。迈克尔·高文馆长、策展人梅根·奥尼尔博士等专家为展览付出了巨大的努力。深圳博物馆、成都金沙遗址博物馆同仁为巡展的成功举办做了大量艰苦细致的工作。在此，我谨代表湖北省博物馆、湖北省文物考古研究所向所有为展览付出辛勤劳动的各界人士表示衷心的感谢！

　　祝展览取得圆满成功！

湖北省博物馆馆长
湖北省文物考古研究所所长

The Maya civilization was an ancient American civilization that developed in an area encompassing southern Mexico, all of Guatemala and Belize, and the western portions of Honduras and El Salvador. It was noted for its brilliant achievements, of the pre-Columbian Americas, in science (astronomy, calendar, engineering and mathematics), agriculture (cultivation of maize, cocoa and tobacco), culture (hieroglyphic script, mythology) and art (sculpture, jadeware and ceramics).

The exhibition represents the extraordinary imagination and understanding of Nature in the Maya civilization. The Maya peoples had a distinguished understanding and division of the universe. Forces of Nature, such as the sun, the moon and rain, were personified as deities. Animals were given divinity, thanks to their features, thus with the ability of transformation. The Maya rulers consolidated their rule, by correlating their names with deities and amplifying their power of divinity through dances, ball games, music and various rituals. The exhibition represents to Chinese visitors, with over 200 exquisite art pieces, the mysterious world view and mythology of the Maya civilization.

All the art pieces on display come from the collection of Los Angeles County Museum of Art (LACMA), and most are on exhibition for the first time. Hubei Provincial Museum and the LACMA had a good cooperation in the 2014-2015 itinerant exhibition "The World of India." LACMA Curator Michael Govan and Associate Curator Dr. Megan O'Neil have worked hard on this exhibition. I would like, on behalf of Hubei Provincial Museum and the Institute of Cultural Relics and Archaeology of Hubei Province, to extend our sincere gratitude to those who have been working hard on this exhibition.

May the exhibition a great success!

Fang Qin
Curator, Hubei Provincial Museum
Director, Institute of Cultural Relics and Archaeology of Hubei Province

　　自19世纪中叶探险家们发现了埋没于墨西哥南部和危地马拉热带雨林中心的宏伟遗迹以来，充满神秘色彩的玛雅文明就不断吸引着世界的目光。雄伟的金字塔、华丽的宫殿、奇诡的雕塑、繁复的象形文字、精密的历法……无不彰显着玛雅文明在建筑、艺术、文字、天文、历法、数学等领域所达到的高度，令世界惊叹。

　　作为中美洲的代表性文明，玛雅文明曾活跃于今墨西哥南部、危地马拉、伯利兹、洪都拉斯西部及萨尔瓦多等地。在前古典中期（约公元前1000年至公元200年），玛雅文明逐渐崛起，这一时期农业迅速发展，人口增多，阶级分化逐渐明显，大型的仪式中心及宗教建筑开始出现。古典期（约公元250年至公元900年）是玛雅文明的鼎盛时期，大型礼仪、政治活动中心及大量城市不断涌现，人口激增，铭文普及，贸易繁荣，文化、政治和艺术等领域的发展都达到巅峰。在后古典期（约公元900年至1524年），玛雅文明从繁盛逐渐走向衰落。虽然玛雅文明已失落在历史的长河中，但这一灿烂文明的创造者——玛雅人却一直繁衍生息于这片土地上。至今，仍有数百万玛雅人在传承玛雅文明古老的风俗，延续其悠久的历史。

　　玛雅文明与古蜀文明虽相隔万里，但二者在文化面貌上却有着许多的相似性。他们都敬畏自然，相信万物有灵，从而塑造出众多充满灵性的形象；他们都重视祭祀，不仅修建祭祀建筑，还以各类珍贵的宝物祭天事神；他们还用自己独特的想象力，创造出许多诡谲神秘的造型艺术……这些共同的精神认知，为我们探讨两地文化的共性留下了广阔的空间。

　　为进一步促进两地文化的交流与探讨，成都金沙遗址博物馆与湖北省博物馆、深圳博物馆携手合作，共同举办"自然的力量：洛杉矶郡艺术博物馆藏古代玛雅艺术品展"，展出美国洛杉矶郡艺术博物馆馆藏的216件（套）玛雅艺术精品，包括各类绘制精美的彩陶、造型生动的雕塑、精雕细琢的装饰品等，带领观众去感受玛雅人独特的文化审美、艺术观念与精神世界，揭示他们对世界和宇宙的理解。此次展览也是这批玛雅艺术珍品在美国以外地区的首次亮相，具有非凡的意义。

　　在此，我谨代表成都金沙遗址博物馆，感谢洛杉矶郡艺术博物馆为本次展览提供的精美展品，感谢湖北省博物馆、深圳博物馆的通力合作，感谢为本次展览的成功举办和图录的编撰付出艰辛努力的朋友与同事！预祝展览圆满成功！

成都金沙遗址博物馆馆长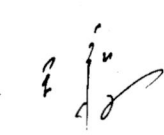

ANCIENT MAYA ARTS FROM THE LOS ANGELES COUNTY MUSEUM OF ART

The mysterious Maya civilization has been a magnet to the world since the mid-19th century, when the explorers discovered the magnificent Maya sites in southern Mexico and in the jungles of Guatemala. The majestic pyramids, the grand palaces, the bizarre sculptures, the complicated hieroglyphs, the exact calendar ... all this suggests the astounding heights that the Maya civilization reached in respect of architecture, art, script, astrology, calendar, mathematics, etc.

As a prominent civilization in Central America, the Maya civilization once thrived in multiple areas including southern Mexico, Guatemala, Belize, western Honduras, and El Salvador. The Middle Preclassic period (c. 1000 BC to 200 AD) saw the gradual rise of the Maya civilization: Agriculture was developing rapidly; population was growing; social stratification gradually became noticeable; massive ritual centers and religious buildings began emerging. In the Classic Period (c. 250 AD to 900 AD), the heyday of the Maya civilization, there emerged large ritual and political centers and a large number of cities, alongside a surging population, the spread of Mayan glyphs, flourishing trade, and the fields of culture, politics, art, etc. all reaching their peaks. The Late Classic Period (c. 900 AD to 1524 AD) saw the gradual decline of the Maya civilization. Though the Maya civilization had disappeared in the river of history, the Maya people, who created this resplendent civilization, have at all times lived on this land. Today, there are still millions of Maya people sticking to the ancient customs from the Maya civilization, carrying its history on.

Though thousands of miles apart, the Maya civilization and the Shu civilization have a lot of similarities in the cultural sense. They both stood in awe of nature, believed in the spirituality of everything, and so created numerous images of spirituality; they both placed high importance on sacrifice, not only building sacrificial monuments but also sacrificing precious treasures of all sorts to the heaven and gods; they created, with their respective unique imagination, countless mysterious sculptures and monuments.... These shared perceptions of spirituality provide us with a broad space for discussion about things the two cultures have in common.

To further promote exchanges and discussion about the two cultures, the Jinsha Site Museum of Chengdu has worked with the Hubei Provincial Museum and the Shenzhen Museum to present the special exhibition, "The Power of Nature: Ancient Maya Art from Los Angeles County Museum of Art". The exhibition, which consists of 216 pieces (sets) of Maya art objects from the Los Angeles County Museum of Art (LACMA) - including beautiful painted pottery, lifelike sculptures and exquisitely carved ornaments, is designed to offer the audience some insights into the unique cultural and artistic notions and the spiritual world of the Maya people, as well as their perceptions of the world and the universe. This exhibition is also the premiere outside the United States of those treasures of Maya art and, therefore, of exceptional importance.

On behalf of the Jinsha Site Museum, I'd like to extend thanks to the LACMA for its providing those beautiful objects, to the Hubei Provincial Museum and the Shenzhen Museum for their concerted efforts made in the collaboration, and to the friends and colleagues for their hard work in the run-up to this event. I wish this exhibition a complete success.

Wang Yi
Director of Chengdu Jinsha Site Museum

自然的力量
FORCES OF NATURE

玛雅文明是世界上唯一一个发源于热带雨林的文明，在巅峰时刻突然万籁俱寂，留下高耸入云的金字塔、广阔无比的球场、令人迷惑不解的文字、记录世界末日的历法……

华夏文明和玛雅文明都是世界上的优秀文明代表，一个是持续时间最长的文明，一个是突然消逝的文明。两者结局不同，但却有着很多相似的地方。两者的文字或许都是意音文字，1955年墨西哥中南部的奥尔梅克文化遗址出土的玉圭，刻有类似甲骨文的符号；都有自然崇拜现象，把巨大力量的自然现象或自然力崇拜为神，如风神、蛇等。古代玛雅人的自然崇拜现象反映出他们的精神世界。

"自然的力量"展览是深圳博物馆首个反映玛雅文明的特展，也是我馆第二次和美国洛杉矶郡艺术博物馆合作引进的重量级展览。精选200余件美洲艺术文物，包括奥尔梅克、萨巴特克和阿兹特克文明的艺术品，集中展现了古代玛雅人对宇宙的理解以及他们与大自然的和谐相处之道。这场艺术盛宴不仅会促进中美两国文化的交流和博物馆际间合作，也将增加中国人民和中美洲地区人民的友谊。

预祝展览取得圆满成功！

深圳博物馆馆长

The Maya civilization is the world's sole civilization that ever originated in tropical forests, which, while at its zenith, perished abruptly, leaving behind the towering pyramids, the big ballcourts, mysterious Maya scripts, and a calendar that foretold the end of the world....

Both the Chinese and the Maya civilizations are the epitome of human civilization, one that has lasted longest, and the other that vanished abruptly. Nevertheless, there are many similarities between them. For instance, they both have a writing system that probably consists of logograms; the jade slabs discovered 1955 at an Olmec site in southern central Mexico were engraved with symbols similar to oracle bone script. In both civilizations there existed practices of nature worship, where awe-inspiring natural phenomena or natural forces were worshiped as gods, e.g. the gods of wind, mountains, thunder, serpent, etc. The ancient Maya people's nature worship was reflective of their inner world.

The exhibition, "The Power of Nature", is the Shenzhen Museum's first exhibition on the Maya civilization, a heavyweight exhibition introduced through its second collaboration with the Los Angeles County Museum of Art, the United States. More than 200 hand-picked objects of artistic and cultural interest, including artworks from the Olmec, Zapotec and Aztec civilizations, are a showcase of how the ancient Maya people perceived the universe and how they lived in harmony with nature. This feast of art will not only boost cultural ties between China and the United States and collaboration between museums in both countries, but also enhance the friendship the Chinese and Central American peoples.

I am confident that this exhibition will be a complete success.

Ye Yang
Director of Shenzhen Museum

自然的力量
FORCES OF NATURE

公元后第一个千年，古老的玛雅文明在墨西哥南部和中美洲兴盛繁衍，并留下了非凡的艺术、建筑、文字遗产。洛杉矶郡艺术博物馆有幸收藏了玛雅艺术及古代美洲其他文化的经典艺术品，种类繁多。我们非常荣幸能与当地社区、观众以及来自其他大陆的博物馆观众分享这些藏品。

通过展示玛雅人重要的艺术和文化遗产，"自然的力量：洛杉矶郡博物馆藏古代玛雅艺术品展"旨在增加人们对历史和其他文化的尊重，促进跨文化理解。"自然的力量"将探讨玛雅艺术家如何描绘被视为超自然实体的自然力量，以及政治领袖如何将其融入艺术、仪式和表演，利用它来获得和展示政治权力。此次展览将会展示古代玛雅人对宇宙的理解以及如何建立与充满能量和超自然力量的自然世界的关系。人类迈入21世纪之后遇到了污染和气候变化等诸多挑战，研究过去和其他文化与环境的关系能使我们懂得人类与自然世界的相互依存，而这已成为人类历史上许多文化的共识。

本馆古代美洲艺术部副主任梅根·奥尼尔亲自策划并领导这次重要的国际性展览，编辑相关出版物，洛杉矶郡艺术博物馆的许多员工积极准备参展艺术品，出版带有精美图版的图录，对此我们表示感谢。我们还要感谢湖北省博物馆、深圳博物馆、成都金沙遗址博物馆的同事，他们为"自然的力量"展览来到中国发挥了重要作用。这已是洛杉矶郡艺术博物馆与中国博物馆的第二次合作，第一次是"印度的世界：美国洛杉矶郡艺术博物馆藏印度文物精品"（2014-2015年）。这些展览有助于在博物馆和国家间搭建起沟通的桥梁，充分利用我们对全球文化的共同兴趣帮助不同民族建立真正的联系。

迈克尔·高文
首席执行官兼沃利丝·安娜伯格基金会行政总裁
洛杉矶郡艺术博物馆

The ancient Maya civilization, which flourished in southern Mexico and Central America in the first millennium CE, left a legacy of extraordinary art, architecture, writing, and calligraphy. LACMA is privileged to hold extensive and exemplary collections of the art of the Maya and of several other cultures of the ancient Americas. We are honored to share these collections with our local communities and visitors, as well as with museum guests on other continents.

By showcasing the significant artistic and cultural legacies of the Maya people, Forces of Nature: Ancient Maya Arts from the Los Angeles County Museum of Art aims to both increase respect for the past and for other cultures and promote cross-cultural understanding. Forces of Nature investigates how Maya artists portrayed natural forces that were perceived as supernatural entities, and how political leaders engaged with these forces in art, ritual, performance, and the acquisition and display of political power. The exhibition thus addresses how the ancient Maya understood their cosmos and shaped relationships with a natural world infused with energy and supernatural power. In the twenty-first century, as we face challenges relating to pollution and climate change, studying the past and other cultures' relationships with the environment reminds us of the interdependence of humans and the natural world, as many cultures over the course of human history have acknowledged.

Thank you to curator Megan E. O'Neil, who conceived and led this remarkable international exhibition and publication, and to the many LACMA employees who prepared the artworks for display and for the exquisitely illustrated catalogue. We are grateful to our colleagues at the Hubei Provincial Museum, Shenzhen Museum and Jinsha Site Museum for taking the lead on Forces of Nature's tour to China. This is LACMA's second collaboration with Chinese museums, the first being India's Universe: Masterworks of the Los Angeles County Museum of Art (2014–15). These exhibitions help us build bridges between museums and countries, capitalizing on our shared interests in global cultures to make genuine connections among diverse peoples.

CEO and Wallis Annenberg Director
Los Angeles County Museum of Art

自然的力量
FORCES OF NATURE

致读者：

洛杉矶郡艺术博物馆所藏"古代美洲艺术"系列艺术品，是由私人历经多年收集而来（而不是考古发掘而来），后为洛杉矶郡艺术博物馆收藏。因此，源出地的判别是在认真研究形制、风格、图像和铭文的基础上作出的。

图片来源：洛杉矶郡艺术博物馆（除非另有说明）。

梅根·奥尼尔、安东尼·迈耶和米歇尔·里奇

Note to Reader:

Pieces in the collection of the Art of the Ancient Americas at LACMA were collected over the years by private parties (rather than excavated by archaeologists) prior to their acquisition by LACMA. Accordingly, identification of locations of origin is based on careful studies of form, style, iconography, and epigraphy.

All photos: PHOTO © Museum Associates/LACMA (unless otherwise noted).

Megan E. O'Neil,
with contributions by Anthony J. Meyer and Michelle E. Rich

专文
ESSAYS

自然的力量：古代玛雅世界的艺术与神灵

梅根·奥尼尔

一 古玛雅及其近邻的自然之力

1. 引论

"自然的力量：洛杉矶郡艺术博物馆馆藏古代玛雅艺术品"展探索了古代玛雅艺术中丰富的超自然世界。展览展出了超过两百件来自洛杉矶郡艺术博物馆的古代美洲艺术藏品，探讨了玛雅艺术家是如何在艺术、仪式和表演中描绘超自然世界，而统治者和王室又是如何将超自然世界与权力的追求与展示相结合。展览侧重小巧的艺术品，尤其是彩陶容器、小型雕像和绿玉珠宝，但也展出了馆藏的部分石碑。图录中的展品出自墨西哥、危地马拉和洪都拉斯的玛雅城市和考古遗址。

如同中美洲其它文化一样，玛雅古典文明时期（公元250-950年）的超自然实体均为太阳、雨、风、闪电或玉米等生长于大地的果实等自然力量的表现。艺术家将天空、水和大地中的这些存在物具象化，表现形式既可以是人形或兽形，也可以是同时具有人、兽特征的想象生物。这些神灵彼此联系、协商和献祭，形成了与自然循环和人际纽带相仿的关系。此外，阴间的神灵在其领域内掌握权力，并与其它领域的神灵交战。16世纪以后记录下来的玛雅故事填补了我们对古典时期图像和文本的理解缺失，这些故事中涉及的人、神和动物都与古代故事中的相差无几，比如其中就解释了宇宙是如何诞生的，而动物又为什么拥有某种特质。

古典时期玛雅国王、王后及宫廷与这一超自然世界在多个层面产生积极的互动。他们沿用这些自然之力的名字——比如基尼什·阿哈瓦（K'inich Ajaw）（太阳脸之主、白昼太阳神）和卡维尔（K'awiil 闪电）——并在仪式和舞蹈中扮作它们的形象，化身为它们。祖先在去世后则变为这些神祇。无论在世时作为统治者，或是死后成为祖先，他们都是真正的自然之力，或转变为太阳、月亮或其它神灵，或是与他们同时出现。统治者的名字和装束也标志人与神之间转变，或促成这种转变。在仪式表演中，在彩陶或石雕所表现的故事中，人类和超自然神灵的行为是相互呼应的，国王可能重生为白昼太阳神或玉米神，而神祇则出现在宫廷场景中；事实上，世俗与超自然世界在本质上是不可分割的。此外，统治者和朝臣也会向祖先和其他超自然神灵供奉柯巴脂熏香、火焰、鲜花和食物。

对于玛雅乃至整个中美洲而言，自然世界是资源的来源，也是危险的起源。谨慎对待自然世界既是生存的关键，同时也是宇宙论中的内在要素。此外，权力也是通过与神祇和自然力量的接触而得以获得和展示。艺术品、建筑是人类彼此间或人与神力沟通的媒介。"自然的力量"展通过那些描绘超自然神灵、人类和动物的文物，以及玛雅人用来与超自然神灵沟通的艺术品，探讨了这种多层面互动。尽管玛雅艺术是展出重点，但精选自奥尔梅克（Olmec）、萨巴特克（Zapotec）和阿兹特克（Aztec）文明的艺术品也在展览之列，用以说明这些观念是如何遍及整个中美洲的。

2. 古玛雅文明

"古代玛雅"指的是16世纪欧洲人到来之前，在墨西哥东南部低地、危地马拉北部、伯利兹和洪都拉斯西部生根发芽的一种文明（图1）。这一文明又称为"古典玛雅"，因为发生在约公元250-950年间的文明繁盛期被称为"古典时期"。但无论是在这一时期之前或之后，玛雅人都曾创作出非凡的杰作；因此这一名称并不足以概括玛雅人延续数个世纪的创造力和艺术创作。例如建筑艺术的杰作就曾在约公元前200年-公元250年的前古典晚期，尤其是在现今的危地马拉地区出现。同样地，大约公元900年，伴随着古典时期南部低地城市的衰落，玛雅文明又在位于墨西哥的尤卡坦半岛发展壮大。后古典时期从大约公元950年开始，此时玛雅聚落继续修建金字塔、制作陶器、书籍和雕塑，遵循神圣历法，使用属于他们的象形文字系统。

洛杉矶郡艺术博物馆藏古代玛雅艺术品
ANCIENT MAYA ARTS FROM THE LOS ANGELES COUNTY MUSEUM OF ART

图1 玛雅地区及部分遗址
Figure 1. Map of Maya region and select sites

直到16世纪西班牙开始入侵这一区域，这些传统才受到严重的破坏。

组成玛雅文明的多个政治体在文化领域都有诸多共通之处——其中包括文字系统、神祇，以及以太阳的视运动为基础的宇宙观。最受爱戴的统治者和包括祖先在内的最受尊崇的超自然神灵，其躯体会被埋葬在具有纪念意义的金字塔内。但玛雅人从未统一为单一的政治体。历史上曾出现的多个玛雅政治体——类似于王国或城邦——不仅拥有各自的首领和守护神，在文字、艺术、建筑、丧葬制度和聚落形态等方面也具有多样化风格。玛雅人使用多种语言，至今在墨西哥和中美洲依然如此。但确实存在一种世代相传的通用语言——现在被称作"玛雅通用语"——这是一种象形文字。统治者被称为库胡尔·阿哈瓦（k'uhul ajaw 圣王），以表明他们具有库胡尔（k'uh 神性）。一些碑文讲述了统治者们缔结联盟，彼此交战的情形，其中也体现了层级关系，即强大王国的统治者任命下属管理小型属地。他们被冠以少见的k'aloomte（领主）头衔，管理大片地区。

玛雅艺术家在历史故事中描绘了大量的人类形象，在神话故事中又表现了无数的神祇和动物形象，而人类与神祇又进行频繁的互动。艺术家们以绘画和雕刻等形式在纪念建筑和可携带的物品上描述这类场景。安置在建筑和广场中的石雕纪念碑展示了王室男女举行宗教和政治仪式的情景。来自彼德拉斯·内格拉斯（Piedras Negras，位于

19

彩陶描绘了王室侍臣在宫廷集会的画面，建筑空间和叙事场景中还包括了柱子、台阶和凳子等（图3）。这一图案反映出古代宫廷中朝气蓬勃的氛围，社交活动、赏赐仪式和歌舞表演（通常是为了赞颂统治者）为宫廷生活增添了不少色彩。陶器所描绘的场景与在帕伦克（Palenque，位于今墨西哥）、蒂卡尔（Tikal，位于今危地马拉）和科潘（Copán，位于今洪都拉斯）古城发现的建筑可以相提并论。陶器还展现出多种感官刺激场景——流动的巧克力酱、罐子中的美酒，以及高足碗里盛满的玉米，还有上面淋着的浓稠酱汁。画面中，统治者和侍臣穿戴五颜六色的织物和羽毛，他们有的翩翩起舞，有的凝视着占卜镜，有的细嗅那芬芳的花香。

3. 中美洲：玛雅及其近邻

玛雅文明位于中美洲这一文化区域。中美洲囊括了墨西哥、危地马拉、洪都拉斯、伯利兹和萨尔瓦多（图4）。尽管该区域拥有丰富的环境、语言和文化多样性，中美洲文化却享有共同的显著特点，包括种植玉米、豆子、南瓜和红辣椒，推崇依据基本方位而确立的宇宙观和相应的颜色，书写体系和圣历，建造阶梯形金字塔，发明模仿星体运动的球类游戏。虽然"中美洲"作为一种地理区域的名称是有用的，但这个地区并非相互孤立，它与其北部（新墨西哥、亚利桑那）和南部（哥斯达黎加、尼加拉瓜和巴拿马）地区诸多繁荣的文化存在重要关联。这些地区相互联系与贸易，无论在物质、观念和宗教方面，还是在艺术和技术发明方面，它们都有千丝万缕的关系。

中美洲最早的文明之一——奥尔梅克文化被许多人认为是中美洲地区的"文化之母"。包括玛雅在内的后期文明都多多少少继承了奥尔梅克文化的体系，无论是宗教、艺术还是计数体系。"奥尔梅克"一词主要来自墨西哥湾附近及墨西哥韦拉克鲁斯（Veracruz）、塔巴斯科（Tabasco）和格雷罗（Guerrero）州的特万特佩克地峡（Isthmus of Tehuantepec）一带的奥尔梅克腹地所发现的遗址。在圣洛伦佐（San Lorenzo，位于今墨西哥韦拉克鲁斯，大约兴盛于公元前1200－公元前900年）和拉文塔（La Venta，位于今墨西哥塔巴斯科，大约兴盛于公元前900－公元前400年）等地，建筑师们依据创世传说场景建造了许多纪念性建筑和雕塑：例如，金字塔底部填埋着多层彩色黏土，而蛇纹石石块是取自起源于海底的山脉。

大约公元前900年以后，奥尔梅克人开始使用石器工具和磨具，以珍贵的绿岩制造小件物品，例如来自危地马拉和洪都拉斯的翡翠和蛇纹石。他们将绿岩打造成与雨水和玉米相关的超自然神灵的形象，并制造仪式性的农用工具，用以播种玉米（展品2.31、2.37，下同）。这些物品呈

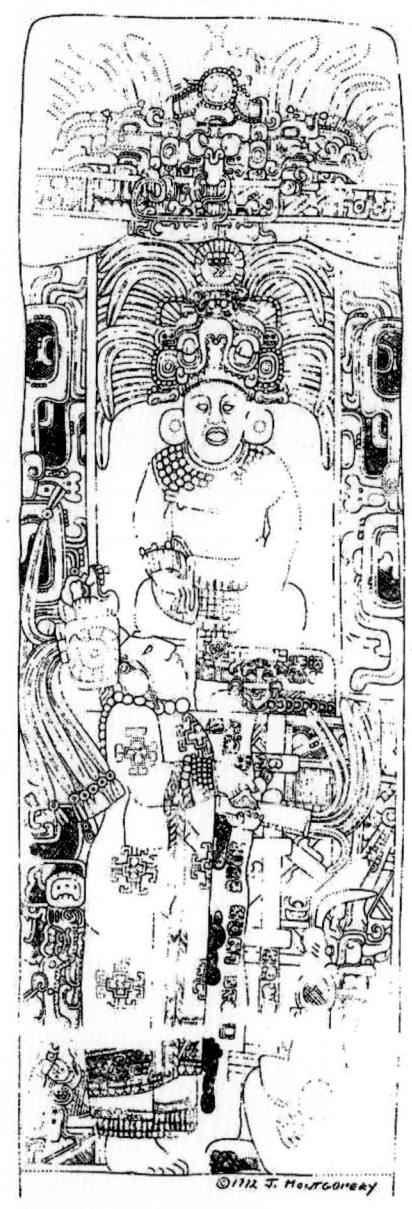

图2　彼德拉斯·内格拉斯第14号石碑（危地马拉，佩滕）

Figure 2. Stela 14, Piedras Negras (Petén, Guatemala)

今危地马拉）的第14号石碑描绘了圣王K'inich Yo'nal Ahk坐在世界树上的场景，装饰在世界树上的宇宙标志则意味着他位于宇宙的中心（图2）。在他登基后的首个新年仪式上，他在世界和社群的复兴中扮演了重要角色。他的母亲作为这次宗教仪式的积极参与者，手持羽状放血器端立于他前方；她的出席对她儿子的行为和权威构成了限制。诚然，大部分统治者由男性担当，但王母和王后在玛雅宗教及政治中也扮演着重要角色，有些女性也会担任统治者。

图3 宫廷场景纹饰陶罐，洛杉矶郡艺术博物馆藏品
Figure 3.Cylinder vessel with palace scene. LACMA M.2010.115.12

冷色调，泛蓝绿色光，这是植物、水和生命之色，象征了这些人们赖以生存的物质。考古学家已经在拉文塔等奥尔梅克遗址和包括赛巴尔（Ceibal，位于今危地马拉佩滕）在内的一些早乎玛雅时期的聚落发现了用于祭祀的绿岩神像和石斧，而这些遗址和聚落依据四个方位、一个中心的样式建造，寓意着这些场所乃宇宙之中心。而那些象征着雨水和玉米的物品有时也被埋在地下，寓意着滋养大地和作物生根发芽。

奥尔梅克文化和奥尔梅克风格也影响了同时期位于中墨西哥的文化（例如，位于墨西哥普埃布拉州的拉斯博卡斯遗址），这些文化都创造了精致的陶器，还从南部引入了这种陶器（3.27、3.29）。中美洲的其他地区在奥尔梅克文化同期也孕育了一些文化，它们可被称为"姐妹文化"，因为其往后发展成为了中美洲几个最重要的文明，包括位于墨西哥瓦哈卡州的萨巴特克文明。

萨巴特克文明兴起于墨西哥的瓦哈卡（Oaxaca）州，其最重要的历史遗址是阿尔班山（Monte Albán）遗址，其大约建于公元前500年，坐落在一处俯瞰瓦哈卡谷地的山坡上。在这一壮观的遗址和其他遗址，萨巴特克人修建了许多宗教、行政和住宅建筑。他们还在其宫殿下方修建了有多个墓室的墓葬，为他们的祖先提供安息之地，阳间与阴间仅有几层之隔。先人以俯卧的姿势置于墓葬的地板上，墙壁上挂着陪葬品，还布满了神灵、祖先和忏悔者的图像和雕塑。地面上放置有陶香炉，其造型为端坐的祖先与掌管雨水、玉米和闪电的神灵（2.40、4.60）。后人会来到这些墓室里，为祖先供奉食物、火焰和香火。在长达一千年的时间里，阿尔班山都是萨巴特克人的主要活动中心，直到14世纪，米斯特克（Mixtec）人占据了这一地区，并用那些旧的墓葬来埋葬他们的先人。

宏伟的特奥蒂瓦坎（Teotihuacan）古城坐落在墨西哥中部的特奥蒂瓦坎谷地，修建于公元1世纪。这座古城是当时美洲地区的最大城市，呈网格化布局，与基本方位和周边的群山相对应。庞大的金字塔沿南北轴拔地而起，城市中心及边缘建有"亡灵之路"，以及适合多户人居住的大型院落住宅。金字塔和住宅区的墙壁上画有彩色壁画，描绘的主题包括神灵（风暴神和羽蛇神），诸如"巨鸟之陨落"（从玛雅地区流传而来的故事）的宗教故事，以及忏悔者的供奉等。

特奥蒂瓦坎曾是一座国际大都会，来自中美洲的移民和游客络绎不绝，从遥远地区进口而来的商品随处可见。产自特奥蒂瓦坎的材料和物品（包括出自帕丘卡附近矿山的绿曜石）在整个中美洲地区贸易流通，在瓦哈卡、韦拉克鲁斯、佩滕、危地马拉高地乃至太平洋沿岸地区，人们从特奥蒂瓦坎进口商品，并受到特奥蒂瓦坎风格的启发而创作了许多艺术品（4.34、4.77）。大约在公元600年，随着特奥蒂瓦坎的衰落，另一支势力脱颖而出，并为特拉斯卡拉（Tlaxcala）、莫雷洛斯州（Morelos）、伊达尔戈（Hidalgo）州和墨西哥中部其他地区（约600-1000年）新政权的兴起清除了障碍。在这些不同地区，艺术家们汲取特奥蒂瓦坎的传统，创造了不拘一格的艺术风格，为包括玛雅地区在内的整个中美洲地区共同的风格和技艺作出了贡献。

卡密拉胡尤（Kaminaljuyú）是危地马拉谷地另一座大都市，大约始建于公元前1500年，持续了超过2500年。这座以土砖建筑为主的雄伟城市现在已经大面积毁坏，并被危地马拉城所覆盖。卡密拉胡尤的艺术家们利用火山岩创造出了杰出的雕塑作品。他们在火山岩上雕刻出人与动物神灵形象，包括美洲虎雨神。一些作品与佩滕地区发现的玛雅2世纪雕塑风格有相似之处。

公元5世纪，佩滕、特奥蒂瓦坎、卡密拉胡尤和太平洋沿岸一带的陶艺家们创造了集该地区艺术风格之大成的作品。尤其是在太平洋海岸的埃斯昆特拉（Escuintla），艺术家们创造了集当地特点和特奥蒂瓦坎风格于一体的三脚圆筒容器和香炉。太平洋海岸是可可豆种植地，因此可

图4 中美洲地图
Figure 4. Map of Mesoameric

可形象在当地艺术品中非常普遍（2.14）。但是，由于太平洋海岸一带的遗址早已被严重破坏，目前我们对该地的历史知之甚少，而且尚不清楚卡密拉胡尤和太平洋海岸一带的古人们使用何种语言。

大约于1325—1521年兴盛的阿兹特克帝国是中美洲最后一个伟大的土著文明。阿兹特克的都城——特诺奇蒂特兰城（Tenochtitlan）是另一个采用网格化布局的古代大都会，但其网格不仅由街道构成，还包括了运河。正是从这里出发，阿兹特克人不断向中美洲扩张。他们与其他文明通商、交战，向其索取贡品，与此同时也融合了这些文明的艺术传统。阿兹特克人信奉雨神——这一形象效仿了特奥蒂瓦坎的风暴神，以及掌管水、玉米和其他自然力量的男女神灵（4.79）。他们以这些神为形象创作石雕，将其供奉于庙宇，或置于泉眼、山洞和其他地点。

1521年，阿兹特克帝国在西班牙入侵者的炮火中衰亡，帝国的都城最终变成了墨西哥城，也是新西班牙总督辖区的都城。其他土著王国和朝代——包括位于库马卡（Q'umarkaj，位于今危地马拉基切省）的基切（K'iche'）玛雅人和位于玛雅潘（Mayapán，位于今墨西哥尤卡坦）的可可姆（Cocom）玛雅人——也都在16世纪被征服。这些王国被西班牙征服后的时期通常被称为殖民时期或总督时期。本书也介绍了这一时期发生的故事，帮助人们了解这些古代图像、文字和建筑所处的背景。

中美洲的历史丰富而多样，但是对自然力量的强烈情感是一个亘古不变的主题，人们长期敬仰并供奉这些神灵，以求得水、食物和其他维持生计的必需品。

4. 玛雅的宇宙

如同中美洲的许多其他文化一样，玛雅主张宇宙是有生命的，充满了代表自然力量（诸如雨和水）的超自然存在。太阳是宇宙中的定位点，而太阳的运动将地球和宇宙划分五个部分，即四个基本方位和一个中心点（图5）。每个部分都具有一种独特的颜色，通常是红、黄、白、黑、绿。宇宙的层次分明，由天空、大地和地下世界组成。白天和黑夜，天体不但在天上运动，而且途经地下世界。祖先们居住在一个世外桃源，称为 Ho Janahb Witz（五花之山），这个芬芳美丽的天堂也是一条通往太阳的道路，沿途繁花似锦，美不胜收。

根据玛雅的创世神话，世界五大部分都以顺时针和逆时针的顺序屹立着大树。这些神话出自玛雅语和西班牙语典籍（16世纪后，以拉丁文字记载），并结合古代传说予以补充。玛雅的城市、建筑、墓葬和雕塑皆以这一结构组织和布局，呈现出显著的圆形或方形（1.1、1.2）。玛雅的仪式也遵循着这一模式，有的追溯太阳由东向西的轨迹，有的则以圆形编队行动。圣巴托洛（San Bartolo，位于今危地马拉）平图拉斯（Pinturas）神庙建筑西墙的壁画描绘了四个青年贵族向四株果树供奉动物和鲜血（刺破自己的生殖器而取血），这四株果树显然象征了四个基本方位，而玉米神则供奉第五株树，可以推断，这株树象征着宇宙中心（图6）。

玛雅人将地球设想为一只乌龟、鳄鱼，或其他漂浮在水域的水生爬行动物。山脉是这只爬行动物崎岖不平的背脊，当它猛然行动时，地震便会发生。根据一些古代神话，以及后征服时期的玛雅和中墨西哥传说，大地和天空是用一只凯门鳄或其他大型爬行动物的躯体塑造的，这只爬行动物被斩首、撕碎，它的血液汇成河流，将人们带入新的宇宙秩序。一些古典时期的图像里会出现与乌龟相似的大地，它看似完整，实则已被震碎，为玉米神的再生开辟通道。许多主张大地"有生论"的传说都具有一个主要观念——大自然或人为地开天辟地，而神灵、人类、祖先或动植物

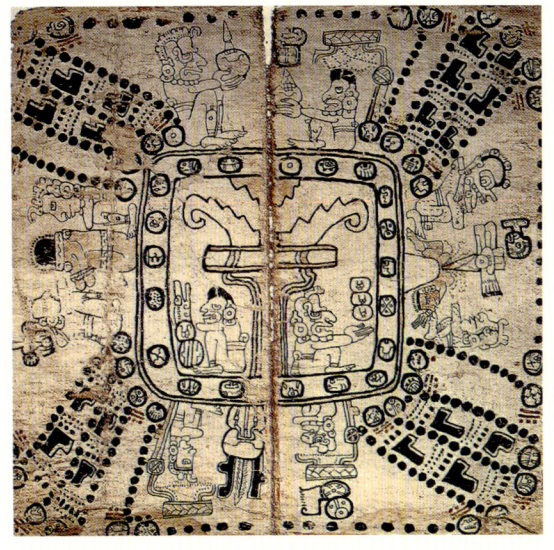

图5 《马德里古抄本》中的宇宙图
Figure 5. Cosmogram from Madrid Codex (also called Trocortesiano Codex), 75–76. Museo de América, Madrid, Spain. Photo: Joaquín Otero Ubeda© Ministerio de Educación, Culturay Deporte

通过这些被开辟的裂口到达另一级宇宙，实现死亡、再生或与超自然存在接触等目的。

在古典时期和后征服时期的传说中，地下世界被描绘为黑暗之地或水下场所。16世纪以基切玛雅语记载的《波波尔·乌》（Popol Vuh）描绘了"西巴尔巴"（基切语Xibalba，指地狱）众神，它们是疾病和死亡之源，其名字也有此类寓意，诸如"第一死神"、"第七死神"、"飞痂"、"聚血"和"脓魔"等，它们也往往与掌管太阳、月亮和玉米的神灵作斗争。古典时期的图像也描绘了地狱之神L神与太阳神、月亮神和玉米神之间的战斗。不过，地下世界也不总是那样阴森。有时，它是一个水下空间，神灵和贵族去世后长眠于此。在前古典时期的圣巴托洛、晚古典时期的蒂卡尔，以及其他地方，"Och ha'"（入水）是死亡的隐喻说法；人们还用跳水或乘独木舟远去的画面，来描绘玉米神（同时也是人类统治者）之死。玉米神亦或人类统治者也正是从这些黑暗水域中转世重生（图18）。

无论是复活、与超自然实体交流，或是其他跨宇宙的活动，都需要通过水或者太阳每天早晨可照射到的其他场所（洞穴、运动场、爬行动物的下颌、蜈蚣的咽喉）来进行。在物理意义和象征意义上，ch'e'en（洞穴）都是山的入口。在玛雅和阿兹特克神话里，玉米和其他食物最初都储存在山上，由神灵和动物帮助人们获取。圣巴托洛遗址北墙的壁画就描绘了该神话的一个版本，即玉米神在一个形似动物、长满鲜花植被的洞穴里接受进贡，贡品是玉米和开花的葫芦（图7）。基切玛雅人将原始山脉称为"Paxil"（裂缝），阿兹特克人则称其为"Tonacatepetl"（生计之山）。洞穴和山脉也是雨神、雷神、闪电神的家园，是人们举行求雨仪式、针对超自然神灵的仪式以及祭祖活动的场所。宇宙

图6 青年贵族供奉宇宙树场景。平图拉斯神庙西墙壁画，圣巴托洛（危地马拉，佩滕）
Figure 6. Young lords make offerings to cosmic trees. West Wall, Pinturas Sub-1, San Bartolo (Petén, Guatemala). San Bartolo Mural, illustration by Heather Hurst, © 2007

图7 玉米神在洞穴里接受贡品——玉米粽子和开花的葫芦。平图拉神庙北墙壁画，圣巴托洛（危地马拉，佩滕）
Figure 7. The Maize God receives corn tamales and a flowering gourd from a cave. North Wall, Pinturas Sub-1, San Bartolo (Petén, Guatemala). San Bartolo Mural, illustration by Heather Hurst, © 2003

中心之树是连通多个宇宙空间的轴心，而建筑物、纪念碑和埋藏的贡品则是与这些宇宙空间连通的途径。类似地，玛雅统治者和祭司通过祭祀仪式而穿越不同的宇宙空间。

玛雅遗址的规划和建筑旨在重现原始景观。每处遗址都建有呈四面阶梯结构的宏伟金字塔。这些金字塔模仿山脉而建，有的甚至一部分就建在了山上，例如帕伦克的碑铭神庙（图8）。这类建筑甚至以"witz"（山）命名。不论从形态还是名称来看，它们都凸显了山的重要意义。一般而言，金字塔的中央石阶可通往上层建筑，其由一间房或多间房组成，通常是一座神殿，用于供奉火焰或举办其他仪式。这些神殿被称为"chan-ch'e'en"（天洞），体现着神话中神灵和祖先的居住地。金字塔还可作为"muknal"（墓丘）：帕伦克碑铭神庙正是作为帕伦克巴加尔大帝的陵墓而建。巴加尔大帝葬于一个石棺内，石棺上除了巴加尔大帝以外，还添加了太阳神、玉米神和闪电神的元素以及蜈蚣的形态。这个上层建筑（即天洞）是纪念巴加尔大帝及其他深受敬仰的祖先和神灵的场所。

崇敬祖先是玛雅宗教和政治生活中不可缺少的内容。后人经常供奉先人，而那些将先人与后人串联起来的碑文为证明统治权的合法性提供了根本途径。在许多地方，人们将统治者依照从王朝创始人起的顺序进行编号，还编制分别用于公私场合的朝代历。在卡拉克穆尔（Calakmul）地区，艺术家们将朝代绘于小型的彩陶上（图9）。位于科潘的象形文字梯列出了跨越四个世纪的统治王朝。这些刻在阶梯上的文字是玛雅世界中现存最长的文字。一步步登上阶梯，你可以阅览每个统治者的生平故事，最顶端的神殿则记载了王朝创始人的丰功伟绩。

在玛雅世界里，对祖先和威力强大的自然现象（即自然力量）的崇敬无处不在。即使你看不见，你也一定能够体会到、聆听到，或是以其他方式予以感知。这些自然的力量体现为阳光、风、雨和闪电等等；艺术家们采用人或动物形态将其具体化，而人们也模仿、恳求它们，用香气和歌声呼唤神灵，并且认为火焰和烟雾就是神灵的化身。根据《波波尔·乌》，上帝最初创造人类的时候，人类可看

图8 从帕伦克（位于今墨西哥恰帕斯）宫殿西南角看过去的碑铭神庙
Figure 8. Temple of the Inscriptions, view from southwest corner of Palace, Palenque (Chiapas, Mexico). Linda Schele Photo Collection, AncientAmericas.org at LACMA. Photo © 2005 David Schele (17020)

得又远又广。但神灵限制了人类的视野，使人类只具有如"照镜子"般的视力。尽管如此，祭司具有"先知"的本领，能够预见世俗之外的事情，不论是通过服用迷幻药而产生的梦境和幻觉，还是通过极端的禁欲，亦或是通过水面倒影、黑曜石或黄铜镜子等方式进行占卜。

一些有关超自然神灵的作品有时只描绘这些超自然存在的一部分，有的仅描绘其轮廓，或将它们描绘成从某个开口中冒出的模样。这些都传递着一个思想——你的所见仅仅是"冰山一角"（2.16、4.60、4.59）。它们有时也被描绘在某个三维的载体上，只有将其翻面，才能看见其余部分的图像（4.64）。这些都是仪式所反映的视觉或物质隐喻，从而告诫人们只有通过仪式，才能更好地看见或感受超自然的世界。这种"可见"与"不可见"的表达是古玛雅艺术家与祭司的重要手段，这些人自如地驾驭并游走于"可见"和"不可见"之间的界限。

5. 艺术与书写

对古典时期的玛雅人来说，艺术和书写是非常神圣的行为，用来描绘和描述人、神和事物，从而让人类与神灵沟通。书吏或艺术家通常被描绘成神灵、人形兔子或猴子等形象，有时也仍保留其人类形象。但即使采用人类形象，他们通常会被赋予超自然的特点，比如其皮肤上具有镜子符号，头戴睡莲装饰物（图10、1.21）。类似地，一个出自

图9 绘有蛇国历代王朝的陶罐，洛杉矶郡艺术博物馆藏品
Figure 9. Cylinder vessel with dynastic list of the Snake Kingdom. LACMA M.2010.115.1. Photo © Museum Associates/ LACMA

蒂卡尔的骨雕描绘了一名画家的形象。画家的手从一个蜈蚣式的通道伸展而出，其寓意是艺术家的手来自另一个世界，这也表明艺术灵感的神圣性。神灵有时也依照工匠来命名。《波波尔·乌》的创作者将创世的神灵取名为"tz'akol"（制框者）、"b'itol"（造形者），这些都是工匠的头衔。这

自然的力量
FORCES OF NATURE

图10 绘有书吏形象的陶罐，洛杉矶郡艺术博物馆藏品

Figure 10. Cylinder vessel with scribes. LACMA M.2010.115.9. Photo © Museum Associates/LACMA

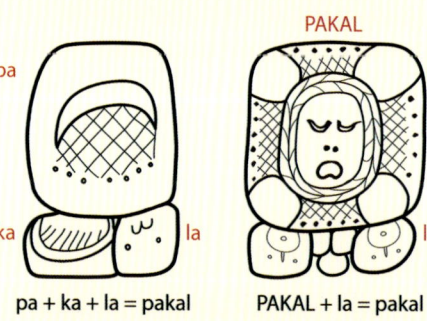

图11 玛雅象形文字"Pakal"（盾）的两种写法。第一种，将该词分为三个音节；第二种，采用词符，有一个音节作为发音说明。"K'inich Janahb Pakal"（向阳花之盾）的名字，即帕伦克的统治者巴加尔大帝，兼用这两种方法进行表述

Figure 11. Pakal ("shield"), written in Mayan hieroglyphs in two ways: one with three syllables, and one with a logogram and syllable used as a phonetic complement. Both were used in the name of K'inichJanahbPakal (Sun-Faced Flower Shield), ruler of Palenque. Illustration by Megan E. O'Neil and Kevin Cain, after drawings by Linda Schele

圣的。而且，神灵也正是通过艺术家之手，才能变得可视化、物质化。

在古玛雅社会，艺术家非常受人尊敬。许多作品描绘了书吏作画或提书、与艺术家交流，或在宫殿中站在统治者身旁的场景。这表明抄写工作本身具有交互性和行为性。书吏被称为"its'at"（智者）。他们有时也会根据具体工作命名，比如"ahtz'ihb"（作家，画家）指用刷子或羽毛笔作画的人士。动词的词源常见于许多彩陶边缘的文字（1.26）。在陶器和石器上雕琢图像和文本之人，其头衔也会出现在作品上。人们曾解读出"yuxul"一词，它源自动词"磨光"。但是，也有人对此持不同看法。

玛雅文字由音节符和词符构成，它们代表古玛雅语的发音，这也是当今玛雅语的前身。一个音节符代表一个音节，音节通常由一个辅音和一个元音组成，两者共同组成词语。例如，pa + ka + la = pakal（盾）。词符即一个词语的符号——有时词符与该词所指代的元素相似。许多玛雅词语以辅音结尾，书吏以一个额外的音节将这个辅音拼写出，但是最后一个元音不发音。音节符还可作为词符的补充，帮助澄清词语所指代的含义，以"pakal"为例，帕伦克的书吏在词符末添加了一个音节"la"（图11）。

书吏通常都训练有素。他们在拼写和书法中体现的创意和创新令人钦佩，他们的图形手稿也备受推崇。然而，并不是所有艺术家都擅长书写。不擅书写的艺术家们则使用所谓的"伪符号"（pseudo-glyphs），它们看起来很像文字，有模有样，却难以辨认（3.8）。

玛雅人采用二十进制的记数体系。圆圈表示1，竖条表示5，两种符号合并使用，可表示20以内的数字。玛雅人还发现了"零"的概念，因此能够在空间记数体系中使用数字，这一体系用于历法和会计。玛雅的历法体系包括一个时长260天的圣历和365天的阳历，两者每52年反复一次。长纪历（Long Count）用于追溯神话中的一个时间节点，对应公元前3114年8月14日。这一天可采用历法循环表示为"4 Ajaw 8 Kumk'u"，或采用长纪历表示为13.0.0.0.0，是一个大约5125年的新循环的起点。如十一神花瓶所体现，在这一天众神创世（tz'akaj k'uh）。玛雅人对早前的周期——神灵诞生并主宰这个世界，以及后世的周期和事件进行了推算。玛雅人还利用这些历法追踪天体运动，记录统治者和其他贵族的大事件。人们还将这一体系用于世俗的目的，例如会计。只可惜，这些文字通常载于纸、竹或其他易腐蚀的材料，未能留存至今。

玛雅的碑文通常呈双栏布局，遵循由上至下、由左至右的顺序书写，字体较大，常见于建筑外墙、内墙、石碑和墓碑，以及一些小件物品，比如陶器、雕像、骨器、贝

些神灵试图用未烧过的陶土和木雕造人，但未能如愿，最后它们发现玉米面才是最理想的材料。《波波尔·乌》依照工匠（尤其是那些与各类材料打交道的工匠）为神灵取名，实际上将神灵与在世的工匠相提并论。无论这些工匠精心打造的是空间、建筑、物品还是图画，他们的作品都是神

壳和翡翠珠宝。彩陶容器的题字往往说明了容器的类型和其内所盛有的物品，如装有"kakaw"（巧克力）或"ul"（玉米粥）的"uk'ib"（酒器），还说明了容器的主人。纪念碑上的题字一般较长，首先列明冗长的日期，再说明与事件相关的天体运动。

彩陶是一种古典时期玛雅代表性的艺术形式，体现出多样的年代和地域风格。洛杉矶郡艺术博物馆所收藏的陶器来自于艺术品市场，而非考古挖掘。但是，我们通常可以研究容器的形态、绘画风格或其上有关人物和政治的文字记录，从而识别出它们的原产地。例如，动物形捉手带盖厚底陶罐是佩滕（Petén）北部和坎佩切（Campeche）南部3至6世纪的典型器物（4.73、4.47）。圆筒形三足陶罐（通常有盖）常见于4至6世纪的玛雅地区，这是受特奥蒂瓦坎城的影响而兴起的（3.12）。

7至9世纪，玛雅艺术家们创造出较高的圆筒陶罐，它们通常无足或无盖，外表有复杂的纹饰。危地马拉北部霍穆尔—纳兰永（Holmul-Naranjo）地区以及伯利兹地区的的容器特点鲜明，通常为红色和橘色，其上描绘着玉米神起舞的画面（2.21）。危地马拉圣何塞（Motul de San José）附近的Ik'王国，其容器通常绘有复杂的图案，呈多种色彩，并且细分为多个子风格，其中就包括"粉色字形风格"（4.1）。出自佩滕北部和坎佩切南部的古抄本风格容器通常以奶油色或白色为背景，图像和文字以黑色和棕色的线条绘制，边缘呈红色（4.60）。这些珍贵的物品在政权内或多个政权之间相互流通。洛杉矶郡艺术博物馆收藏的容器为了解古代玛雅神话提供了丰富的资源，但是只有结合考古遗址挖掘出来的材料一同研究，我们才能充分领悟其中的奥妙。

虽然没有任何一部古典时期的抄本典籍幸存，但我们可以通过陶器上的图案一探究竟。它们被描绘成以美洲虎毛皮作为封面的一叠叠纸张（1.21）。现存的四本后古典时期玛雅典籍——《德累斯顿古抄本》（Dresden Codex）、《马德里古抄本》（Madrid Codex）、《巴黎古抄本》（Paris Codex）和《格罗里尔古抄本》（Grolier Codex）——为对比研究提供了便利（图5、图13、图16、图17）。这些树皮纸典籍以白色或奶油色为背景，其图案和字体以黑色线条绘制，边缘呈红色——这与晚古典时期的"古抄本"风格如出一辙。古典时期的典籍很可能兼有古抄本风格和后古典时期风格的特点，并记载了大量的神圣图案和文字。

二 超自然实体：天、地、水和地下世界

1.引论

"库胡尔（k'uh）"一词通常译为"神"或"神灵"，

图12 十一神陶瓶，洛杉矶郡艺术博物馆藏品
Figures 12. Vase of the Eleven Gods (two views). LACMA M.2010.115.14. Photos © Museum Associates/LACMA Conservation Center by Yosi Pozeilov

指具有神圣本质或神圣存在。"库胡尔"如果用于描述某个人、建筑或事物，则表明他们被赋予了神圣本质。玛雅的神灵通常与某种宇宙领域（天，地和地下世界）相关，但是它们可以在宇宙领域之间穿梭。有的神灵每天都可以施展这一本领，有的一年一次，而有的却只能借助于仪式。

艺术家们描绘了一系列人形和兽形的玛雅神灵。有的神灵显得很年轻，朝气十足，如玉米神，有的则显得很老迈，满脸皱纹，牙齿脱落，嘴部凹陷。图案上总是有许多蛛丝马迹——有的呈螺旋上升状，有的具有方形瞳孔（拥有非同寻常的视力），有的存在镜子符号，有的身上金光闪闪——从中不难看出，这些神灵是超自然个体。它们是人与动物结合的产物，但在画面中总是在从事人类活动，包括就坐于王座、写书或抱小孩。可以说，人类和神灵的世界是相互映射、相互交织的，神灵的举止与人类大同小异，人类则将自己打扮成神灵的模样。

许多学者试图对众多玛雅超自然个体加以分类，虽然他们取得了一定的收获，但这项工作却非常棘手，因为玛雅的神话错综复杂。学者保罗·斯尔赫斯（Paul Schellhas）在后古典时期的古抄本中发现了一些比较独特的神灵，并用字母表中的字母加以标记，比如A神、B神等等。人类学家卡尔·陶布（Karl Taube）则对古典时期的神灵加以鉴别，而其他学者试图破译这些神灵在古代的名称。然而，玛雅神话为这方面的努力带来了多个难题。第一，神灵总是有多个化身，而且有时成双成对出现，有时又四个一组出现；它们颜色不同，特点不同，但与宇宙的四分结构对应。

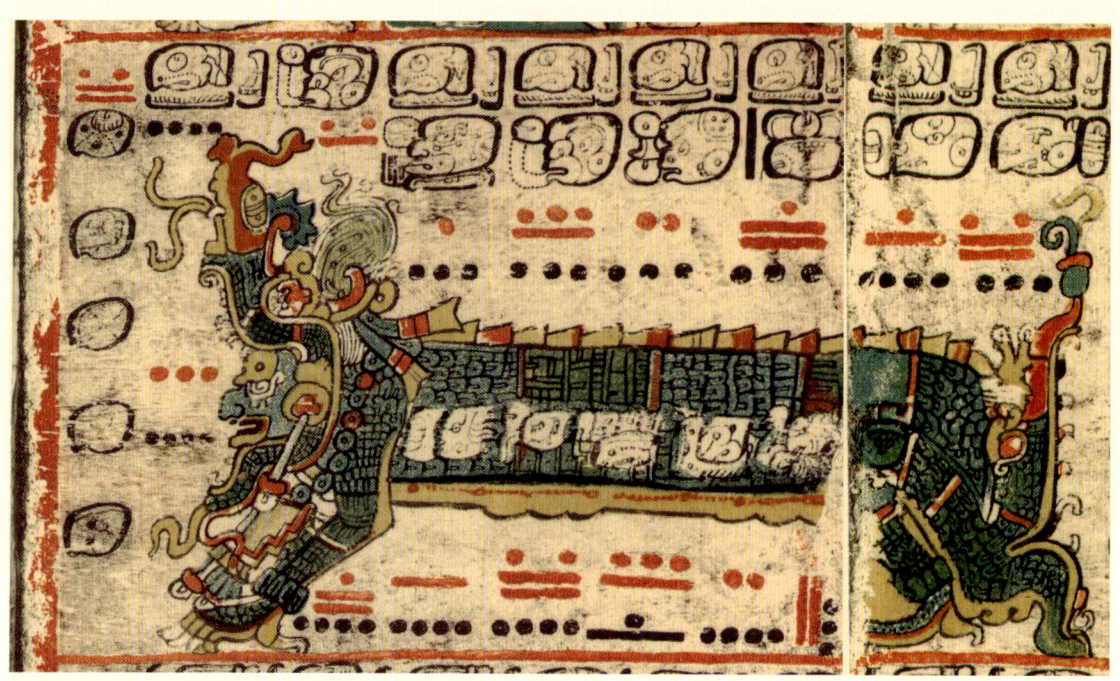

图13 形似鳄鱼的Itzam Kokaaj（又称为伊察姆纳），《德累斯顿古抄本》
Figure 13. Itzam Kokaaj (or Itzamna) in crocodile, Dresden Codex (SächsischeLandesbibliothek Dresden Mscr. Dresd. R 310), 4b–5b (detail). Photograph of Ernst Förstemann facsimile courtesy Art of the Ancient Americas at LACMA

其次，一个神灵可能会与另一个神灵合并，汲取后者的物理特征或是力量，西蒙·马丁将这个概念称为"神话合成"。最后，玛雅人用一个说法来形容神灵——"pik k'uh"，它表示"八千神灵"，也表示"一大群神灵"，这表明神灵是数不胜数的。

2. 古老的天神和地神

伊察姆纳（依据16世纪的记录，又称为D神）是居住在天上的一个重要古神。他是一位创世神，代表智慧、书写和知识（图13）。他存在于宇宙，呈人和鸟的形象，并结合了多个超自然个体。以人形出现时，他身着玛雅祭司的服装，一些图像描绘了他登基的场景，动物和其他神灵皆臣服于他，与宫殿里人类统治者及其朝见者的场景非常相似。他还往往与开天辟地的大鳄鱼相联系，体现着他在创世中扮演的角色。以鸟形出现时，他是"Yax Kokaaj Muut"——当今学者将其称为"至尊鸟神"。

在早期神界，N神（一位古老神灵，可能是D神的另一个化身）时常以乌龟或无脊椎贝类动物等为背景现身。他还会以托天者的形象出现，有时分为四个化身，分别居于天空的四个角。后征服时期的文字将这位托天者称为"帕瓦吞（pawatun）"或"巴克布（bakab）"；在古典时期，"巴克布"这个名称指一种贵族头衔，持有这一头衔的人都是显要人物。

3. 太阳神与月亮神

在古玛雅人的设想中，有多个超自然神灵代表了太阳，它们体现着太阳从白天到黑夜、从天上到地下以及在一个太阳年内的运动轨迹。基尼什·阿哈瓦（白昼太阳神）是一位成年男性，他有着方形瞳孔、大鼻子、T型门牙，脸上还有"k'in"（太阳）的标记。当太阳在黑夜移动到地下世界，掌管太阳的神灵就变成了地下世界的美洲虎神。有时，他的脸上有着"akbal"（夜晚或黑暗）标记。他同时也是火焰之神和战争之神，其脸上有盾牌装饰。白昼太阳神和美洲虎神可能分别主宰了"太阳神"的东方和西方特点。另一个掌管太阳的神灵是面部有鲨鱼图案的鲨鱼太阳神，其经过一条形似蜈蚣的通道，通过东方水域从地下世界现身。

月亮女神是一位年轻女性，通常与代表性的新月一同出现，怀抱一只可能是她孩子的兔子。年纪稍长一些的是生育、医药和占卜女神伊希切尔，她是一名接生婆，在某些场景中与月亮女神一同出现。在某些描述天神战胜冥神的场景中，太阳和月亮神与L神（贸易之神）等冥神斗争。在一个彩绘陶瓶上，冥神L神被脱去了他代表性的斗篷和帽子，顺从地跪在加冕的月亮女神和兔子面前，月亮女神手持他的帽子（图15）。这一场景与另一个神话相关，在这一神话中兔子偷了L神的华服，可能是另一个天神战胜冥神的故事。

《波波尔·乌》中讲述了双子英雄的冒险经历。他们是年轻的猎人和球手，由于最终会成为升起的太阳和月亮，他们也被认为是太阳神和月亮神。在古典时期的图画里，双子英雄（Hunahpu 和 Xbalanque）和他们的父亲（玉米神）参与了打败 L 神和其他黑暗之神的斗争。此外，在古代和后征服时代的神话故事中，双子英雄的原始行为之一就是打败了代表新生太阳的大鸟。

4. 水、雨、风暴和闪电

水（ha'）以不同的形式存在，包括雨、风暴、积水和云层，与水相关的有雷电等气候现象。农业需要水分滋养，且人类生活和洪水、飓风、冰霜和干旱等破坏性天气均需要水分，雷电等气候现象与之相关，并且对于维持这些水分的平衡至关重要。由于雨水、风暴、闪电和玉米在自然界中相互影响，它们的化身也有相似的特征，这表明化身会根据不同的环境和气候现象交叉、重合与分离。

雨神、暴风雨、闪电和雷神恰克以四种形式出现，代表不同的方向和颜色。他通常被赋予一个人体的形象，长着一张人脸或蛇形脸，上唇很长（图16）。他的名字（在古典时期的铭文和后征服时代的文本中）代表不同种类的雨和相关的现象，例如初雨、气雾和天空中的火焰（闪电）。恰克在每种化身中都代表了水，并栖身在不同的领域：他可能在天上、云层中或可以形成雨云的洞穴中。恰克通常使用鹅卵石、斧头或蛇来生成闪电或献祭（2.11）。

风（ik'）是自然界必要而危险的基础力量。风为降雨扫清道路并带来了积雨云层。风的象形文字呈 T 字形，这一词也代表了人体中的生命气息。然而飓风或暴风等可能造成火灾，产生破坏。

闪电神卡维尔被赋予人形，右脚为蛇（图17）。其蛇形脸的前额上有一面镜子，生起一团炽烈的火焰（2.15）。卡维尔是闪电的化身，可劈开土地，令玉米生长，因此他可能以玉米粒的形式出现或具有玉米神的特征。因为他具有在宇宙各个层级创造联系的能力，他也与出生、统治者就位和召唤祖先等转换过程相联系。卡维尔是异形火石中最常刻画的神，火石由燧石制成，燧石被认为是闪电击中地面的产物（1.4）。

特奥蒂瓦坎风暴神是墨西哥中部雨神、风暴神和闪电神等的同源体，戴着一个特有的毒牙面具。另一个与之相关的是阿兹特克的特拉洛克。在卡密拉胡尤，风暴神的形象是一只美洲虎（2.14）。

5. 大地果实：玉米和巧克力

玉米是一种粮食作物，年轻的玉米神前额倾斜，长出玉米穗轴，是一位主神。他的生命周期与田野中的玉米相似，其形象代表了生长、死亡和重生的过程。他进入水中或被斩首则将死亡，与农民折弯玉米杆中断植物生长，和在将穗从杆上折下之

图14 太阳神香炉，洛杉矶郡艺术博物馆藏品
Figures 14. Censer stands with solar deities. LACMA M.2010.115.426, .427. Photo © Museum Associates/ LACMA

图15 饰有月亮女神和其他神灵图案陶罐，洛杉矶郡艺术博物馆藏品
Figure 15. Rollout photograph of Cylinder Vase with Moon Goddess and Other Celestial Beings. LACMA M.2010.115.628 (Catalogue Number 2.9). Image © Museum Associates/LACMA Conservation Center by Yosi Pozeilov

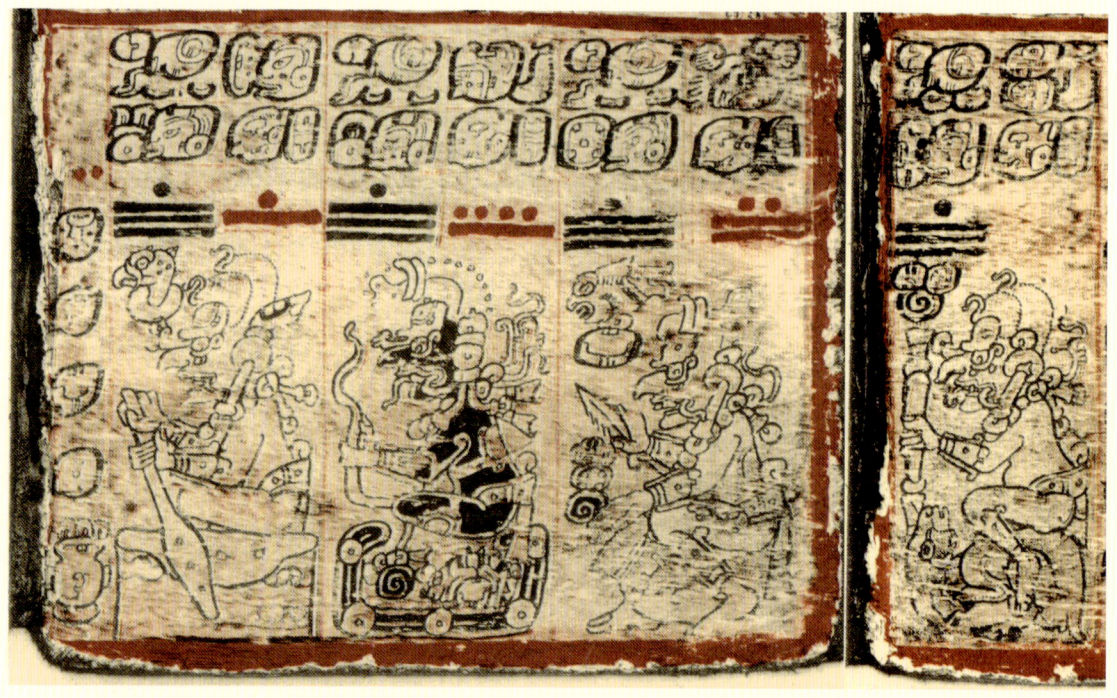

图16 雨神恰克的四种化身，《德累斯顿古抄本》
Figure 16. Quadripartite manifestations of Chahk, Dresden Codex (Sächsische Landesbibliothek Dresden Mscr. Dresd. R 310), 29c–30c (detail). Photograph of Ernst Förstemann facsimile courtesy Art of the Ancient Americas at LACMA

前令玉米粒变硬的行为相似。玉米神在龟状大地的球场或裂缝中重生（4.42），或从黑暗的原始水域中升起（图18）。

重生后的玉米神由侍女服侍穿衣，手臂向外伸展，优雅地翩翩起舞，如同随风摇摆的玉米秆。脚跟微微抬起说明是在跳舞，但在某些场景中，用羽毛装饰的玉米神从地上一跃而起，如同一只鸟一般。在圆筒形陶罐上，玉米神的不同化身与超自然的小矮人一同跳舞；玉米神背负巨大的羽状后背架，装有无数作物及不同的超自然动物。他们通过跳舞来使世界获得新生（2.20、2.21）。

Kakaw（巧克力）来自于可可树上的可可豆，是另一种重要食品，是流行于中美洲贸易中的奢侈品。玉米与可可树的传说紧密相连；在某些传说中，可可树是从玉米神身体中长出来的果树之一。洛杉矶郡艺术博物馆藏品中一个花瓶描绘了第一颗可可树从一个超自然男性身体中生长出来的情景。闪电神卡维尔指向这棵原生树和上面繁盛的可可豆。在这一神话中，有可能是闪电劈开了地面，令第一棵可可树得以生长（2.27）。

巧克力被用作饮品，与玉米等混合饮用，并用香料和鲜花调味，同时也作为调味品，和盛在素面和彩色餐盘和酒器中的玉米粉蒸肉及其他食物一起食用。在今天的玛雅仪式中，巧克力只是普通的祭祀品，但在古典时期则可能是献给神和祖先的珍贵礼物。

6. 神蛇

蛇在玛雅神话中以多种形式出现，但通常具有神性并且是通向其它宇宙之境的载体。有些神蛇具有响尾蛇和剧毒枪头蛇等毒蛇或无毒但食肉的大蟒蛇的外观特征。它们是用来象征转化的理想生物，因为它们通常会蜕皮，而这一过程常与重生和更新联系在一起。而且它们在地上、地下、树上和水中等不同的环境中活动，类似于跨越宇宙空间的仪式。蛇身和蛇口因此成为了通过出生、死亡、重生或召唤在不同空间中移动的载体。玛雅艺术家将蛇与其它生物结合在一起来强调这种穿越不同空间的能力。例如，有羽毛的蛇具备蛇和鸟的双重特征，能穿越天际、地面和水面；喉部是蜈蚣的蛇是太阳和祖先重生的载体。

睡莲蛇的身体部分是蛇，生活在水中。其头部或头饰中长着睡莲叶子或花朵，在水生环境中出现（1.25）。睡莲在陆地水体的表面开花，这是地表与地下相连接的通道，因此与变化相关。然而，睡莲蛇在变化中的作用还可能与美洲白睡莲茎的致幻作用相关。

7. 黑暗之神与梦神

冥神处于地下世界，通常与年轻的主神或天神竞争。L神在古代的名字未被解密，是一位年长的冥神，他抽雪茄，还是贸易和烟草之神（图19）。某些图画描绘了冥神在地下宫殿或洞穴中加冕的场景（图12a和b）。在其他图画中，他与基尼什·阿哈瓦、月亮女神、玉米神或其他年轻的神战斗（图15）。这些图画与古典时期双子英雄战胜西巴尔巴神（死神）的图画同源，与天神战胜冥神、光明战胜黑暗相关。它们也可能描绘了夜晚天空中变化的星象或从旱季到雨季时新生的玉米开始发芽的变化。

其他的黑暗之神和梦境之神，在夜间寻欢作乐、散播疾病（2.23、2.59）。这些具有神性的生物有着一张统治者的面孔，被一张美洲虎毛皮半掩着，这与睡眠和梦境相关。一些神以统治者的所属物品命名，可能是在他们的睡梦中游荡的个性中的另一面，他们可以在不同的境域内活动。这些超自然体被描绘成具有人形和不同动物的特征或者嘴中长出其它物体的生物（2.58）。尽管他们中的有些看起来很可爱或可笑，有些却被描绘成拿着一盘人骨或眼球从眼

图17 绘有闪电神卡维尔的陶罐，洛杉矶郡艺术博物馆藏品
Figure 17. Cylinder vessel with lightning deity K'awiil. LACMA M.2010.115.3. Photo © Museum Associates/LACMA

图18 饰有玉米神从原始水域中出现的陶盘，洛杉矶郡艺术博物馆藏品
Figure 18. Plate with the Maize God emerging from primordial waters. LACMA M.2010.115.5. Photo © Museum Associates/LACMA

窝中凸出的可怕生物。其中一些的名字与源于16世纪的玛雅疾病相似。事实上，这些神可能是人格化的疾病，他们被当作诅咒送去伤害竞争对手，这是一种与公然的军事进攻同时发生的辅助性的超自然战争，纪念石雕或建筑上的图像和铭文记载了军事战争。这些拿着灌肠工具或吸烟的神可能在摄取导致变形或做梦的致幻药。

三 玛雅艺术和宗教中的动物

古典时期的玛雅艺术和宗教中随处可见动物的身影，

自然的力量
FORCES OF NATURE

图19 L神像，位于帕伦克东侧柱十字神庙（墨西哥，恰帕斯）
Figure 19. God L, Temple of the Cross East Jamb, Palenque (Chiapas, Mexico). Drawing by Linda Schele © David Schele (SD-176)

动物以多种形式出现在不同场景中，且其形象独具创意、丰富多样。同样地，《波波尔·乌》详述了人类和动物之间的多种交互关系，显示了动物与人类具有共同的起源，既产生冲突，又相互合作。当造物神创造这些动物时，他们将动物命名为"森林的守护者"，但由于动物不能说出神的名字或崇拜神，神对它们感到失望。因此，他们创造了可以崇拜神和命令动物的人类，动物则变成了人类的食物。此外，在神创造人类的多次实验中，一些失败的创造物则变成了蜘蛛猿等动物。行为不得体的人类（或拟人神）也被变成了猴子。

在某些时候，动物与人类（或拟人的超自然体）发生冲突。西巴尔巴神使用蝙蝠恐吓和击败了双子英雄。与此同时，猎人双子英雄猎杀的对象之一是骄傲的七金刚鹦鹉。七金刚鹦鹉自称是太阳，而双子英雄要将其击败才能使新生的太阳升起。然而，他们猎杀动物的行动毫无疑问为猎杀其他动物为食赋予了特权。

动物也帮助了双子英雄和他们的家族繁衍生息。它们帮助双子英雄的母亲在只有一株玉米的田地中收集了一整袋的玉米，从而向他们的祖母证明了他们母亲的价值。尽管动物们一开始挑衅双子英雄，每晚都将他们的玉米地变成森林，但动物们后来开始帮助他们。在棒球比赛中，长鼻浣熊带了可以代替胡纳赫普头的壁球，兔子四处跳动来分散对手的注意力，从而使胡纳赫普得以取回他的头。最后，当双子被打败时，他们请求动物将他们的骨头研碎并撒进水中，在水中他们变成了鲶鱼并得到再生。在人形和动物形中变换因此成为了重生和再生的媒介，在仪式变换中也可运用这一操作，使人类具备动物的特征，从而在某些环境中继续存活。

古代铭文中对此记载的并不详细，但玛雅艺术中多种多样富有创意的动物画像表明这些故事也在古代玛雅流传。《波波尔·乌》的故事可能从早前几个世纪就开始流传，因为前古典时期和古典时期的图画叙述了类似的故事。例如，彩陶上带吹箭筒的猎人形象与双子英雄的形象相似，小型陶器和纪念性建筑中的图画描述了至尊鸟神的坠落。动物被描绘成典型的动物行为，例如吃东西或挠腋窝，但它们也经常被拟人化，戴项链、头巾和缠腰带，和从事跳舞、说话等人类活动，或展示敌人被斩下的头颅（3.4、3.7、3.16）。某些图画看起来很幽默，因为它们将动物置于不寻常但并非不可能的环境中，而其它图画将人类比作猴子等生物，这些生物在创造人类之前充当了人类，因此这些图画强调了两者的相似性。

玛雅统治者通过命名和变装将自己与动物相联系。科潘 K'inich Yax K'uk' Mo' 的名字意为第一只太阳面孔的绿咬鹃金刚鹦鹉，代表与太阳相关的多彩华美的热带鸟类（图21）。帕伦克 K'inich Kan Bahlam 的名字意为天空中以太阳为脸的美洲虎，不仅指凶猛的夜行捕食者，也指天空中的太阳。统治者、武士和其他贵族通常身着动物头饰，包括美洲虎、鳄鱼、蛇、鹿和鸟。在玛雅时代的整个中美洲地区，从古代到现在——顶级食肉动物美洲虎由于行动隐秘、力量巨大而使人崇拜和惧怕。因此它们常常是战争和较高社会地位的象征，用来展示政治权力和精神力量。

玛雅人将动物用作食物和宗教祭祀品。他们吃鹿、火鸡、狗、鱼和其它动物，并穿着动物毛皮制成的衣物，穿美洲虎毛皮制成的短裙，戴绿咬鹃华丽的羽毛制成的头饰以及河流和海洋中的贝类制成的珠宝。考古学家已经挖掘出无数用作祭祀品的鹿、海牛和鸟骨、贝壳、黄貂鱼刺和其它物种的遗骸,许多壁画和陶器上的图画描述了人类和神正在用这些动物祭祀。其中有圣巴托洛前古典时代彩绘壁画上年轻君主在宇宙树前用鹿、火鸡和鱼献祭的场景,后古典时代现存的四本玛雅书籍之一《德累斯顿古抄本》描绘了神在装扮一新的树前献祭的场景。

动物是神话传说中普遍存在的元素。例如,月亮女神的孩子是一只兔子,它帮助天神战胜了黑暗之神。神可能具有动物的特征,通常由人类和多种动物杂糅而成。蛇和蜈蚣是在宇宙之境穿行的超自然载体,蝴蝶被认为是复活的祖先。鱼、鳄鱼、乌龟和青蛙等水生物和鸬鹚等水鸟因为近水而受到重视。这不仅是因为水是生命和食物之源,还因为人们认为水下有一个冥界。例如,鸬鹚象征着重生,因为它们常钻进水中又从水中出现。

本展览将动物分成天空、地面和水中的动物,但许多动物经常在宇宙的不同境域穿行。此外,玛雅艺术和宗教中出现的真实和复合动物都具备在天空、树上、陆地、水中和地下等不同环境中生活和移动的能力。水鸟在水中和天空中生活,鳄鱼可在水中和地面爬行,蛇在水中、树上和地下都可自由移动。这些动物经常在神话故事中出现。事实上,在不同环境中穿行的能力类似于穿越不同的宇宙之境,并在其间建立联系。这是玛雅宗教和政治的基本观念,在中美洲的其他地方,如奥尔梅克艺术中也有所反映。

四 国王和王后的神圣仪式

1. 引论

古典时期的玛雅国王和王后以及宫廷成员通过多种方式积极从事与动物和超自然世界相关的活动。人们充分利用自然资源:饮用从天空中降落的雨水来滋润他们的身体,用地面的石头来建造房屋,用森林中的木头来生火,用地下的颜料粉刷墙壁,用动物的骨头制作工具。自然的力量赋予宇宙生机,既维持了人类社会的运行又对人类社会构成了挑战。因为人类的生存取决于资源的平衡,鉴于自然力量具有哺育和破坏的伟大性,人们非常敬畏自然力量。实际上,在整个中美洲地区,领袖和祭司举行祭献和其他仪式,努力维持宇宙界的平衡。

因此,在许多地方,这一富有生机的宇宙观在权力语境中得到运用。领袖展示这些自然力量并在它们之间建立联系,从而证明自己的权力。这些力量可以维持子民的生活,但也可能很危险,并被统治者用来唤起子民的尊崇与畏惧。在1996年的一篇开创性论文中,碑铭研究家斯蒂芬·休斯顿(Stephen Houston)和大卫·斯图尔(David

图20 绘有与蛇国相关的神的陶罐,洛杉矶郡艺术博物馆藏品
Figure 20. Cylinder vessel with wahy entities associated with the Snake Kingdom. LACMA M.2006.41. Photo © Museum Associates/LACMA

图21 刻有K'inich Yax K'uk' Mo'名字的灰泥板(洪都拉斯,科潘马尔加里塔)
Figure 21. Stucco panel with name K'inich Yax K'uk' Mo', Margarita facade, Copán (Honduras). Photograph Early Copán Acropolis Project, courtesy Loa Traxler

Stuart)特探讨了玛雅统治者如何将自己与神相联系,并展示了建立这种联系的多种方法。其中一种方法是使用库胡尔(k'uhul神性)称号,称号说明了他们具有神性;他们使用神的名字并模仿神;他们供奉神并建造神的塑像,神见证了他们的行为,因而认可了他们的统治。

2. 命名和日历纪年

除了使用动物名称外,玛雅贵族还使用神的名字命名,这毫无疑问是为了获取他们的权力和某种特殊力量。其中最为常用的是太阳神的称号或名字,包括帕伦克统治者K'inich Janahb Pakal和K'inich K'an Joy Chitam所取的K'inich(太阳脸)的称号等等。使用这一称号暗示此人充满了能量和其它太阳的属性(图22a)。其它名称还有Itzam Kokaaj Bahlam,这一名称与造物神的智慧、创造力和美洲虎相关(图22b)。与闪电神K'awiil和Yopaht相关的名字意为强大而危险,但对于生命不可或缺,因为

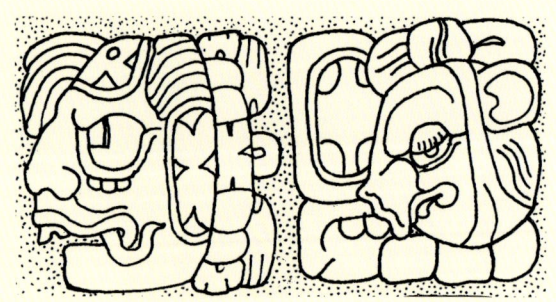

图22a K'inich K'an Joy Chitam的名字
Figure 22a. Name of K'inich K'an Joy Chitam. Detail of Palace Tablet, Palenque. Detail of drawing by Linda Schele © David Schele (SD-121)

图22b 陶罐上Itzam Kokaaj Bahlam的名字，洛杉矶郡艺术博物藏品
Figure 22b. Name of Itzam Kokaaj Bahlam on a cylinder vessel. LACMA M.2010.115.573. Photo © Museum Associates/LACMA

闪电将大地劈开，令玉米和其它植物得以生长。与此相关的名称包括Tikal的Sihyaj Chan K'awiil（天空之子卡维尔K'awiil）、Quiriguá的K'ahk'Tiliw Chan Yopaht（在空中燃火的闪电）和Yopaht Bahlam（闪电美洲虎），Yopaht Bahlam是洛杉矶郡艺术博物馆藏一件陶器的所有者（1.21）。与水神相关的名称有Machaquilá统治者Sihyaj K'in Chahk（太阳之子Chahk）和Sihyaj Chan Chahk（天空之子Chahk），Sihyaj Chan Chahk的名字刻在洛杉矶郡艺术博物馆的一件陶器上（4.76）。这种通过命名与神产生的联系在统治者死后将继续下去并转化为自然力量。

玛雅贵族还使用历法将他们自身与神的生日和行为相联系。在帕伦克寺庙的碑文上，K'inich Janahb Pakal的即位日期是一百万年前一位神的生日。此外，许多地方的贵族在重大事件的纪念日举行仪式，在他们和与这些日期相关的祖先和神之间建立联系（4.69）。

3. 音乐、舞蹈和扮演

音乐和舞蹈是古代玛雅生活和仪式中不可或缺的元素。k'ayom（歌者）是玛雅精英的称号，歌曲是献给祖先和其它超自然神灵的祈祷词或献祭品。古典时期的图画描绘了有可能在葬礼中演奏鼓、响铃和哨子等乐器的场景，舞蹈和仪式祭典同时进行，乐器在演奏完后被随葬在坟墓中。在石碑和陶罐的图像中，跳舞可由ahk'oot（"舞蹈"的动词词根）一词或由一个人物踮起的脚尖或优雅的手势表示。

音乐和舞蹈表演不仅是一种娱乐，也是扮演超自然神灵并与之沟通的方式，音乐和舞蹈使玛雅贵族运用和呈现了超自然力量。纪念碑、陶像和陶罐等许多媒介描绘了统治者和其他贵族扮演动物或玉米神等超自然神灵跳舞的图画。有些图画可以明显看出其中的人物身着戏服，而其他图画中舞者和其扮演的神不可分辨。

着戏装的人可变成他们的服装所代表的神，且戏装促成了这一转化。在某些人物的旁边写着u-baah-ila'n（"这是扮演……的图画"），其后跟着超自然神灵和扮演者的姓名。雅科奇兰（Yaxchilán，位于今墨西哥）地区的一根浮雕门楣描绘了一位身处弯月形涡纹中的女性，表明她已经变成了祖先；文字和头饰也显示她身着睡莲蛇的服装（图23）。统治者身着玉米神服装的图像通常模棱两可，有可能是统治者自己的画像也可能是他们在扮演玉米神。但这种转化不一定由图像刻画，也有可能记录在文字中。一个查马（Chamá）风格的陶罐上标明其所有者是太阳神的扮演者Wuk Chapaht K'inich Nohol Yok'in；这一短语可能表明在扮演活动结束后太阳神仍附身在其体内（图24）。

有歌舞的超自然活动的另一作用是社会融合，因为公共表演能够吸引来自分散居住地的人们，使人们感受到他们是圣主（k'uhul ajaw）统治下的更大社区的一部分。

4. 球赛运动

球赛运动是玛雅地区另一项活跃的宗教仪式，在整个中美洲地区，球赛对于宗教、政治和社会凝聚都具有重要意义。事实上，球赛图画不仅描绘了运动员，还有音乐家和观众，考古记录还证明了人们会在球场周围举行宴会。不同地区的球赛规则各不相同，墨西哥的某些地区仍然有多种打法。在古代中美洲，球赛运动通常在以两座平行的长条低矮建筑为边界的球场内进行。为保护自己不受像球的撞击，球员身着厚重的垫料和装备，还在腰间绑上一种U型轭。在礼仪中使用的这种装备由绿岩和其它珍贵石头制成（4.44），可能是授予给运动员的奖品或礼物。事实上，在某些墓中曾经发现一些石轭。墨西哥韦拉克鲁斯州的城市是了解古典时期球赛装备和图像的主要来源。埃尔塔欣（El Tajín，位于今墨西哥韦拉克鲁斯）留存有许多球场及运动员在礼仪和神话中的图像。

5. 纪念神和祖先的建筑、雕像和供品

玛雅贵族还通过建造房屋与超自然体产生连结，他们在房屋中祭祀祖先和供奉神灵雕像。帕伦克14号神庙中的一块浮雕石灰岩嵌板描绘了贵族妇女Tz'akbu Ajaw举着一座卡维尔雕像的画面（雕像可能由木头或灰泥制成）；从她手中垂下的纺织物说明这座雕像之前被包装或捆束，这与当代玛雅牧师将宝石和其它物品放在圣包中的做法类似（图25）。帕伦克铭文中也叙述了与照料和装扮神灵雕像相关的王家仪式。古典时期和后古典时期的图画显示了人和神通过食物和生火向神灵、神灵雕像和祖先献祭的画面。例如，《德累斯顿古抄本》中的一个场景是通过无头鸟和香炉向一棵装扮成恰克的树祭祀。这份手抄本中的其它图画也描绘了用鹿肉或蜥蜴肉做成的玉米粉蒸肉作献祭食品（图26）。

生火和燃烧树脂和树胶是献祭的其它基本程序。许多古代铭文和图画中叙述了火供仪式，如纳兰霍（Naranjo）统治者Aj Wosal（4.70）在战争后在香炉中焚烧树胶的场景。考古遗址中经常可见焚烧后变黑的香炉和烧焦的松树变成的木炭。焚烧松树、柯巴脂和其它树脂产生的烟雾和香气是向神灵和祖先献祭的代表性食物，并且是与他们沟通的方式。

贵族也会切割他们的身体来采集鲜血，向神灵和祖先献祭。放血通常是召唤仪式中不可分割的一部分。玛雅纪念碑的雕刻、绘画和小型陶器和雕像上描绘了放血和召唤仪式，这些仪式将神灵和祖先召唤回现实世界。波南帕克的一面彩绘墙（墨西哥恰帕斯）描绘了一群妇女从舌头中拉出一根采血的绳子，采血是房间中进行的仪式的一部分。临近的雅科奇兰中23号遗址中的一块石雕楣梁描绘了另一位王室妇女K'abal Xook正以相似的方式取血，同一座建筑中的另一块楣梁描述了在仪式中召唤而来的战神。战神的到来认可了妇女的丈夫就任统治者。

服用烟草、酒和致幻剂也有助于召唤、扮演、礼制仪式的举行以及与超自然神灵的连结。玛雅人抽雪茄或服用粉末状和液态烟草。高剂量的烟草可能产生幻觉。居住在泽套和索西的现代玛雅人在医疗和仪式中使用烟草，古代玛雅人可能也有类似的做法。玛雅人还在净化仪式中服用发酵龙舌兰酒（龙舌兰汁液）、蜂蜜、巴尔切树皮，和蘑菇、睡莲（美洲白睡莲）、曼陀罗和木曼陀罗花等致幻剂，这些东西可引发呕吐，带来狂喜和迷幻的体验。

图23 饰有月形涡纹中的女性祖先扮演睡莲蛇的浮雕楣梁，洛杉矶郡艺术博物藏品

Figure 23. Carved lintel with female ancestor in lunar cartouche and impersonating the Water Lily Serpent. LACMA AC1992.76.1. Photo © Museum Associates/ LACMA

图24 写有祭文的陶碗局部，洛杉矶郡艺术博物藏品

Figure 24. Detail of Cylindrical Bowl with Dedication Text. LACMA M.2010.115.824 (Catalogue Number 1.24). Photo © Museum Associates/ LACMA

图25 举着一座卡维尔像的Tz'akbu Ajaw，帕伦克第14号庙宇嵌板细节图（墨西哥，恰帕斯州）

Figure 25. Lady Tz'akbu Ajaw holding a K'awiil effigy. Detail of panel from Temple XIV, Palenque (Chiapas, Mexico). Detail of drawing by Linda Schele © David Schele (SD-150)

五 经久不衰的传统

图26 向装扮成恰克的一棵石头树献祭，《德累斯顿古抄本》
Figure 26. Offering to a stone tree dressed as Chahk, Dresden Codex (Sächsische Landesbibliothek Dresden Mscr. Dresd. R 310), 25c. Photograph of Ernst Förstemann facsimile courtesy Art of the Ancient Americas at LACMA

在一千多年来，尽管在不同的时间和空间有不同的信仰和表述，古玛雅文明与动物世界和祖先敬奉紧密相连。虽然在过去的五个世纪中，玛雅文化、政治、宗教和人口发生了重大变化，许多这类传统仍然延续至今。西班牙探险家首次于1507年进入尤卡坦半岛，但遭到了玛雅人的驱逐。当征服者和牧师在16世纪中期在尤卡坦半岛站稳脚跟后，他们开始镇压当地人的神灵信仰并传播基督教。为此，他们破坏了玛雅庙宇、神灵雕像和书籍并惩罚试图保护它们的人。在玛雅人居住的其它地方和整个新西班牙辖区都发生了奴役等类似的压迫。疾病和瘟疫（欧洲人带来）的入侵加剧了文化破坏，令对天花等疾病无免疫力的土著人口数量锐减。

尽管早期发生了这些悲剧和之后长达几个世界的压迫，今天的玛雅人仍在他们的祖居地繁衍生息，并分散居住在墨西哥中部、美国和欧洲等地区，仍有三十多种玛雅语言（和其它方言）在使用。玛雅文化在过去的几个世纪发生了很大变化，宗教仪式也有了改变，许多人开始信奉基督教，将基督教信仰和传统玛雅和其它宗教信仰相结合。与此同时，许多传统玛雅仪式和信仰也得以留存。玛雅妇女仍使用背带式织布机纺织惠毕尔（huipil，一种自头部套穿的连衣裙），这种纺织技术已有超过一千年的传统（4.15）。在墨西哥和危地马拉的教堂中，与圣胡安·查姆拉这个教堂一样，玛雅人身着惠毕尔制成的衣服，打扮成天主教圣人的样子，与帕伦克铭文中描述的及中世纪欧洲的习俗类似。玛雅牧师仍然使用260天的圣历来指导个人行动和宗教仪式，包括祖先敬奉。此外，玛雅社区仍然举行宗教和政治性质的舞蹈，特别是在春天与新年相关的节日中（当然舞蹈和服装也有了重要创新和变化）。洞穴、山脉、泉水和其它自然景观持续充当了向祖先献祭和与之沟通的重要地点，火仍然是祈祷者的基本媒介——不仅是与祖先沟通的方式，还是将食物、树脂、蜡烛和烟草等供奉给祖先和其它神灵的途径。

这些现存的传统和仪式被证明是理解古代玛雅的丰富知识源头，为艺术、铭文和考古记录提供了新颖的研究视角。例如，当代玛雅语言的使用者对于解读古代文字具有重要作用。玛雅文化、语言和艺术的从古至今的创造力和多样性应该被人们所了解和纪念，尤其是在贫穷、全球化和其它力量的威胁令它们难以为继的情况下。

图27 陶罐上绘有通过太阳蜈蚣载体重生的祖先，洛杉矶郡艺术博物馆藏品
Figure 27. Cylinder vessel with an ancestor being reborn from the solar centipede portal. LACMA M.2010.115.21. Image © Museum Associates/LACMA Conservation Center by Yosi Pozeilov

6. 死后向神灵和祖先的转化

死亡虽然是必然要经历的转化事件，但不一定是最终的；因为玛雅贵族在死后会变成祖先。在这些转化过程中，他们变成大自然的某个部分如太阳、月亮、玉米和闪电而得到重生。正如《波波尔·乌》中的双子英雄重生为太阳和月亮，蒂卡尔（Tikal）31号石碑记录了祖先 Yax Nuun Ayiin 变成白昼太阳神，雅科奇兰和周边地区的王后则作为月亮女神出现在雕刻于楣梁和其它建筑元素上的月形涡纹中。他们通过多种载体重生，包括通过每天早上从东方升起的太阳的蜈蚣喉咙得到重生，他们居住在花山，按照花期即太阳在天空的运行轨迹来移动（图27）。事实上，他们成为了自然的力量。

Forces of Nature: Art and Divinity in the Ancient Maya World

Megan E. O'Neil

Forces of Nature among the Ancient Maya and their Neighbors

Introduction

Forces of Nature: Ancient Maya Arts from the Los Angeles County Museum of Art explores the rich world of the supernatural in ancient Maya art. Featuring more than two hundred works from LACMA's collection of the Art of the Ancient Americas, the exhibition and the catalogue investigate how artists portrayed the supernatural world and how rulers and royal courtiers engaged with that world in art, ritual, and performance, as well as in the acquisition and display of power. The exhibition's focus is on portable works, particularly painted ceramic vessels and figurines and greenstone jewelry, though also included are stone monuments from the LACMA collection. The catalogue further situates these objects in relation to architecture and monuments excavated in Maya cities in Mexico, Guatemala, and Honduras.

As in other Mesoamerican cultures, Classic-period (250–950 CE) Maya supernatural entities were manifestations of forces of nature such as the sun, rain, wind, and lightning, and fruits of the earth such as maize. Artists visualized these beings of sky, water, and earth in anthropomorphic and zoomorphic form and as fantastic creatures with both human and animal characteristics. These entities communicated, negotiated, and made offerings to one another, forming relationships that mimicked natural cycles and human bonds. In addition, underworld beings held power in their respective realms and battled entities of other realms. Maya stories recorded in the sixteenth century and later complement our understanding of Classic-period images and texts, for they relate tales of humans, deities, and animals that are similar to the ancient narratives, explaining, for example, how the universe came into existence or why animals have certain traits.

Classic-period Maya kings, queens, and royal courts actively interacted with this supernatural world in multifaceted ways. They took the names of forces of nature—including K'inichAjaw (Sun-Faced Lord, the diurnal sun god) and K'awiil (lightning)—and dressed as and embodied them in rituals and dances. After death, ancestors transformed into such deities. As living rulers and as ancestors, they truly were forces of nature, having turned into—or merged with—the sun, moon, and other entities, and their names and costume elements both signaled and enabled those transformations. In ritual performances and in narratives painted on clay or sculpted in stone, the actions of humans and supernatural entities are shown to mirror each other, for kings may be reborn as the diurnal sun or the Maize God, and deities may be arrayed in palace scenes; in fact, these worlds were effectively inseparable. Additionally, rulers and their courts made offerings of copal incense, fire, flowers, and food to their ancestors and other supernatural entities.

For the Maya, and throughout Mesoamerica, the natural world was a source of both nourishment and danger. Careful engagement with the natural world was crucial for survival and an inherent part of indigenous cosmologies. Furthermore, power was acquired and displayed through engagement with deities and natural forces. Artworks, buildings, and site plans were some of the media through which humans interfaced with one another and with divine forces. Forces of Nature investigates these multifaceted interactions through objects that depict supernatural entities, humans, and animals and through works that the Maya used to communicate with supernatural entities. Although the primary focus is Maya art, select artworks from the Olmec, Zapotec, and Aztec civilizations also are presented in the exhibition and the catalogue to demonstrate how these concepts appear throughout greater Mesoamerica.

Ancient Maya Civilization

"Ancient Maya" refers to the civilization that thrived in the lowlands of southeastern Mexico, northern Guatemala, Belize, and western Honduras before the arrival of Europeans in the region in the sixteenth century (figure 1). This civilization is also called the "Classic Maya," a term based on designating the Classic period as the time of the flourishing of civilization, circa 250–950. However, Maya people created extraordinary works both before and after this date range; thus, that naming system does not do justice to the many centuries of creativity and art-making of the Maya people. For example, extraordinary works of art and architecture were created during the Late Preclassic period, circa 200 BCE–250 CE, particularly in present-day Guatemala. Likewise, contemporaneous with and following the decline of Classic-period cities of the Southern Lowlands circa 900, Maya civilization flowered in the Yucatán Peninsula in Mexico. During the Postclassic period, beginning circa 950, Maya communities continued to build pyramids, make ceramics, books, and sculptures, track the sacred calendar, and use their hieroglyphic writing system. These practices were severely curtailed when the Spanish invaded those regions in the sixteenth century and later.

The many polities comprising the Maya civilization shared myriad aspects of culture—among them, a writing system, deities, and a cosmology based on cardinal directions determined by solar movements. Most honored living rulers and worshiped supernatural entities, including ancestors whose bodies were interred in monumental pyramids. Yet the Maya were never united under a single political system. There were multiple polities—akin to kingdoms or city-states—and these had their own distinct leaders and patron deities, as well as diversity in styles of writing, art-making, architecture, burial practices, and settlement patterns. Multiple Mayan languages were spoken, as they are in Mexico and Central America today. Nonetheless, there was a common ancestral language—known today as "Common Mayan"—used for hieroglyphic writing.[1] Rulers were called k'uhulajaw (sacred lord), indicating that they were infused with k'uh (sacred essence). Inscriptions provide narrations about rulers making alliances and conducting war with one another, and there were hierarchical relationships in which rulers of larger, more powerful kingdoms installed subordinate leaders in smaller sites.[2] Those bearing the rare title k'aloomte' governed over larger areas.

Maya artists rendered numerous images of humans in historical narratives, deities or animals in mythological narratives, and humans interacting with deities. Artists painted, carved, or otherwise illustrated these scenes on monumental structures as well as on portable objects. Carved stone monuments installed in buildings and plazas show royal men and women performing religious and political ceremonies. Stela 14 from Piedras Negras (Guatemala) depicts the k'uhulajaw K'inich Yo'nal Ahk seated in a scaffold adorned with cosmological symbols that place him at the center of the universe (figure 2). In his first new-year ceremony after acceding to rulership, he takes an active role in renewing the world and the community. His mother, a dynamic participant in this sacred rite, stands before him, holding a feathered bloodletter; her presence sanctions her son's actions and authority. Indeed, although most rulers were men, royal mothers and queens played important roles in Maya religion and politics, and some women also served as rulers.

Polychrome ceramics illustrate royal courtiers gathered in palace settings, with pillars, stairs, and benches forming architectural spaces and framing narrative scenes (figures 3a and b). Such tableaux demonstrate the vibrant nature of ancient palaces, which were enlivened with social interactions, gift-giving ceremonies, and music and dancing, often to honor the ruler. [3] These depicted spaces are comparable to buildings found in ancient cities such as Palenque (Mexico), Tikal (Guatemala), and Copán (Honduras). Pictorial narratives demonstrate that these were multi-sensorial environments in which cylinder vessels overflow with foaming chocolate, jars hold sweet alcoholic beverages, and footed bowls are replete with tamales covered in rich sauces. In these scenes, rulers and courtiers dressed in colorful textiles and feathers speak and dance with one another, gaze into divinatory mirrors, and sniff aromatic flowers.

Mesoamerica: The Maya and Their Neighbors

The Maya homelands are part of a larger cultural region called Mesoamerica, which encompasses Mexico, Guatemala, Honduras, Belize, and El Salvador (figure 4). Although inhabiting an area of great environmental, linguistic, and cultural diversity, Mesoamerican cultures share significant features.[4] These include the domestication of maize, beans, squash, and chili peppers; a cosmos organized by the cardinal directions, with associated colors; a writing system and sacred calendar; stepped pyramids; and a ballgame characterized by movements emulating celestial bodies. Although "Mesoamerica" is useful as a category, the region was not isolated and had important relations with the vibrant cultures to the north (in New Mexico and Arizona) and south (in Costa Rica, Nicaragua, and Panama), with whom they communicated and traded, sharing material goods, imagery, and religion, as well as innovations in art and technology.

The Olmec culture, among the earliest civilizations of Mesoamerica, is considered by many to be Mesoamerica's "Mother Culture," as later civilizations—such as the Maya—adopted aspects of Olmec religious, artistic, and notational systems. The

---

1. Stephen D. Houston, John Robertson, and David Stuart, "The Language of Classic Maya Inscriptions," *Current Anthropology* 41, no. 3 (2000): 321–56.
2. For more information on Maya geopolitics, see Simon Martin and Nikolai Grube, *Chronicles of the Maya Kings and Queens* (London and New York: Thames & Hudson, 2008).
3. Stephen D. Houston and David Stuart, "Peopling the Classic Maya Court," in *Royal Courts of the Ancient Maya, Volume 1, Theory, Comparison, and Synthesis*, eds. Takeshi Inomata and Stephen D. Houston (Boulder, CO: Westview Press, 2001), 54–83.
4. These were identified by Paul Kirchhoff, "Mesoamérica: sus límites geográficos, composición étnica y caracteres culturales," *Acta Americana* 1 (1943): 92–107.

name Olmec refers principally to the archaeological sites in the Olmec heartland on the Gulf Coast and in the Isthmus of Tehuantepec in the Mexican states of Veracruz, Tabasco, and Guerrero. At sites such as San Lorenzo (Veracruz, Mexico), which flourished circa 1200–900 BCE, and La Venta (Tabasco, Mexico), which thrived circa 900–400 BCE, builders constructed monumental architecture and sculptures that emulated landscapes of creation: for instance, a pyramid built atop buried layers of colored clay and serpentine blocks is the primordial mountain emerging from the sea.

After about 900 BCE, the Olmec used stone tools and abrasives to craft small items from precious greenstones such as jadeite and serpentine imported from Guatemala and Honduras. They carved greenstones into images of supernatural entities related to rain and maize and crafted ceremonial forms of agricultural tools made for planting maize seeds (Catalogue Number 2.31; Catalogue Number 2.37). Luminescent and in shades of blue and green, the colors of plants, water, and life, the materials embodied these life-giving substances.[5] Archaeologists have found greenstone deity images and celts in offering caches in Olmec sites like La Venta and at early Maya settlements including Ceibal (Petén, Guatemala), where they were arranged according to the four directions and the center, establishing these locales as cosmic centers. Embodying rain and maize, these objects also were planted underground, both to nourish the earth and to germinate.

"Olmec" or "Olmec-style" also is applied to contemporaneous cultures in Central Mexico (at sites including Las Bocas, in Puebla, Mexico, for example) that created exquisite carved ceramics and imported such ceramics from the south (Catalogue Number 3.27; Catalogue Number 3.29). Cultures contemporaneous with the Olmec developed in other parts of Mesoamerica and can be considered "sister cultures," for they developed into several of Mesoamerica's most important civilizations, including the Zapotec civilization in Oaxaca.

The Zapotec civilization thrived in the Mexican state of Oaxaca, and its most important site, Monte Albán, was founded about 500 BCE on a hilltop overlooking the Oaxaca Valley. At this striking location and at other sites, the Zapotecs constructed religious, administrative, and residential structures; underneath their palaces, they built multiroom tombs as homes for their ancestors, layering the worlds of the living and the ancestors. The deceased were laid prone on tomb floors, and walls held offering niches and were painted or carved with images of deities, ancestors, and penitents. On the floor were censers whose modeled ceramic forms portrayed seated ancestors and deities of rain, corn, and lightning (Catalogue Number 2.40; Catalogue Number 4.60). Descendants visited these tombs to make offerings of food, fire, and incense to their ancestors. Monte Albán was a principal Zapotec center for more than a millennium, but in the fourteenth century, Mixtec people took over the dramatic site and used the older tombs to bury their dead.

The great city of Teotihuacan was founded in the first century CE in the Teotihuacan Valley in Central Mexico. Constructed on a grid oriented both to the cardinal directions and to surrounding mountains, Teotihuacan grew into the largest city in the Americas in its day. Enormous pyramids arose along the prominent north-south axis, the Street of the Dead, and large, multifamily residential compounds were built in the city center and periphery. Painted on the walls of the pyramids and residential compounds were polychrome murals portraying deities such as the Storm God and Feathered Serpent, religious narratives like the fall of the Great Bird (a story also known from the Maya region), and penitents making offerings.[6]

Teotihuacan was a cosmopolitan city, with immigrants and visitors from throughout Mesoamerica and goods imported from far-flung places. Materials and objects from Teotihuacan, including green obsidian from the nearby Pachuca mines, were traded across Mesoamerica, and in Oaxaca, Veracruz, the Petén, highland Guatemala, and the Pacific Coast, people imported Teotihuacan goods and created artworks inspired by Teotihuacan forms (Catalogue Number 4.34; Catalogue Number 4.77). Following the fall of Teotihuacan circa 600, a power vacuum cleared the way for emerging new polities in Tlaxcala, Morelos, Hidalgo, and elsewhere in Central Mexico (circa 600–1000). In these diverse locations, artists developed eclectic styles that drew from Teotihuacan traditions and participated in shared styles and techniques from across Mesoamerica, including the Maya region.

Kaminaljuyú, another grand metropolis, was constructed in the Valley of Guatemala beginning about 1500 BCE and was occupied for more than 2,500 years. This magnificent city of adobe architecture has been largely destroyed or covered by Guatemala City. Kaminaljuyú artists made extraordinary sculptures out of volcanic rock onto which they carved images of humans and zoomorphic deities, including the jaguar rain deity (Catalogue Number 2.14). Some are comparable to second-century Maya sculptural styles in the Petén.

In the fifth century, ceramic artisans in the Petén, Teotihuacan, Kaminaljuyú, and the Pacific Coast created works that integrated artistic styles from these regions. This is especially apparent in Escuintla, along the Pacific Coast, where artists produced tripod cylinder vessels and theater-style censers with local and Teotihuacan-style imagery. Cacao imagery is common

5. Karl A. Taube, "The Symbolism of Jade in Classic Maya Religion," *Ancient Mesoamerica* 16(2005): 23 - 50; Karl A. Taube, "Lightning Celts and Corn Fetishes: The Formative Olmec and the Development of Maize Symbolism in Mesoamerica and the American Southwest," in *Olmec Art and Archaeology: Social Complexity in the Formative Period*, in Studies in the History of Art 58, eds. John E. Clark and Mary Pye (Washington, DC: National Gallery of Art, 2000): 297 - 337.
6. Jesper Nielsen and Christophe Helmke, "The Fall of the Great Celestial Bird: A Master Myth in Early Classic Central Mexico," *Ancient America* 13 (2015).

7. Oswaldo Chinchilla Mazariegos, "Human Sacrifice and Divine Nourishment in Mesoamerica: The Iconography of Cacao on the Pacific Coast of Guatemala," *Ancient Mesoamerica* 27 (2016): 361–75.

8. Karl A. Taube, "Flower Mountain: Concepts of Life, Beauty, and Paradise among the Classic Maya," *RES: Anthropology and Aesthetics* 45 (Spring 2004):69–98.

9. Karl A. Taube, William Saturno, David Stuart, and Heather Hurst, *The Murals of San Bartolo, El Petén, Guatemala, Part 2: The West Wall*, in *Ancient America* 10 (Barnardsville, NC: Center for Ancient American Studies, 2010).

10. Karl A. Taube, "Where Earth and Sky Meet: The Sea in Ancient and Contemporary Maya Cosmology," in *Fiery Pool: The Maya and the Mythic Sea*, eds. Daniel Finamore and Stephen D. Houston (Salem, MA: Peabody Essex Museum, 2010), 204; Erik Velásquez García, "The Maya Flood Myth and the Decapitation of the Cosmic Caiman," *The PARI Journal* 7, no. 1 (2006):1–10.

11. PopolVuh: Sacred Book of the Quiché Maya People, transl. Allen-Christenson, electronic version of original 2003 publication (2007). Mesoweb: www.mesoweb.com/publications/Christenson/PopolVuh.pdf. The PopolVuh was recorded centuries after the Classic period. Maya cultures had experienced drastic changes over those centuries, especially with the arrival of Europeans and Christianity, but there are important parallels between the Classic-period and sixteenth-century narratives.

in artworks from the Pacific Coast, a cacao-growing region (Catalogue Number 4.79).[7] Because the Pacific Coast sites have been heavily looted, our historical knowledge of them remains limited, and we do not know what languages the ancient people of Kaminaljuyú or the Pacific Coast spoke.

The Aztec Empire, the last, great indigenous civilization of Mesoamerica, flourished from about 1325 to 1521. The Aztec capital, Tenochtitlan, was another gridded cosmopolitan city, but its grid was composed not only of streets but also of canals. From here the Aztecs expanded across Mesoamerica, trading with or conquering other civilizations, from which they demanded tribute and appropriated those cultures' artistic traditions. They worshiped a rain deity, Tlaloc, whose form emulated the Teotihuacan Storm God, and male and female deities of water, maize, and other forces of nature (Catalogue Number 2.38). They created stone sculptures of these entities and placed them in temples and at springs, caves, and other landscape locations.

In 1521, the Aztec Empire fell to Spanish invaders, and its capital eventually was transformed into the City of Mexico and the capital of the viceroyalty of New Spain. Other indigenous kingdoms and dynasties—including the K'iche' Maya at Q'umarkaj (El Quiché, Guatemala) and the Cocom Maya at Mayapán (Yucatán, Mexico)—were likewise conquered in the sixteenth century. The period following the Spanish Conquest of these kingdoms is generally referred to as the Colonial Period or the Viceregal Period. This catalogue includes references to stories recorded during this period that shed light on ancient images, texts, and archaeological contexts.

Mesoamerica's history is rich and diverse, but one constant was an intense engagement with forces of nature, as people worked to honor and propitiate these entities in hopes of being compensated with water, food, and other necessities to sustain life.

The Maya Cosmos

The Maya, as did many Mesoamerican cultures, perceived the cosmos to be essentially animate, infused by supernatural beings that were manifestations of natural forces, such as rain and water. The movements of the sun, the primary orienting entity of the cosmos, organize the earth and cosmos into a five-part structure associated with the cardinal directions plus the center (figure 5). Each part has a related color, usually red, yellow, white, black, or green. The cosmos also is layered, comprising sky, earth, and underworld. Celestial entities travel across the sky in the day and night and also journey to the underworld. Ancestors live in a celestial paradise known as Ho Janahb Witz (Five Flower Mountain), a fragrant, paradisiacal place that is also the flowery road of the sun's path.[8]

Maya creation stories, known both from Mayan- and Spanish-language accounts (which were recorded in Latin letters in the sixteenth century and later) and reconstructed from ancient sources, tell of trees erected in the five parts of the world in a clockwise or counterclockwise order. Maya cities, buildings, tombs, and sculptures were organized and arranged according to this structure, which could be articulated in circular or squared form (Catalogue Number 1.1; Catalogue Number 1.2). Ritual performance also followed this plan, tracing the east-west solar path across the sky or moving in circular formation. The painted murals on the West Wall of the San Bartolo (Guatemala) Pinturas Sub-1 building illustrate four young lords offering animals and blood (from their pierced penises) to four fruit trees that undoubtedly relate to the cardinal directions; and the Maize God makes an offering to a fifth tree, presumably that of the center (figure 6).[9]

The Maya envisioned the earth as a turtle, crocodile, or other aquatic reptile floating in the primordial waters. Mountains are the ridges on the reptile's bumpy back, and earthquakes happen when the creature moves abruptly. In some ancient and Post-Conquest Maya and Central Mexican narratives, the earth and sky are created from the body of a caiman or other large reptile that is decapitated or otherwise torn apart, producing a flood of water or blood and ushering in a new cosmic order.[10] In several Classic-period images, the turtle earth appears to be whole but is cracked open for the Maize God's rebirth. Indeed, an overarching conception is of an animate earth that contains natural or man-made openings through which deities, humans, ancestors, plants, and animals move to traverse the cosmic levels, either for death, rebirth, or contact with supernatural beings.

During the Classic period, and in Post-Conquest narratives, the underworld is represented as a place of darkness or an aquatic locale. The *PopolVuh*, recorded in the sixteenth century in the K'iche' Mayan language, describes the Lords of Xibalba (the K'iche' underworld) as beings of sickness and death, with names like One Death, Seven Death, Flying Scab, Gathered Blood, and Pus Demon, who battle entities associated with the sun, moon, and maize.[11] Classic-period images depict analogous battles between God L, an underworld deity, and deities of the sun, moon, and maize. Yet the underworld is not always menacing; it is also the watery place that deities and nobles enter when they die. *Och ha'* (water-entering) is one metaphor for death, and in scenes from Preclassic San Bartolo, Late Classic Tikal, and elsewhere, the dead or dying Maize God (doubled with the human ruler) is shown diving into water or entering via canoe. It is from these dark waters that the resurrecting Maize God or human rulers are reborn (figure 18).

Resurrection, contact with supernatural entities, or other movement across cosmic realms takes place through water and other portals such as caves, ballcourts, reptilian jaws, or the solar centipede maw, the portal through which the sun emerges every morning.[12] Caves—called ch'e'en—also were physical and symbolic entrances to mountains. In Maya and Aztec mythology, maize and other foods were originally stored in mountains, and animals and deities helped humans acquire them. The San Bartolo North Wall mural pictures one version of this myth, showing the Maize God receiving a bowl of corn tamales and a flowering gourd from an animate, zoomorphic cave sprouting plants and flowers (figure 7).[13] The K'iche' Maya called this primordial mountain Paxil (Split), and the Aztecs called it Tonacatepetl (Mountain of Sustenance). Caves and mountains also were the homes of rain, thunder, and lightning deities and the locales for rain ceremonies and other communication rites with supernatural entities and ancestors.[14] The tree at the center of the universe is another axis mundi that joins cosmic realms, and buildings, monuments, and buried offerings can establish links connecting them. Likewise, Maya rulers and ritual specialists could traverse cosmic realms through ritual performance.

Maya site-planning and architecture re-created these primordial landscapes. Prominent in each site were pyramids, generally four-sided terraced structures. These emulated mountains, and some, such as the Temple of the Inscriptions at Palenque, were partially built on mountains (figure 8). This type of building was named *witz* (mountain); thus their shapes and their names emphasized mountains. Generally a central stairway led to a superstructure composed of one or more rooms, often including a shrine where fire and other ceremonies were performed. Named *chan-ch'e'en* (sky-cave), these shrines also embodied mythological places where deities and ancestors dwelled.[15] A pyramid also could be a *muknal* (burial-hill): the Temple of the Inscriptions was made to hold the tomb of K'inichJanahbPakal of Palenque, who was interred in a sarcophagus on which Pakal is rendered with aspects of the sun, maize, and lightning deities and emerging from the centipede maw. The superstructure—or sky-cave—was a place for venerating Pakal and other cherished ancestors and deities.

Venerating ancestors was an essential part of Maya religion and politics. Descendants frequently made offerings to their ancestors, and numerous inscriptions connecting the actions of the living to those of their predecessors provided a fundamental way to demonstrate legitimization for rulership. Furthermore, at several sites, rulers were numbered in order of rule from a dynasty founder, and dynastic lists were created for public and private contexts. In the Calakmul region, artists painted dynastic lists on small polychrome ceramic vessels (figure 9). The Hieroglyphic Stairway of Copán lists the ruling dynasty over four centuries. Carved into the stairway risers, it is the longest extant text of the Maya world.[16] A person ascending the stairway traversed accounts of rulers' lives, culminating in the shrine honoring the founder.

Ancestors and powerful natural phenomena—forces of nature—were present in the Maya world and could be felt, heard, or otherwise perceived even when not visible. These were manifest in solar light, wind, rain, and lightning; when artists materialized them in anthropomorphic and zoomorphic form; or when people impersonated or conjured them, using aromas and song to call deities who took form in smoke and fire. According to the PopolVuh, when the gods first created man, they could see far and wide, but the deities soon dulled their vision, blinding them "like breath upon the face of a mirror."[17] Nevertheless, priests were "seers" who could see beyond the quotidian world, whether in dreams and visions induced by hallucinogens, during extreme physical abstinence, or by using divination tools such as the murky, reflective surfaces of water or obsidian or pyrite mirrors.

Renderings of supernaturals portrayed them sometimes as only partially visible, in a cartouche or emerging from an open maw, signaling that what is seen is only a glimpse of what exists (Catalogue Number 2.16; Catalogue Number 4.60; Catalogue Number 4.59). Alternatively, they are represented on a three-dimensional form that must be turned to reveal the remainder of the image (Catalogue Number 4.64). These are visual or physical metaphors of the ritual action required to view and experience more of the supernatural world. In these ways, both the seen and the unseen were important modes for Classic-period Maya artists and ritual specialists, who straddled and accentuated the permeable border between the seen and unseen.

Art and Writing

For the Classic-period Maya, art and writing were sacred acts used to depict and describe people, deities, and actions, and to connect humans to the divine. Scribes or artists are represented in the form of deities, anthropomorphic rabbits or monkeys, and humans. However, even when portrayed as human, they display characteristics associating them with the supernatural, such as mirror signs on their skin or water lilies in their headdresses (figure 10 and 1.21). Likewise, a carved bone from Tikal features a painter's hand emerging from a solar centipede portal, indicating the artist's hand comes from the otherworld and suggesting that artistic inspiration is divine. Deities can be named as artisans

12. Karl A. Taube, "Maws of Heaven and Hell: The Symbolism of the Centipede and Serpent in Classic Maya Religion," in Antropología de la Eternidad: La Muerteen la Cultura Maya, eds. A. Ciudad Ruiz, M. H. Ruz Sosa, and M. J. Iglesias Ponce de León (Madrid; Mexico: Sociedad Española de Estudios Mayas and Centro de Estudios Mayas, Universidad Nacional Autónoma de México, 2002).
13. William A.Saturno, Karl A. Taube, and David Stuart,The Murals of San Bartolo, El Petén, Guatemala, Part 1: The North Wall, in Ancient America 7 (Barnardsville, NC: Center forAncient American Studies, 2005).
14. Evon Z.Vogt and David Stuart, "–Some Notes on Ritual Caves among the Ancient and Modern Maya," in In the Maw of the Earth Monster: Mesoamerican Ritual Cave Use, eds. James E. Brady and Keith M. Prufer (Austin: University of Texas Press, 2005), 155–85; James E. Brady, "Uncovering the Dark Secrets of the Maya—The Archeology of Maya Caves," in Maya: Divine Kings of the Rainforest, ed. Nikolai Grube (Potsdam, Germany: H. F. Ullmann, 2012), 296–307.
15. Vogt and Stuart, "Some Notes on Ritual Caves," 156.
16. WilliamFash, "Dynastic Architectural Programs: Intention and Design in Classic Maya Buildings at Copán and Other Sites," in *Function and Meaningin Classic Maya Architecture*, ed. Stephen Houston (Washington, DC: Dumbarton Oaks, 1998), 223–70.
17. *PopolVuh*, transl. Christenson, 188.

18. DavidStuart, "Hieroglyphs on Maya Vessels," in *The Maya Vase Book, A Corpus of Rollout Photographs of Maya Vases, Volume 1*, ed. Justin Kerr (New York: Kerr Associates, 1989), 149–60.

19. DavidStuart, *Ten Phonetic Syllables. Research Reports on Ancient Maya Writing* 14 (Washington, DC, Center for Maya Research, 1987); Michael Coe, *Breaking the Maya Code*, 3rd ed. (New York: Thames & Hudson, 2012).

20. MichaelCarrasco, "From Field to Hearth: An Earthly Interpretation of Maya and Other Mesoamerican Creation Myths," In *Pre-Columbian Foodways: Interdisciplinary Approaches to Food, Culture, and Markets in Ancient Mesoamerica*, eds. John Edward Staller and Michael Carrasco (New York: Springer, 2010), 601–34.

21. For more on regional styles, see Dorie Reents-Budet, *Painting the Maya Universe: Royal Ceramics of the Classic Period* (Durham, NC: Duke University Press, 1994); Mary Ellen Miller and Megan E. O'Neil, *Maya Art and Architecture*, 2nd ed. (New York: Thames & Hudson, 2014): 182–209; Bryan R.Just, *Dancing into Dreams: Maya Vase Painting of the Ik' Kingdom* (Princeton, NJ: Princeton University Art Museum, 2012).

too. The authors of the *PopolVuh* describe the creator deities as *tz'akol*(framer) and *b'itol*(shaper), titles of artisans. These deities attempted to shape people from unfired clay and carved wood but failed, finally settling on maize dough as the ideal material. By naming them artisans, particularly ones who experimented with materials, the *PopolVuh* links them to living artisans who re-created divine work whenever they crafted spaces, buildings, objects, and images. Moreover, it is often through the artist's hand that deities are made visible and material.

Artists were esteemed members of ancient Maya society. Depictions of scribes painting or pointing to books, communicating with other artists, or standing near a ruler in a palace scene indicate the interactive and performative nature of scribal work. They were called its'at (wise person). Or they were named by their practice: for example, *ahtz'ihb* (writer, painter) referred to those who painted with a brush or quill pen. The verb root also appears in dedication statements painted on the rims of many polychrome vessels (Catalogue Number 1.21; Catalogue Number1.24; Catalogue Number1.25; Catalogue Number 1.27).[18]There also are titles for those who carved images and texts onto ceramic vessels and stone sculptures (Catalogue Number 1.26). Some have deciphered the word as yuxul, which may derive from the verb for "polish," but this reading is debated.

Mayan hieroglyphic writing is composed of syllabograms and logograms that represent sounds from Common Mayan, ancestral to Mayan languages spoken today. A syllabogram stands for a syllable, generally a combination of a consonant and a vowel, and these were joined together to form words; for example, *pa + ka + la = pakal*(shield). A logogram—a sign that stands for a word—sometimes resembles the element to which it refers. Many Mayan words end with a consonant; scribes spelled this consonant with an extra syllable, but the last vowel is silent. Syllabograms also complement logograms and clarify which word is intended, as when Palenque scribes added the syllable *la* at the bottom of the logogram for *pakal*(figure 11).

Scribes were highly trained, creativity and innovation in spelling and calligraphy were prized, and the graphic nature of the script was celebrated.[19] Nonetheless, there were artists who did not know how to write and made what we call "pseudo-glyphs," which look like texts and carried the prestige of writing but are not legible (Catalogue Number 3.8).

The Maya used a vigesimal (based on the number twenty) numbering system. Circles standing for one and bars standing for five were put together in numbers up to twenty. The Maya discovered the concept of zero, which allowed them to manipulate numbers in a place-based notation system employed for calendars and accounting. Calendar systems included a 260-day sacred calendar and a 365-day solar calendar that together repeated every 52 years. The Long Count tracked dates from a day in mythological time that correlates with August 14, 3114 BCE. That date, written as its Calendar Round date of 4 Ajaw 8 Kumk'u or with its Long Count date of 13.0.0.0.0, was the start of a new temporal cycle of about 5,125 years; on this date, as recounted on the *Vase of the Eleven Gods,tz'akajk'uh* (the gods were ordered) (figure 12a). The Maya envisioned earlier temporal cycles, in which deities were born and acceded to rulership,[20]and cycles and events in the distant future, as recounted at Palenque. The Maya used these calendars both to track celestial bodies and to record events in the lives of rulers and other nobles. This system was probably exploited for mundane purposes of accounting, although such texts, likely written on paper, bamboo, or other perishable materials, have not survived.

Maya inscriptions, generally read from top to bottom and left to right in paired columns, were inscribed and painted in large formats, in contexts such as building exteriors, interior walls, and stone and wood monuments, as well as on small items including ceramic vessels and figurines, bone implements, and shell and jadeite jewelry. Dedication texts name the building or thing, the date installed, and the person who dedicated or owned it. Dedication texts on polychrome ceramic vessels usually identify the vessel type and contents, such as *uk'ib* (drinking vessel) for kakaw (chocolate) or *ul*(maize gruel), and the owner. Dedication texts on stone monuments customarily are longer, beginning with a lengthy date tying the event to the movements of celestial entities.

Polychrome ceramics, comprising a distinctive Classic Maya art form, were made in diverse temporal and regional styles. The ceramics in the LACMA collection came through the art market, not from archaeological excavations, but we frequently can identify region of origin by studying the vessel shape, painting style, or textual references to persons or polities. For example, lidded basal-flange cache vessels in the form of animals are characteristic of third- to-sixth-century ceramics from the northern Petén and southern Campeche (Catalogue Number 4.73; Catalogue Number 4.47). Tripod cylinder vessels, often with lids, were made in the Maya region during the fourth through sixth centuries, following extensive contact with Teotihuacan (Catalogue Number 3.12).

Maya artists from the seventh to ninth centuries created taller cylinder vessels, usually without feet or lids, and painted or carved complex pictorial narratives around their exteriors. Distinctive vessels from the Holmul-Naranjo region in northeast Guatemala and northwest Belize are characterized by a red and orange palette and scenes of the dancing Maize God

(Catalogue Numbe 2.21). The intricate pictorial narratives of Ik'-kingdom vessels, from near Motul de San José, Guatemala, are illustrated in multiple colors and made in several sub-styles, including the Pink Glyphs Style (Catalogue Number 4.1).[21] Codex-style vessels, painted with cream or white backgrounds, black and brown lines for images and texts, and red borders, come from the northern Petén and southern Campeche (Catalogue Number 4.60).[22] These prized portable items were shared within and across polities. The vessels in the LACMA collection comprise a rich source for understanding ancient Maya mythology but must be understood in relation to materials excavated from archaeological sites.

No Classic-period codices (books) survive, but they are portrayed on vessels as stacked pages covered by jaguar pelts (Catalogue Number 1.21). The four surviving Postclassic Maya books—*Dresden Codex, Madrid Codex, Paris Codex, and Grolier Codex*— offer useful comparisons (figures 5, 13, 16, 27). These bark-paper books are painted with white or cream backgrounds, black lines for images and texts, and red borders, the same palette as the Late Classic–period vessels called "codex-style." Classic-period books probably were similar to both codex-style vessels and Postclassic books and held abundant sacred imagery and texts.

Supernatural Entities of Sky, Earth, Water, and Underworld

Introduction

The word k'uh, often translated as "god" or "deity," means sacred essence or sacred entity.[23] K'uhul, when used as an epithet for people, buildings, and things, indicated that they were energized by this sacred essence. Maya deities were generally associated with one of the cosmic realms of sky, earth, or underworld, but they moved throughout the cosmos, either on a daily or an annual basis or during conjuring rituals.

Artists illustrated an array of Maya deities with anthropomorphic and zoomorphic characteristics. Some, like the Maize God, appear youthful, and others are aged, with wrinkled faces and sunken mouths resulting from tooth loss. They frequently bear clues, such as spiral or squared pupils (for special vision), signaling that they are supernatural, or mirror signs on their skin to show their shininess. Or, they are human-animal hybrids, though they often are portrayed performing human activities, including sitting on a throne, writing in a book, or holding a child. Indeed, the worlds of humans and gods mirrored and overlapped, with gods acting like humans, and humans dressed as gods.[24]

Scholars' efforts to categorize the plethora of Maya supernatural entities have proven productive yet tricky, due to the complexity of Maya theology. Scholar Paul Schell has identified distinct deities in Postclassic codices, giving them letters of the alphabet, such as God A or God B. Anthropologist Karl Taube identified their Classic-period counterparts, and others have deciphered their ancient names.[25] But Maya theology challenges such endeavors in several ways. First, deities had multiple manifestations and could exist in pairs or groups of four, each with different colors and characteristics, in alignment with the quadripartite structure of the cosmos.[26] Second, deities could merge with one another, taking on physical characteristics and powers of others, a concept epigrapher Simon Martin calls "theosynthesis."[27] Moreover, one phrase for Maya gods, pikk'uh, literally "eighhousand gods" but meaning a "multitude of gods," suggests they are not quantifiable.[28]

Aged Deities of Sky and Earth

A major aged deity inhabiting the sky, ItzamKokaaj (also known as God D or Itzamna, as recorded in the sixteenth century) is a creator god associated with wisdom, writing, and knowledge (figure 13). Pervasive throughout the universe, he appears in anthropomorphic and avian form and blends with multiple supernatural entities.[29] In anthropomorphic form, he wears the garb of Maya priests, and some images show him enthroned, with animals and other divinities in deference before him, much like palace scenes with human rulers and visitors. He also is associated with the earth- and sky-crocodiles, which relates to his role in world creation. In avian form, he is YaxKokaajMuut (nicknamed the Principal Bird Deity by scholars today).[30]

Itzam Kokaaj

An earth deity, God N (an aged entity who may be another manifestation of God D) frequently emerges from portals such as a turtle or mollusk shell. But he also appears as a sky-bearer, at times in quadripartite manifestations at the earth's four corners. Post-Conquest texts refer to this sky-bearer as *pawatun* or *bakab*; the *bakab* appellation is used as a noble title in the Classic period, likely associating its bearers with this important figure.

Solar and Lunar Deities

The ancient Maya envisioned multiple solar entities whose manifestations embodied the sun on its journey over the course of a day and night, from the sky to the underworld and back again, and over the course of a solar year. K'inich Ajaw, the diurnal solar deity, is a mature male with squared pupils, large nose, T-shaped front tooth, and *k'in* (sun) signs on his face. The Jaguar God of the Underworld is the sun at night as it moves through the underworld and sometimes has *akbal*

22. RichardHansen, Ronald L. Bishop, and Federico Fahsen, "Notes on Maya Codex-style Ceramics from Nakbe, Petén, Guatemala," Ancient Mesoamerica 2, no 2(1991): 225–43; Sylviane Boucher and YolyPalomo, "Discriminación Visual como-determinante de estilo y asignación-tipológica de la cerámicaceódice de Calakmul, Campeche," Estudios de culturamaya 39 (2012): 99–132.

23. StephenHouston and David Stuart, "Of Gods, Glyphs, and Kings: Divinity and Rulership among the Classic Maya," Antiquity 70 (1996): 289–312;DavidStuart, "The Gods of Heaven and Earth: Evidence of Ancient Maya Categories of Deities," in Homenaje a Alfredo López Austin (unpublished manuscript, 2012): 7–8.

24. Mary EllenMiller and Simon Martin, Courtly Art of the Ancient Maya (San Francisco: Fine Arts Museums of San Francisco, 2004), 5.

25. PaulSchellhas, Representation of Deities of the Maya Manuscripts, Papers of the Peabody Museum of American Archaeology and Ethnology, Harvard University4, no. 1 (1904);Karl A. Taube,The Major Gods of Ancient Yucatan(Washington DC: Dumbarton Oaks, 1992).

26. Stuart, "The Gods of Heaven and Earth," 5–6.

27. SimonMartin, "The Old Man of the Maya Universe: A Unitary Dimension to Ancient Maya Religion," in Maya Archaeology 3, eds. Charles Golden, Stephen Houston, and Joel Skidmore (San Francisco: PrecolumbiaMesoweb Press, 2015), 186–227.

28. Stuart, "The Gods of Heaven and Earth," 15.

29. KarenBassie-Sweet, *Maya Sacred Geography and the Creator Deities* (Norman, OK: University of Oklahoma Press, 2008),137; Martin, "The Old Man of the Maya Universe."

30. Nielsen and Helmke, "The Fall of the Great Celestial Bird."

31. Karl Taube and Stephen Houston, "Masks and Iconography," in *Temple of the Night Sun: A Royal Tomb at El Diablo, Guatemala*, eds. Stephen Houston, Sarah Newman, Edwin Román, and Thomas Garrison (San Francisco: Precolumbia Mesoweb Press, 2015), 213.

32. Susan Milbrath, *Star Gods of the Maya. Astronomy in Art, Folklore, and Calendars* (Austin: University of Texas Press, 1999), 141.

33. Nielsen and Helmke, "The Fall of the Great Celestial Bird."

34. Ana García Barrios, *Chaahk, el dios de la lluvia, en el periodo clásico maya: aspectos religiosos y políticos*, PhD dissertation (Madrid: Universidad Complutense, 2009), 170, 183, 205; Kasper Wrem Anderson and Christophe Helmke, "The Personifications of Celestial Water: The Many Guises of the Storm God in the Pantheon and Cosmology of Teotihuacan, Contributions in New World Archaeology 5 (2013): 170, 183; James Doyle, "Creation Narratives on Ancient Maya Codex–Style Ceramics in the Metropolitan Museum," *Metropolitan Museum Journal* 51 (2016): 42–63.

35. Karl A. Taube, "The Breath of Life: The Symbolism of Wind in Mesoamerica and the American Southwest," in *The Road to Aztlan: Art from a Mythic Homeland*, eds. Virginia M. Fields and Victor Zamudio-Taylor (Los Angeles: Los Angeles County Museum of Art, 2001), 104.

36. Bassie-Sweet, *Maya Sacred Geography and the Creator Deities*, 103; Nicholas P. Dunning and Stephen Houston, "Chan Ik: Hurricanes as a Disruptive Force in the Maya Lowlands," in *Ecology, Power, and Religion in Maya Landscapes*, eds. C. Isendahl and B. L. Persson (Berlin: Verlag Anton Saurwein, 2011), 58–67.

37. John E. Staller and Brian Stross, *Lightning in the Andes and Mesoamerica: Pre–Columbian, Colonial, and Contemporary Perspectives* (New York: Oxford University Press, 2013), 124.

38. Bassie-Sweet, *Maya Sacred Geography and the Creator Deities*, 20.

(night or darkness) signs on his cheeks. He also is a god of fire and warfare, and his face adorns war shields. K'inich Ajaw and the Jaguar God of the Underworld may be eastern and western aspects of the Sun God, respectively. Another solar deity (today known as the Shark Sun God) has shark features and rises from the underworld via the eastern waters through a portal shaped like a centipede maw.[31]

The Moon Goddess is a young woman, often depicted with a characteristic lunar crescent and holding a rabbit, which may be her child. The older Ix Chel,[32] a goddess of childbirth, medicine, and divination, is an aged midwife and appears in some scenes with the moon goddess. Solar and lunar deities also were portrayed in narratives of conflict with other supernatural entities, such as God L, in scenes that recount the victory of celestial beings over underworld ones. On one polychrome ceramic vessel, the underworld deity God L, submissive and stripped of his characteristic cloak and hat, kneels before the enthroned moon goddess and rabbit, who holds God L's hat (figure 15). This scene relates to a larger myth in which the rabbit has stolen God L's finery, a narrative presumably about the triumph of celestial bodies over underworld entities.

The Hero Twins—the youthful male hunters and ballplayers whose adventures are narrated in the *Popol Vuh*—also may be considered solar and lunar entities, for ultimately they rise as the sun and the moon. In Classic-period images, the Hero Twins (Hunahpu and Xbalanque) and their father (the Maize God) are among the beings who battle God L and other lords of darkness. Furthermore, in both ancient and Post-Conquest narratives, one of the Hero Twins' primordial acts is the defeat of the Great Bird, which prefigures the rising of a new sun.[33]

Water, Rain, Storms, and Lightning

Entities of water (*ha'*) in various forms—including rain, storms, pools, and clouds—and associated atmospheric phenomena of thunder and lightning were interrelated and crucial to maintaining balance between the nourishing moisture needed for agriculture and sustaining human life and destructive elements such as floods, hurricanes, frost, and drought. Because rain, storms, lightning, and maize overlap in nature, the anthropomorphic embodiments of these appear with similar characteristics, which indicates a conception that these entities overlapped, merged, and separated according to different circumstances and atmospheric phenomena.

Chahk, deity of rain, rainstorms, lightning, and thunder, is manifest in quadripartite form and is associated with the four directions and their colors. He generally is rendered with an anthropomorphic body and a human or serpentine face with a long upper lip (figure 16). His names (in Classic-period inscriptions as well as in Post-Conquest texts) refer to different types of rain and related phenomena, such as first rain, morning fog, and fire in the sky (lightning).[34] Chahk is water in all its forms and inhabits multiple realms: he can be celestial, in the clouds, or in a cave, where rain clouds are formed. Chahk frequently wields a hand-stone, axe, or serpent to generate lightning or to make sacrifices (Catalogue Number 2.11).

Wind (*ik'*) was another fundamental force of nature that was both necessary and dangerous. Wind clears the way to bring rains and carries rain-bearing clouds.[35] The hieroglyph for wind, a T-shaped form, also was the word for the breath of life in the human body. Yet too much wind, in the form of hurricanes or windstorms that create fire hazards, could be devastating.[36]

K'awiil, the lightning god, is rendered in anthropomorphic form, with a human body whose right leg is a serpent (figure 17). A fiery torch emerges from a mirror in the forehead of his serpentine face (Catalogue Number 2.15). As the embodiment of lightning, K'awiil breaks open the earth for maize growth, and he thus can appear with maize kernels or Maize God characteristics. Because of his ability to create connections among the levels of the universe, he is associated with transformative processes such as birth, rulership accession, and ancestor conjuring. K'awiil is the supernatural entity most commonly portrayed in eccentric flints, which are made from chert, one of the materials thought to result from lightning striking the earth (Catalogue Number 1.4).[37]

The Teotihuacan Storm God, the Central Mexican cognate of these deities of rain, storms, and lightning, wears a characteristic fanged mask. A related being was known as Tlaloc among the Aztec. At Kaminaljuyú, the storm god took the form of a jaguar (Catalogue Number 2.14).

Fruits of the Earth: Maize and Chocolate

Maize was a staple food, and the youthful Maize God, whose sloping forehead evokes a corncob, was a principal deity. His life cycle mimics that of corn in the fields, and images picture that cycle of vitality, death, and rebirth. He dies by entering water or by being decapitated, which is comparable to the act of maize farmers who bend the stalk to cut off the food supply and allow the kernels to harden before removing the ear from the stalk.[38] The Maize God's rebirth is through a ballcourt or a crack in the turtle earth (Catalogue Number 4.42), or he rises out of the dark, primordial waters (figure 18).

Following rebirth the Maize God is dressed by maidens, and he dances gracefully, with arms outstretched, as if he is a corn stalk swaying in the wind. A simple lifting of the heels can indicate dancing, but in some scenes, the feather-bedecked Maize God leaps off the earth, as if a bird. On cylinder vessels, different manifestations of the Maize God and supernatural dwarfs dance together; the maize gods wear enormous feathered backracks holding mountains of creation occupied by different supernatural animals (Catalogue Number 2.20; Catalogue Number.2.21).[39] They perform this dance to renew the world.

Kakaw (chocolate), which comes from pods on the *Theobroma cacao* tree, was another important foodstuff, and a luxury good traded across Mesoamerica (figure 19). The mythology of maize and cacao are closely related; in some conceptions, cacao is one of the fruit trees that grow from the Maize God's body.[40] One vessel in the LACMA collection illustrates the birth of the first cacao tree from the body of a supernatural male figure. The lightning god K'awiil points toward this primordial tree and its abundant cacao pods. In this myth, it probably is lightning that breaks open the earth so that the first cacao tree can emerge (Catalogue Number 2.27).

Chocolate was consumed as a drink, mixed with substances such as corn and flavored with spices and flowers, and also as a sauce on corn tamales and other foods that were served in plain and painted plates and drinking vessels. A common offering in Maya rituals today, chocolate likely was a valued gift for gods and ancestors during the Classic period.

Supernatural Serpents

Serpents are portrayed in myriad forms in Maya art but generally appear as supernatural entities and portals to other cosmic realms. Some supernatural serpents bear physical characteristics of venomous snakes, such as rattlesnakes and the deadly fer-de-lance, or non-venomous but predatory boa constrictors. They are ideal creatures for metaphors of transformation because they regularly shed their skin, which is a process associated with rebirth and renewal, and because they move through different environments—on the earth, underground, in trees, and in water—which can be likened to ritual transformation or conveyance across cosmic realms. The serpent body and mouth thus were portals for movement between realms via birth, death, resurrection, or conjuring. Maya artists accentuated this ability to cross realms by combining serpents with other creatures. The feathered serpent, for example, had serpentine and avian characteristics and could transcend sky, earth, and water; and the serpent with a centipede maw was the portal for the rebirth of the sun and ancestors.

The Water Lily Serpent is part serpentine but associated with aquatic environments. With a water lily pad or flower emerging from its head, or in its headdress, this creature appears in compositions suggesting a watery context (Catalogue Number,1.25).

Water lilies flower at the surface of terrestrial bodies of water, liminal places envisioned at the intersection of earth and underworld, and thus are associated with transformation. However, the role of the Water Lily Serpent in transformation also may relate to the psychoactive qualities of the water lily stalk of *Nymphaea ampla*.[41]

Entities of Darkness and Dreaming

Underworld entities are depicted in subterranean palaces and often in contention with young lords or celestial entities. God L, whose ancient name has not been deciphered, was an aged underworld denizen as well as a cigar-smoking deity of trade and tobacco (figure 19). In some images, he is enthroned in an underworld palace or cave (figures 12a and b). Alternatively, he battles with K'inich Ajaw, the Moon Goddess, the Maize God, or other young deities (figure 15). These images, Classic-period cognates of the Hero Twins battling the Lords of Xibalba, are about the triumph of celestial bodies over underworld deities and of light over darkness. They also may refer to varying stellar patterns in the night sky or to the changes that occur when moving from the dry to the wet season, when the new maize begins to sprout.[42]

Other denizens of darkness, *wahy* entities, cavort in the night and spread sickness (figure 20; Catalogue Number 2.23; Catalogue Number 2.59). The hieroglyph for these *wahy* creatures is a face of *ajaw* (ruler) that is half-covered by a jaguar pelt, and relates to sleeping and dreaming. Some *wahy* beings are named as belonging to rulers and may have been their alter egos who wandered during sleep and cavorted in alternate realms.[43] These supernatural entities are depicted as human skeletons, as zoomorphic creatures with characteristics of multiple animals, or as creatures from whose gaping mouths emerge other bodies (Catalogue Number 2.58). Although some seem cute or humorous, others are portrayed as frightening beings holding plates of human bones or with eyeballs protruding from their sockets. Some of their names are analogous to those of diseases described in sixteenth-century Maya sources. Indeed, these *wahy* entities may have been personified illnesses sent as curses to harm rivals,[44] a form of supernatural warfare that took place alongside—and complemented—the overt military aggression that is known from images and inscriptions on monumental stone sculpture and architecture. The rendering of *wahy* entities holding enema tools or smoking tobacco may relate to the ingestion of hallucinogens to induce altered states and dreaming.

Animals in Maya Art and Religion

Animals, ubiquitous in Classic-period Maya art

---

39. Karl Taube, "The Maya Maize God and the Mythic Origins of Dance," in The Maya and Their Sacred Narratives: Text and Context in Maya Mythologies, Acta Mesoamericana 20, eds. G. Le Fort, R. Gardiol, S. Matteo, and C. Helmke (Markt Schwaben, Germany: Anton Saurwein, 2007), 41–52; Alexandre Tokovinine, Place and Identity in Classic Maya Narratives (Washington, DC: Dumbarton Oaks, 2013), 115–17.

40. Simon Martin, "Cacao in Ancient Maya Religion. First Fruit from the Maize Tree and Other Tales from the Underworld," in Chocolate in Mesoamerica: A Cultural History of Cacao, ed. Cameron L. McNeil (Gainesville: University Press of Florida, 2009), 154–83.

41. J. Andrew McDonald and Brian Stross, "Water Lily and Cosmic Serpent: Equivalent Conduits of the Maya Spirit Realm," *Journal of Ethnobiology* 32, no.1 (Spring/Summer 2012): 74–107.

42. Miller and Martin, Courtly Art of the Ancient Maya, 58–63.

43. Stephen D. Houston and David Stuart, "The *Way* Glyph: Evidence for 'Co-essences' among the Classic Maya," Research Reports on Ancient Maya Writing 30 (Washington, DC: Center for Maya Research, 1989).

44. Nikolai Grube and Werner Nahm, "A Census of Xibalba: A Complete Inventory of WAY Characters on Maya Ceramics," in The Maya Vase Book, Volume 4, ed. Justin Kerr (New York: Kerr Associates, 1994), 686–715; Christophe Helmke and Jesper Nielsen, "Hidden Identity & Power in Ancient Mesoamerica: Supernatural Alter Egos as Personified Diseases," *Acta Americana* 17, no. 2 (2009): 49–98.

and religion, appear in myriad forms and contexts and in an extraordinarily creative range of portrayals. Comparably, the *Popol Vuh* recounts a variety of interactions between humans and animals that reveal shared origins and show humans and animals acting both in conflict and in cooperation. When the creator gods made the animals, they named them "guardians of the forest," but the gods were disappointed when the animals could not speak the gods' names or worship them. Thus, they created humans who were able to worship the gods and command the animals, which would become food for them. Plus, during their multiple experiments in creating humans, some of the failed creations were turned into animals like spider monkeys. Humans (or anthropomorphic deities) who did not behave properly also were transformed into monkeys.

In some cases, animals and humans (or anthropomorphic supernaturals) were in conflict. The Lords of Xibalba used bats to threaten—and defeat—the Hero Twins. At the same time, the Hero Twins were hunters, and one of their victims, the prideful Seven Macaw, claimed to be the sun and had to be defeated for the new sun to emerge. However, their actions as hunters of animals undoubtedly constituted a charter for hunting other animals for food.[45]

Animals also helped the Hero Twins and their family prevail. They assisted the Hero Twins' mother in proving her value to their grandmother by gathering a net full of maize, even though there was only one maize ear in the field.[46] And although the animals initially challenge the Hero Twins by turning their maize field into a forest each night, they later come to their aid. The coati brought the squash that would stand in for Hunahpu's head in the ballgame, and the rabbit hopped away as a distraction so that Hunahpu could retrieve his head. Finally, when the Twins are defeated, they ask that their bones be ground and thrown into the water, and from there they become catfish and are reborn. Moving between anthropomorphic and zoomorphic form is thus the medium for rebirth and survival and also may be associated with practices of ritual transformation in which humans take on qualities of animals to survive certain situations.

We do not have this level of detail from ancient inscriptions, but the diversity of creative animal portrayals in Maya art suggests that such stories were told among the ancient Maya as well. The Popol Vuh stories may have been passed down from prior centuries, for Preclassic- and Classic-period images illustrate similar narratives. For example, scenes of blowgun hunters on polychrome ceramics are close to those of the actions of the Hero Twins, and images on portable ceramics and monumental structures depict the downfall of the Principal Bird Deity.[47] Animals are shown engaging in typical animal-like activities, such as eating or scratching an armpit, however, they are frequently personified, wearing necklaces, headdresses, and loincloths and performing human-like acts, dancing, speaking, or displaying a victim's decapitated head (Catalogue Number 3.4; Catalogue Number 3.7; Catalogue Number 3.16). Some of these likely were considered humorous, for they present animals in unusual—if not impossible—contexts, while others compare humans to creatures like monkeys, who were humans from a prior era of creation, and thereby accentuate their similarities.

Maya rulers and other nobility connected themselves with animals through naming and costuming. The name K'inich Yax K'uk' Mo' of Copán translates as Sun-Faced First Quetzal Macaw and invokes colorful tropical birds related to the sun (figure 21). The name of K'inich Kan Bahlam of Palenque translates as Sun-Faced Sky-Jaguar, referring not simply to the powerful nocturnal predator but to one in the sky. Rulers, warriors, and other nobles are often rendered wearing animal headdresses, including jaguars, crocodiles, serpents, deer, and birds. Wearing these animal forms allowed humans to take on characteristics of those animals. In the Maya area—and throughout Mesoamerica, from ancient times to the present—jaguars are admired and feared for their stealth, strength, and role as apex predators. For this reason, they are symbols of warfare and high social status and exploited for displays of political and spiritual power.[48]

The Maya also used animals for food and religious offerings. They ate deer, turkey, dog, fish, and other creatures, and they dressed in animal products, wearing skirts made of jaguar pelts, headdresses of the resplendent feathers of the quetzal bird, and jewelry from river and ocean shells. Archaeologists have excavated countless offerings of deer, manatee, and bird bones, shells, stingray spines, and other species' body parts,[49] and many images rendered on murals, codices, and ceramics illustrate people and deities making such offerings. These range from young lords making offerings of a deer, turkey, and fish in front of cosmic trees in the Preclassic painted murals at San Bartolo to the deities making offerings before dressed trees in the Dresden Codex, one of four surviving Maya books from the Postclassic period (figures 6 and 26).

Animals also are pervasive in mythological narratives. For example, the child of the moon goddess is a rabbit who helps the celestial deities triumph over the lords of darkness. Deities can have animal characteristics and often are hybrids of humans and multiple animals. Serpents and centipedes are supernatural portals for movement across cosmic realms, and butterflies are perceived as resurrected ancestors. Creatures of the water such as fish, crocodiles, turtles, and frogs, and waterbirds like

---

45. *Popol Vuh*, transl. Christenson, 63–66, 73–77, 106, 130–35.

46. *Popol Vuh*, transl. Christenson, 123–27.

47. Michael D. Coe, "The Hero Twins: Myth and Image," in The Maya Vase Book: A Corpus of Rollout Photographs of Maya Vases, Volume 1 (New York: Kerr Associates, 1989), 161–84.

48. Nicholas J. Saunders, "Predators of Culture: Jaguar Symbolism and Mesoamerican Elites," World Archaeology 26, no. 1 (1994), 105.

49. Mary DeLand Pohl, "The Ethnozoology of the Maya: Faunal Remains from Five Sites in Petén, Guatemala," in Excavations at Seibal, Department of Petén, Guatemala 17, no. 3, ed. Gordon R. Willey (Cambridge, MA: Peabody Museum of Archaeology and Ethnology, 1990), 143–74.

cormorants are valued for their relationship to water; this is not simply because water is a source of life and food but more so because it is perceived as the aquatic underworld. For instance, cormorants carry symbolism of rebirth, since they regularly dive into and emerge from the water.

This exhibition divides animals into creatures of sky, earth, and water, but many animals regularly move across these realms of the universe. In addition, throughout Maya art and religion, real and hybrid animals were chosen for their abilities to live in and traverse different environments, such as sky, trees, land, water, and underground: waterbirds live in water and in the sky; crocodiles traverse water and land; and serpents move freely in water, through trees, on land, and underground. Such creatures appear frequently in mythological narratives. Indeed, being able to cross multiple environments is analogous to traversing cosmic realms and creating links among them, which is a fundamental aspect of Maya religion and politics that is also seen elsewhere in Mesoamerica, for example, in Olmec art.

Divine Rites of Kings and Queens

Introduction

Classic-period Maya kings, queens, and members of royal courts actively engaged animals and the supernatural world in myriad ways. People utilized natural resources to their advantage: they drank water from the sky to nourish their bodies, and they used stone from the earth to build houses, wood from the forest to burn cooking fires, pigments from underground to paint walls, and bones from animals to make tools. Forces of nature animated the universe and both sustained and challenged human society. Because human survival depended on a balance of resources, and given the sublime nature and power of natural forces to nurture as well as destroy, humans fervently revered them. Indeed, throughout Mesoamerica, leaders and other ritual specialists performed propitiatory and other rites as efforts to maintain balance in the cosmos.

Consequently, in many places forces of this animate universe were appropriated into the rhetoric of power. Leaders displayed and manipulated connections with these natural forces as proof of their own power. The actions of these forces could sustain their people, yet they also could be dangerous and were employed to stoke both reverence and fear. In a groundbreaking 1996 essay, epigraphers Stephen Houston and David Stuart explored how Maya rulers situated themselves in relation to the divine, demonstrating that rulers exploited multiple strategies to link themselves with the divine. Among others, they used the k'uhul (holy) title, which indicated they were perceived to be divine; they took on names of deities and impersonated them; and they possessed gods or god effigies who witnessed their actions—and thereby authorized their rule.[50]

Naming and Calendar Anniversaries

In addition to using animal names, Maya nobles' names included those of deities, undoubtedly to draw upon their power and specific strengths. Especially prominent were titles or names of solar deities, including the title K'inich (sun-faced), assumed by Palenque rulers K'inich Janahb Pakal and K'inich K'an Joy Chitam, among others. Use of this title implied that one was imbued with heat and other solar qualities (figure 22a).[51] Others were named Itzam Kokaaj Bahlam, which connected them to the creator deity's wisdom and creative power as well as to jaguars (figure 22b). Those associated with entities of lightning like K'awiil and Yopaht were considered powerful and dangerous but also necessary for life, since they crack open the earth for maize and other plants to emerge.[52] These include Sihyaj Chan K'awiil (Sky-Born K'awiil) from Tikal, K'ahk' Tiliw Chan Yopaht (Lightning That Makes Fire in the Sky) of Quiriguá, and Yopaht Bahlam (Lightning Jaguar), who is named as the owner of a vessel at LACMA (Catalogue Number 1.21). Among those linked with water entities are Sihyaj K'in Chahk (Sun-Born Chahk), a ruler from Machaquilá,[53] and Sihyaj Chan Chahk (Sky-Born Chahk), named on a vessel at LACMA (Catalogue Number 4.76). These correlations with deities continued as rulers died and were transformed into forces of nature.

Maya nobility also made calendrical calculations to link themselves with the births and actions of deities. On the Palenque Temple of the Inscriptions tablets, the accession of K'inich Janahb Pakal is connected to the birth of a deity more than a million years earlier.[54] Furthermore, nobles at many sites performed rites on anniversaries of important events to associate themselves with ancestors and deities who acted on those dates (Catalogue Number 4.69).

Music, Dance, and Impersonation

Music and dance were intrinsic elements of ancient Maya life and ritual. The word k'ayom (singer) was used as a title for Maya elite, and songs were prayers or offerings to ancestors and other supernatural beings. Classic-period images portray musical instruments like drums, rattles, and trumpets in scenes with dancers and ritual processions, and rattles, whistles, and drums were deposited in graves, perhaps after being played at funerals. In images on stone monuments and ceramic vessels, dance can be signified by the word ahk'oot (verb root for "dance") or by a figure's raised heel or elegant hand gestures.[55]

Performed not only for entertainment but also for

50. Houston and Stuart, "Of Gods, Glyphs, and Kings," 289–312.
51. Pierre Robert Colas, "K'inich and King: Naming Self and Person among Classic Maya Rulers," *Ancient Mesoamerica* 14, no. 2 (2003): 269–83.
52. Matthew Looper, *Lightning Warrior: Maya Art and Kingship at Quiriguá* (Austin: University of Texas Press, 2003), 140.
53. Stuart and Houston, "Of Gods, Glyphs, and Kings," 296.
54. David Stuart and George Stuart, *Palenque: Eternal City of the Maya* (London and New York: Thames & Hudson, 2008), 169.
55. Nikolai Grube, "Classic Maya Dance: Evidence from Hieroglyphs and Iconography," *Ancient Mesoamerica* 3 (1992): 206–18; Matthew Looper, *To Be Like Gods: Dance in Ancient Maya Civilization* (Austin: University of Texas Press, 2009).

56. Andrea Stone, "Aspects of Impersonation in Classic Maya Art," in *Sixth Palenque Round Table, 1986*, ed. Virginia M. Fields (Norman, OK: University of Oklahoma Press, 1991), 194–202; Houston and Stuart, "Of Gods, Glyphs, and Kings," 297–300; Stephen Houston, David Stuart, and Karl Taube, *The Memory of Bones: Body, Being, and Experience Among the Classic Maya* (Austin: University of Texas Press, 2006), 270–74.

57. Julie Nehammer Knub, Simone Thun, and Christophe Helmke, "The Divine Rite of Kings: An Analysis of Classic Maya Impersonation Statements," in The Maya and Their Sacred Narratives: Text and Context in Maya Mythologies, Acta Mesoamericana 20, eds. G. Le Fort, R. Gardiol, S. Matteo, and C. Helmke (Markt Schwaben, Germany: Anton Saurwein, 2007), 187.

58. Takeshi Inomata, "Plazas, Performers, and Spectators: Political Theaters of the Classic Maya," Current Anthropology 47, no. 5 (2006): 806, 815–18.

59. Marc Zender, "Sport, Spectacle and Political Theater: New Views of the Classic Maya Ballgame," originally pub. in *The PARI Journal* 4, no. 4 (2004): 10–12.

60. Rex Koontz, "Ballcourt Rites, Paradise, and the Origins of Power in Classic Veracruz," in *Pre-Columbian Landscapes of Creation and Origin*, ed. John E. Staller (New York: Springer, 2008).

61. Stuart and Houston, "Of Gods, Glyphs, and Kings," 302–7.

62. Stuart and Stuart, *Palenque: Eternal City of the Maya*, 167.

63. Stephen Houston and Karl Taube, "An Archaeology of the Senses: Perception and Cultural Expression," *Ancient Mesoamerica* 10, no. 2 (2000): 271–73; Christopher T. Morehart, David L. Lentz, and Keith M. Prufer, "Wood of the Gods: Ritual Use of Pine (*Pinus spp*) by the Ancient Lowland Maya," *Latin American Antiquity* 16, no. 3 (2005): 255–74; David Stuart, "'The Fire Enters His House': Architecture and Ritual in Classic Maya Texts," in *Function and Meaning in Classic Maya Architecture*, ed. Stephen D. Houston (Washington,

engagement with and impersonation of supernatural entities, music and dance enabled Maya nobles to tap into and embody supernatural forces. Images of rulers and other nobles dancing and dressed as animals or supernatural beings such as the Maize God are depicted in many media, including stone monuments and ceramic figurines and vessels. Some show a figure clearly in costume, while on others, the identity of the dancer and the impersonated entity are fused.[56]

Costumed individuals may transform into the entities whose accoutrements they wear, and the costume may facilitate that transformation. Next to some figures is the phrase *u-baah-il a'n* ("it is the image in impersonation of"), followed by the name of a supernatural and then the name of the person embodying that being. A carved lintel from the Yaxchilán region depicts a female in a lunar cartouche, showing that she has transformed into an ancestor; the text and her headdress also denote that she appears in the guise of the Water Lily Serpent (figure 24). Images of rulers dressed as the Maize God are often ambiguous and double as portrayals of both the rulers themselves and the impersonated deity. But these transformations were not always illustrated and instead could be recorded textually. The owner of a Chamá-style cylinder vessel is named as an impersonator of Wuk Chapaht K'inich Nohol Yok'in, a version of the solar deity; the incorporation of this impersonation phrase may indicate that the divine presence remained in his persona following the impersonation event (figure 24).[57]

Complementing these supernatural associations involved in music and dance were their respective roles in social integration, for public performances could attract people from dispersed settlements and make them feel part of larger communities ruled by the *k'uhul ajaw*.[58]

Ballgame

The ballgame was another vibrant ritual in the Maya area and across Mesoamerica that was significant for religion, politics, and social cohesion. Indeed, images of the ballgame portray not only players but also musicians and spectators, and the archaeological record provides evidence of feasting around ballcourts.[59] Varieties of the ballgame were played in different regions, and some communities in Mexico still play versions of the game. In ancient Mesoamerica, it was generally played on a court defined by two long, low, parallel buildings. To protect themselves from the rubber ball, players wore extensive padding and equipment, including a U-shaped yoke on the waist. Ceremonial versions of this piece of equipment, made of greenstones and other precious stones (Catalogue Number 4.44), may have been offered as trophies or gifts to ballplayers. Indeed, some stone yokes have been found in tombs. Cities in the Mexican state of Veracruz were major sources of innovation for ballgame equipment and imagery in the Classic period. El Tajín (Veracruz, Mexico) features multiple ballcourts and pictorial narratives of ballplayers in ceremonial and mythological contexts.[60]

Buildings, Effigies, and Offerings Honoring Deities and Ancestors

Maya nobility also engaged with supernatural entities by constructing buildings in which they venerated ancestors and curated deity effigies.[61] A carved limestone panel from Palenque Temple XIV depicts the noblewoman Tz'akbu Ajaw holding a K'awiil effigy (perhaps made of wood or stucco); the textile wrapping falling out of her hands implies that this effigy was typically wrapped or bundled, which is analogous to contemporary Maya priests' holding precious stones and other items in sacred bundles (figure 25). Palenque texts also recount royal rituals relating to the caring for and dressing of deity effigies.[62] Classic- and Postclassic-period images show both humans and gods making offerings of food and fire to deities, deity effigies, and ancestors. For example, a scene in the *Dresden Codex* portrays an offering of a beheaded bird and a censer to a stone tree dressed as Chahk. Other images in the codex portray gifts of foods such as tamales with deer or iguana meat (figure 26).

Stoking fire and burning tree resins and rubber were other fundamental aspects of offerings. Fire rituals are recounted in many ancient inscriptions and illustrated in pictorial narratives like the scene of the Naranjo ruler Aj Wosal burning rubber in a censer following a warfare campaign (Catalogue Number 4.70). Blackened censers are common finds in archaeological sites, as is charcoal from burned pine. The smoke and fragrant aromas from burning pine and copal and other tree resins were symbolic food offerings for deities and ancestors and served to open lines of communication with them.[63]

Nobles also cut their bodies to draw blood for offerings to deities and ancestors. Bloodletting was frequently integral to conjuring rites. Performed by women and men to bring deities and ancestors into their world, bloodletting and conjuring rites were depicted in Maya monumental sculpture and in painting and on portable ceramic vessels and figurines. One painted wall at Bonampak (Chiapas, Mexico) portrays a group of women drawing cords through their tongues to draw blood, as part of the festivities displayed elsewhere in the room. A carved stone lintel from Structure 23 at the neighboring site of Yaxchilán (Chiapas, Mexico) portrays another royal woman, Lady K'abal Xook, drawing blood in a similar fashion, and a second lintel in the same building depicts the war deity that is conjured in this rite. This conjured deity's presence sanctions her husband's accession to rulership.

Consuming tobacco, alcohol, and hallucinogens

also facilitated conjuring and impersonation rites, ritual visions, and other ways of engaging with the supernatural. The Maya ingested tobacco via cigars, powdered snuff, or in liquid form. Tobacco in high doses can provoke altered states. The contemporary Tzeltal and Tzotzil Maya use tobacco for healing and ritual contexts, and the ancient Maya likely did so as well.[64] The Maya also ingested fermented pulque (maguey sap), honey, and balché tree bark, as well as hallucinogens including mushrooms in the *Psilocybe* genus, water lilies (*Nymphaea ampla*), and datura and *Brugmansia* flowers, in purifying rites involving vomiting and to induce ecstatic and entheogenic experiences.[65]

Transformation into Deities and Ancestors after Death

Death, though the ultimate transformative event, was not necessarily final; for after death, Maya nobility became ancestors. In these transformations, they were reborn with aspects of forces of nature, such as the sun, moon, maize, and lightning. Just as the Hero Twins of the *Popol Vuh* rose as the sun and the moon, the ancestor Yax Nuun Ayiin transformed into the diurnal sun god, as conveyed on Tikal Stela 31, and queens at Yaxchilán and environs appear as the moon goddess in lunar cartouches carved onto lintels and other architectural elements (figure 23). They are reborn through portals of various kinds, including the centipede maw from which the eastern sun rises every morning, and they inhabit Flower Mountain and travel along the floral paradise that is the solar path across the sky (figure 27).[66] Indeed, they truly are forces of nature.

Enduring Traditions

Over the course of more than a millennium, the ancient Maya civilization practiced intense engagement with an animate world and veneration of ancestors, albeit with a diversity of beliefs and expressions across space and time. Many of these traditions persist today, despite substantial changes to Maya culture, governance, religion, and demographics over the last five centuries. Spanish explorers first tried to enter the Yucatán in 1507, but Maya people repelled them. When conquerors and priests gained a foothold in the mid-sixteenth century, they began to quell worship of native deities and beliefs and spread Christianity. To these ends, they destroyed Maya temples, deity effigies, and books and punished the people who tried to preserve them. Similar patterns of oppression, which also included enslavement, took place elsewhere in the Maya homelands and across New Spain. The destruction of culture was worsened by waves of illness and epidemics (carried by Europeans), which decimated indigenous populations that did not have immunity to diseases such as smallpox.

Despite these early tragedies and subsequent centuries of oppression, Maya people today live and thrive in their ancestral homelands and in diaspora in Central Mexico, the United States, and Europe, and more than thirty Mayan languages (and additional dialects) are still spoken. Maya culture has vastly changed over the centuries, and religious practices have been altered too, with many people practicing Christianity, a religion that combines Christianity with traditional Maya beliefs, or other religions. At the same time, numerous traditional Maya practices and beliefs endure. Maya women weave textiles such as *huipiles* (a woman's traditional dress or tunic) on backstrap looms, as they have for more than a millennium (Catalogue Number 4.15). In churches in Mexico and Guatemala like the one in San Juan Chamula (Chiapas, Mexico), Maya people dress Catholic saints in layers of these textiles, catering to them in ways that are analogous to those described in the Palenque Inscriptions, as well as to Medieval European practices. Maya priests still follow the 260-day sacred calendar to guide personal actions and religious practice, including ancestor veneration.[67] In addition, Maya communities continue to organize dances for religious and political purposes, particularly those related to new-year festivals in the spring (although there have been, of course, great innovation and transformation in the dances and costuming).[68] Caves, mountains, springs, and other landscape features continue to be significant loci for offerings to and communication with ancestors and the animate universe, and fire remains a fundamental medium for such prayers—both to open lines of communication and to transform food, tree resins, candles, and tobacco into nourishment for ancestors and other divine entities.[69]

These persisting traditions and practices have proven fruitful sources of knowledge for understanding the ancient Maya past, providing fresh insights into the artistic, epigraphic, and archaeological records. For example, the role of speakers of contemporary Mayan languages was crucial to the decipherment of the ancient script. The creativity and diversity of Maya cultures, languages, and arts—from the ancient past to the present—should be known and celebrated, especially in the face of poverty, globalization, and other forces that threaten their survival.

DC: Dumbarton Oaks, 1998), 373–425.

64. Kevin P. Groark, "'Elder Brother Tobacco':Traditional Nicotiana Snuff Use among the Contemporary Tzeltal and Tzotzil Maya of Highland Chiapas, Mexico" (forthcoming), in *Breath and Smoke: Tobacco among the Maya*, eds. Keith Eppich and Jennifer A. Loughmiller-Cardinal (Albuquerque: University of New Mexico Press, 2017).

65. Peter A.G.M. De Smet, *Ritual Enemas and Snuffs in the Americas* (Dordrecht: Foris Publications, 1985); W. A. Emboden, "Nymphaea Ampla and Other Mayan Narcotic Plants," *Mexicon* 1 (1979): 50–52; F. J. Carod-Artal, "Alucinógenos en las culturas precolombinas mesoamericanas," *Neurología* 30 (2015): 44.

66. David Stuart, "Birth of the Sun: Notes on the Ancient Maya Winter Solstice," *Maya Decipherment* (Dec. 29, 2015), https://decipherment.wordpress.com/2015/12/29/birth-of-the-sun-notes-on-the-ancient-maya-winter-solstice/.

67. Barbara Tedlock, *Time and the Highland Maya*, rev. ed. (Albuquerque: University of New Mexico Press, 1993).

68. Garret W. Cook, Thomas A. Offit, and Rhonda A. Taube, *Indigenous Religion and Cultural Performance in the New Maya World* (Albuquerque: University of New Mexico Press, 2013).

69. Evon Z. Vogt, *Tortillas for the Gods: A Symbolic Analysis of Zinacanteco Rituals* (Cambridge, MA: Harvard University Press, 1976); Evon Z. Vogt, "Persistence of Maya Tradition in Zinacantan," *Ancient Americas: Art from Sacred Landscapes*, ed. Richard Townsend (Chicago, Munich: Art Institute of Chicago; Prestel Verlag, 1992), 60–69; Vogt and Stuart, "Some Notes on Ritual Caves"; Stuart, "The Fire Enters His House"; Morehart et al., "Wood of the Gods"; Groark, "Elder Brother Tobacco."

蒂卡尔神庙

第一部分　玛雅的宇宙
PART I The Maya Cosmos

一、玛雅的宇宙

太阳是玛雅宇宙的主要参照物,日出日落的方向确定了东西向,其垂线为南北向。太阳行进的路径将宇宙划分为四个部分,此外还有大地的中心。玛雅的城市、建筑、坟墓和雕塑均按照这种结构构建,整体呈圆形或方形。仪式表演也遵循这种编排方式,追寻着太阳每天的东西运动轨迹,或以圆形模仿太阳一年运动的轨迹。

珍贵的器物也会沿用这种结构。一件小型石雕祭坛模仿了这种五分式宇宙组织,顶部中心为始祖的面孔,侧面为四个涡纹,形状酷似天空的半球穹顶;其中一个涡纹饰描绘了一块石头冉冉升起,正是这个祭坛要表达的主题(展品1.2)。一个陶盒也模仿了宇宙结构,这是一种罕见的陶器,不过外形为长方体而非正方体(展品1.1)。三面刻有玛雅宇宙六大神,均为人形和鸟形。长边的中心位置刻有铭文,铭文的开头部分应刻在盒盖上,但它已经遗失;陶盒的年代可追溯至公元5世纪中期。盒盖形似屋顶,整体看上去便是一座房子或神庙,这个盒子可被用来存放珍贵的书籍或其他王室物品。

梅根·奥尼尔

The Maya Cosmos

The sun is the primary orienting entity of the Maya cosmos, with the east-west path defined by the sun's rising and setting on the equinoxes and, perpendicular to this, the north-south axis. The solar path divides the universe into a quadripartite form, plus the earth's center. Maya cities, buildings, tombs, and sculptures were organized in accordance with this configuration, which could be articulated in circular or squared form. Ritual performance also followed this plan, tracing the east-west daily solar path or moving in circular formation to emulate the sun's yearly journey.

Precious things also could exemplify this structure. A small carved stone altar, with an ancestor's face at its top center and four cartouches on its sides, models this five-part cosmic organization, and its shape echoes the sky's hemispheric dome; one of the cartouches shows the raising of a stone, certainly referring to the dedication of this very altar (1.2). A four-sided ceramic box, a rare form for ceramic vessels, also emulates the cosmic structure, although it is rectangular rather than square (1.1). Carved on three sides are six major deities of the Maya cosmos, in anthropomorphic and avian form. At the center of one long side is an inscription; the beginning of this text was inscribed on a now-missing lid, but it can be reconstructed to a mid-fifth-century date. The lid likely was crafted into the shape of a roof in order to make this box a house or temple. This box could have been used to store a valued book or other royal possessions.

—MEO

洛杉矶郡艺术博物馆藏古代玛雅艺术品
ANCIENT MAYA ARTS FROM THE LOS ANGELES COUNTY MUSEUM OF ART

本件陶盒三面刻有玛雅宇宙六大神，均为人形和鸟形。

1.1 浮雕陶盒 | **1.1 Carved Box with Deities**

出自危地马拉佩滕北部，玛雅文明 | Guatemala, Northern Petén, Maya

公元450–550年 | 450–550 CE

釉陶，烧后施彩绘 | Slip-painted ceramic with post-fire pigment

27.3 × 45.1 × 35.6厘米 | 27.3 × 45.1 × 35.6cm

自然的力量
FORCES OF NATURE

本件为浮雕的石球。顶端描绘了身披美洲虎皮的祖先面孔。其中一个侧面是神灵托举这一块石头的场景。根据玛雅创世神话，猎户座的三颗星星构成的三角形是宇宙的诞生之初。玉米神等神灵将三块石头安放的行为，就是创世行为。玛雅人将宇宙视为炉膛，因此在家内的炉膛中，也会安放三块石头。

1.2 浮雕石球
出自伯利兹、危地马拉或墨西哥，玛雅文明
公元200–450年
石灰岩
22.4 × 25.4 × 25.4厘米

1.2 Carved Sphere
Belize, Guatemala, or Mexico, Maya
200–450 CE
Limestone
22.4 × 25.4 × 25.4cm

二、可见与不可见

玛雅人将黑曜石和燧石打磨成刀状物、斧头和矛尖，制作成为镜子和异形制品等奢侈品和礼仪用品（不是工具）。这些物体通过暴露、隐藏和透露超自然境界展示了"可见与不可见"的概念。玛雅和其他中美洲文明的贵族会将镜子戴挂于身，镜子也则是玛雅宫殿里经常出现的饰物；黑曜石镜的黑色表面反射出的模糊光线会被用来占卜。阿兹特克人的镜子有穿孔，以便与贵族服饰系绑，常有制作过程中留下的贝壳状裂纹；这些图案在背面非常清晰，但在抛得很光的正面稍微暗淡，不过仍可看见，它们会在发亮但又浑浊的反光表面产生一种波纹效果（展品1.20）。

玛雅人常把燧石和黑曜石敲成古怪的形状，制作成节杖手柄或放入献祭地窖，外形非常抽象，有的像动物，有的像人（展品1.12、1.16、1.18）。其中一个典型的例子就是地狱之口，传说太阳从蜈蚣咽喉中升起，蜈蚣的咽喉好似一个洞口（展品1.3）。一个怪人是闪电神卡维尔，侧面还露出了多张面孔。另一个是站立着的闪电神，从他的头部、背部和腹部显示出多张面孔（展品1.4）；这些面庞有的并不写实，介于自然主义和抽象主义之间，凸显了艺术家在将超自然实体塑造为人形时的创造力。闪电化身的存在与燧石的特性有关，燧石摩擦时产生的火花，被玛雅人想象成了闪电。

梅根·奥尼尔

Seen and Unseen

Obsidian and chert were crafted into blades, choppers, and spear points and made into luxury and ceremonial items such as mirrors and "eccentrics" (non-tool forms). These objects engaged with ideas of the seen and unseen by revealing, yet also concealing, and by providing glimpses into the supernatural realm. Maya and other Mesoamerican nobles wore mirrors on their bodies, and mirrors were frequent accoutrements in Maya palaces; the dark surface of obsidian mirrors produced murky reflections used for divination. One Aztec mirror, which has perforations for attachment to a noble's costume, bears conchoidal fractures resulting from its manufacture; these patterns, which are distinct on the back and fainter but still visible on the highly polished front, create a ripple effect in the shiny yet murky reflective surface (1.20).

The Maya knapped chert and obsidian into eccentric forms. Made to be hafted onto scepters or to be deposited in offering caches, they can be abstract, zoomorphic (1.12, 1.16, 1.18), or anthropomorphic. One exquisite example is the open mouth of the underworld, the centipede maw through which the sun rises, which is also evocative of a cave opening (1.3). From the sides emerge faces of K'awiil (lightning), who appears on other eccentrics. Another depicts a standing K'awiil with additional faces emerging from his head, back, and groin (1.4); these additional faces, partially unformed, oscillate between naturalism and abstraction, highlighting the role of the artist to make supernatural entities visible to humans. The presence of the embodiment of lightning relates to the materiality of chert, which creates spark when struck and is imagined as the product of lightning strikes.

—MEO

自然的力量
FORCES OF NATURE

1.3 口形燧石

出自伯利兹、危地马拉、洪都拉斯或墨西哥，玛雅文明

公元600–900年

燧石

16.5 × 19.8 × 1.3厘米

1.3 Eccentric Flint in Form of an Open Mouth

Belize, Guatemala, Honduras, or Mexico, Maya

600–900 CE

Chert

16.5 × 19.8 × 1.3cm

1.4 人形燧石

出自伯利兹、危地马拉、洪都拉斯或墨西哥，玛雅文明
公元600-900年
燧石
25.4×6.4×1.3厘米

1.4 Anthropomorphic Eccentric Flint

Belize, Guatemala, Honduras, or Mexico, Maya
600-900 CE
Chert
25.4 × 6.4 × 1.3cm

1.5 人形燧石

出自伯利兹、危地马拉、洪都拉斯或墨西哥，玛雅文明
公元600-900年
燧石
11.4×5.1×1.3厘米

1.5 Anthropomorphic Eccentric Flint

Belize, Guatemala, Honduras, or Mexico, Maya
600-900 CE
Chert
11.4 × 5.1 × 1.3cm

1.6 人形燧石

出自伯利兹、危地马拉、洪都拉斯或墨西哥，玛雅文明
公元600-900年
燧石
14×5.1×1.3厘米

1.6 Anthropomorphic Eccentric Flint

Belize, Guatemala, Honduras, or Mexico, Maya
600-900 CE
Chert
14 × 5.1 × 1.3cm

1.7 异形燧石
出自伯利兹、危地马拉、洪都拉斯或墨西哥，玛雅文明
公元600–900年
燧石
14.7 × 5.8 × 1.3厘米

1.7 Eccentric Flint
Belize, Guatemala, Honduras, or Mexico, Maya
600–900 CE
Chert
14.7 × 5.8 × 1.3cm

1.8 人形燧石
出自伯利兹、危地马拉、洪都拉斯或墨西哥，玛雅文明
公元600–900年
燧石
15.2 × 5.8 × 1.3厘米

1.8 Anthropomorphic Eccentric Flint
Belize, Guatemala, Honduras, or Mexico, Maya
600–900 CE
Chert
15.2 × 5.8 × 1.3cm

1.9 人形燧石
出自伯利兹、危地马拉、洪都拉斯或墨西哥，玛雅文明
公元600–900年
燧石
13.5 × 5.1 × 1.3厘米

1.9 Anthropomorphic Eccentric Flint
Belize, Guatemala, Honduras, or Mexico, Maya
600–900 CE
Chert
13.5 × 5.1 × 1.3cm

1.10 人形燧石

出自伯利兹、危地马拉、洪都拉斯或墨西哥，玛雅文明

公元600–900年

燧石

10.9 × 5.1 × 1.3厘米

1.10 Anthropomorphic Eccentric Flint

Belize, Guatemala, Honduras, or Mexico, Maya

600–900 CE

Chert

10.9 × 5.1 × 1.3cm

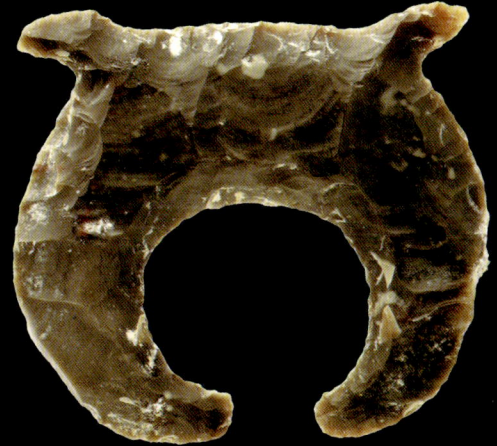

1.11 异形燧石

出自伯利兹、危地马拉、洪都拉斯或墨西哥，玛雅文明

公元600–900年

燧石

4.6 × 5.1 × 1.3厘米

1.11 Eccentric Flint

Belize, Guatemala, Honduras, or Mexico, Maya

600–900 CE

Chert

4.6 × 5.1 × 1.3cm

1.12 虫形燧石

出自伯利兹、危地马拉、洪都拉斯或墨西哥，玛雅文明

公元600–900年

燧石

8.9 × 6.4 × 1.3厘米

1.12 Eccentric Flint in Form of an Insect

Belize, Guatemala, Honduras, or Mexico, Maya

600–900 CE

Chert

8.9 × 6.4 × 1.3cm

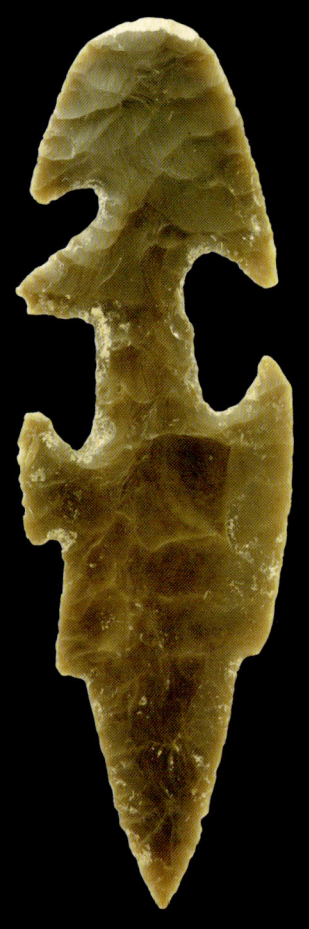

1.13 异形燧石

出自伯利兹、危地马拉、洪都拉斯或墨西哥，玛雅文明
公元600–900年
燧石
15.2 × 5.6 × 1.3厘米

1.13 Eccentric Flint

Belize, Guatemala, Honduras, or Mexico, Maya
600–900 CE
Chert
15.2 × 5.6 × 1.3cm

1.14 异形燧石

出自伯利兹、危地马拉、洪都拉斯或墨西哥，玛雅文明
公元600–900年
燧石
12.2 × 5.8 × 1.3厘米

1.14 Eccentric Flint

Belize, Guatemala, Honduras, or Mexico, Maya
600–900 CE
Chert
12.2 × 5.8 × 1.3cm

1.15 人形燧石
出自伯利兹、危地马拉、洪都拉斯或墨西哥，玛雅文明
公元600-900年
燧石
13.2 × 5.1 × 1.3厘米

1.15 Anthropomorphic Eccentric Flint
Belize, Guatemala, Honduras, or Mexico, Maya
600-900 CE
Chert
13.2 × 5.1 × 1.3cm

1.16 节肢动物形燧石
出自伯利兹、危地马拉、洪都拉斯或墨西哥，玛雅文明
公元600-900年
燧石
19.8 × 5.6 × 1.3厘米

1.16 Eccentric Flint in Form of an Arthropod
Belize, Guatemala, Honduras, or Mexico, Maya
600-900 CE
Chert
19.8 × 5.6 × 1.3cm

自然的力量
FORCES OF NATURE

1.17 异形燧石
出自伯利兹、危地马拉、洪都拉斯或墨西哥，玛雅文明
公元600–900年
燧石
15.2 × 5.8 × 1.3厘米

1.17 Eccentric Flint
Belize, Guatemala, Honduras, or Mexico, Maya
600–900 CE
Chert
15.2 × 5.8 × 1.3cm

1.18 蝎形燧石
出自伯利兹、危地马拉、洪都拉斯或墨西哥，玛雅文明
公元600–900年
燧石
12.7 × 5.6 × 1.3厘米

1.18 Eccentric Flint in Form of a Scorpion
Belize, Guatemala, Honduras, or Mexico, Maya
600–900 CE
Chert
12.7 × 5.6 × 1.3cm

1.19 异形燧石 | 1.19 Eccentric Flint

出自伯利兹、危地马拉、洪都拉斯或墨西哥，玛雅文明
公元600–900年
燧石
19.1×5.1×1.3厘米

Belize, Guatemala, Honduras, or Mexico, Maya
600–900 CE
Chert
19.1×5.1×1.3cm

1.20 石镜 | 1.20 Mirror

出自墨西哥，墨西哥谷，阿兹特克文明
公元1325–1521年
黑曜石
10.2×10.2×1厘米

Mexico, Valley of Mexico, Aztec
1325–1521 CE
Obsidian
10.2×10.2×1cm

三、艺术和文字

艺术和文字对古代玛雅人来说非常神圣，被用来描绘人、神和记事，将人类与神联系起来。书吏是受过专门训练的人士，非常受人尊敬，有些还受到王室成员的青睐。彩绘陶器常常描绘书吏坐着书写或指着书册的场景，堆叠的纸上覆盖着美洲虎皮（展品1.21、1.22）。这些书吏有的是人形，有的被塑造成为兔、猴或神灵，但即使是人形也表现出了超自然的特征。书吏书写、手指书册、与他人交谈或者立于统治者之旁的场景，暗示着文字工作的互动性和表演性。

玛雅书写系统是由代表单词和音节的符号组成，这些符号构成了今天许多玛雅语言的表音雏形。经常出现在彩陶边缘的文字多用来说明容器功能（比如饮水杯或盘子）以及装饰类型，比如是涂绘（展品1.21、1.27，1.25、1.24）或是雕刻（展品1.26）。文字也会说明容器盛放的东西，比如巧克力（展品1.25、1.24）或玉米粥（展品1.21、1.27）。有的文字说明主人的名字和头衔，还有些是书吏的名字（展品1.23）。书法变体和创造性的装饰符号非常重要，书吏研究出了多种装饰符号，增加了玛雅文字的动感。

画家使用的工具包括画笔、鹅毛笔和贝壳漆罐（展品1.21），他们将颜料储存在模制小瓶中（展品1.22）。

梅根·奥尼尔

Art and Writing

Art and writing, sacred to the ancient Maya, were used to visualize and describe people, deities, and events and connect humans to the divine. Scribes were highly trained individuals and held in great esteem; some were favored members of royal courts. Painted ceramic vessels represent seated scribes painting or gesturing to books, shown as stacked pages covered with a jaguar pelt (1.21, 1.22). Scribes are portrayed as humans, anthropomorphized rabbits or monkeys, or deities; however, even when portrayed as human, they display characteristics suggesting a supernatural nature. Scenes of scribes who paint or point to books, communicate with others over a book, or stand near a ruler hint at the interactive and performative nature of scribal work.

The Mayan writing system is composed of signs representing words and syllables used to phonetically convey words in a language ancestral to the many Mayan languages spoken today. Frequently painted on the rims of polychrome ceramics is a dedication text identifying the vessel type, such as drinking cup or plate, and the decoration type, whether painted (1.21, 1.27, 1.25, 1.24) or carved (1.26). It also names the contents, such as chocolate (1.25, 1.24) or maize gruel (1.21, 1.27), and the owner's name and titles. Some name the scribe (1.23). Calligraphic variations and creativity in rendering signs were prized, and scribes developed multiple ways of rendering signs, which were often personified in "full-figure" forms, making Maya writing animate.

Painters used tools including paintbrushes, quills, and shell paint-pots (1.21) and stored pigments in small, mold-made bottles (1.22).

—MEO

本件绘有书吏坐像，口沿处书写有一周玛雅文字。书吏在玛雅社会中备受尊敬，而且至少有一部分书吏出身王族。玛雅古典时代晚期的陶器常常在口沿处饰有装饰性的文字，这些文字曾被认为是一种纯粹的装饰，但经过研究，现在可以确定这些文字是描述不同种类陶器及其用途、陶器拥有者的名字和头衔，甚至包括书吏的名字。这件陶器上的文字表明其所有者为Yopaht Bahlam，功能是用来盛放玉米粥。

本件为抄本风格陶器。玛雅的书籍档案书写在无花果树皮制成的纸上。由于入侵美洲的西班牙人认为玛雅传统信仰为异端，来到当地的天主教神父大规模焚毁了玛雅文书。目前所知，仅有四部古抄本保留至今，其中最著名的的是现藏于德国的《德累斯顿古抄本》，记载了玛雅的宗教祭祀周期。

1.21 书吏坐像纹陶罐

出自危地马拉佩滕北部或墨西哥坎佩切南部，玛雅文明

公元650–800年

釉陶

13.5 × 10.2厘米

1.21 Codex-style Cylinder Vessel with Scribes

Guatemala or Mexico, Northern Petén or Southern Campeche, Maya

650–800 CE

Slip-painted ceramic

13.5 × 10.2cm

1.22 书吏坐像纹陶瓶

出自危地马拉或洪都拉斯，玛雅文明

公元600–900年

彩绘釉陶

8.9 × 6.4 × 3.8厘米

1.22 Bottle with Seated Scribe

Guatemala or Honduras, Maya

600–900 CE

Slip-painted ceramic with post-fire pigment

8.9 × 6.4 × 3.8cm

类似本件的这种小瓶为模制陶器，用于盛放彩绘用的矿物颜料。

自然的力量
FORCES OF NATURE

1.23 睡莲蛇纹陶罐
出自危地马拉佩滕北部，玛雅文明
公元650–850年
釉陶
24.9 × 10.2厘米

1.23 Cylinder Vessel with Water Lily Serpent
Guatemala, Northern Petén, Maya
650–850 CE
Slip-painted ceramic
24.9 × 10.2cm

本件口沿上的文字说明其功能是盛放巧克力。其所有者是太阳神的扮演者Wuk Chapaht K'inich Nohol Yok'in。

玛雅象形文字由音节符和词符构成，它们代表古玛雅语的发音，这也是当今玛雅语的前身。一个音节符代表一个音节，音节通常由一个辅音和一个元音组成，两者共同组成词语。

1.24 玛雅文字陶碗

出自危地马拉上维拉帕斯、查马或邻近地区，玛雅文明

公元600–800年

釉陶

21.6 × 28.7厘米

1.24 Cylindrical Bowl with Dedication Text

Guatemala, Alta Verapaz, Chamá or vicinity, Maya

600–800 CE

Slip-painted ceramic

21.6 × 28.7cm

自然的力量
FORCES OF NATURE

本件绘有睡莲蛇纹饰,口沿上的文字说明其功能是盛放巧克力。

1.25 睡莲蛇纹陶罐

出自危地马拉佩滕,可能是蒂卡尔或佩滕湖地区,玛雅文明

公元700–800年

釉陶

20.3 × 10.9厘米

1.25 Cylinder Vessel with Water Lily Serpent

Guatemala, Petén, possibly Tikal or Petén Lakes region, Maya

700–800 CE

Slip-painted ceramic

20.3 × 10.9cm

自然的力量
FORCES OF NATURE

1.26 睡莲蛇纹陶罐

出自伯利兹、危地马拉或墨西哥,玛雅文明

公元600-900年

釉陶

21.6 × 14厘米

1.26 Cylinder Vessel with Water Lily Serpent

Belize, Guatemala, or Mexico, Maya

600–900 CE

Slip-painted ceramic

21.6 × 14cm

1.27 玛雅文字陶碗

出自危地马拉佩滕北部或墨西哥坎佩切南部，玛雅文明

公元650–800年

釉陶

10.7 × 18.5厘米

1.27 Codex-style Bowl with Dedication Text

Guatemala or Mexico, Northern Petén or Southern Campeche, Maya

650–800 CE

Slip-painted ceramic

10.7 × 18.5cm

Mixco Viejo遺址

第二部分　天空、大地、水中和地下的超自然实体

PART II Supernatural Entities of Sky, Earth, Water, and Underworld

一、年长的天神与地神

以拟人手法呈现的玛雅神具有年龄特征，有些神灵很年轻，有些年长些。居于天上的一位重要年长的神是伊扎姆·卡卡伊（Itzam Kokaaj）（也被称为伊察姆纳），他是智慧和文字的创造者。他是一位驼背老人，牙齿已掉光，长着方形瞳孔和大鼻子，内斜视，嘴巴凹陷。在一些图像中，动物和其他神灵向主神供奉祭品，场景非常像世俗的宫殿（展品2.1、2.2）。其中有双子英雄和一位矮人正在供奉鸟和兔的场景（展品2.3）。多位统治者都是以伊扎姆·卡卡伊命名，从而使自己与智慧和创造力产生了联系。当以鸟形出现时，伊扎姆·卡卡伊代表的便是鸟神之首亚克斯·卡卡伊·穆特（Yax Kokaaj Muut），他身穿珠宝，头戴花箍。他居于世界树的顶端，但必须被击落树下，为新太阳的诞生作准备（展品3.2、2.4、3.1）。

神N长着大鼻子，满脸皱纹，嘴巴凹陷，常戴着一块头巾，与其他老神不同的是他长着一双杏仁眼。作为地神，他常出现于乌龟、贝壳（展品2.5）或鳄鱼等动物的空腔处。他还会站在地的四角撑起天空，以免它塌陷。殖民时期称他为"巴卡贝"（bakab），也是古典期的贵族头衔，这些贵族由此与这个主神联系在了一起。

梅根·奥尼尔

Aged Deities of Sky and Earth

Maya deities rendered in anthropomorphic form bear characteristics indicating age, with some deities youthful and others aged. A major aged deity inhabiting the sky is Itzam Kokaaj (also called Itzamna), the creator god associated with wisdom and writing. In anthropomorphic form he is a hunchbacked, toothless old man with squared pupils and crossed eyes, large nose, and sunken mouth. In some images, animals and other divinities make offerings to the enthroned deity, much like human palace scenes (2.1,2.2). In one, a Hero Twin and a dwarf present birds and rabbits as tribute (2.3). Multiple rulers took Itzam Kokaaj's name, thus making a connection to the deity's wisdom and creative power. In avian form, he is Yax Kokaaj Muut, the Principal Bird Deity, and wears jewelry and a flowered headband. This being lives at the top of the World Tree but must be defeated—and fall from the tree—to prepare for the birth of the new sun (3.2,2.4,3.1).

The aged deity God N, or Pawatun, has a large nose, wrinkled face, and sunken mouth and often wears a net head scarf; unlike other aged deities, he has almond-shaped eyes. An earth deity, he frequently emerges from portals such as a turtle, mollusk shell (2.5), or crocodile. He also holds up the sky at the earth's four corners, keeping the sky from collapsing. Colonial texts refer to this sky-bearer as bakab, which is used as a Classic-period noble title, associating such nobles with this important deity.

—MEO

洛杉矶郡艺术博物馆藏古代玛雅艺术品
ANCIENT MAYA ARTS FROM THE LOS ANGELES COUNTY MUSEUM OF ART

奇琴伊察羽蛇金字塔

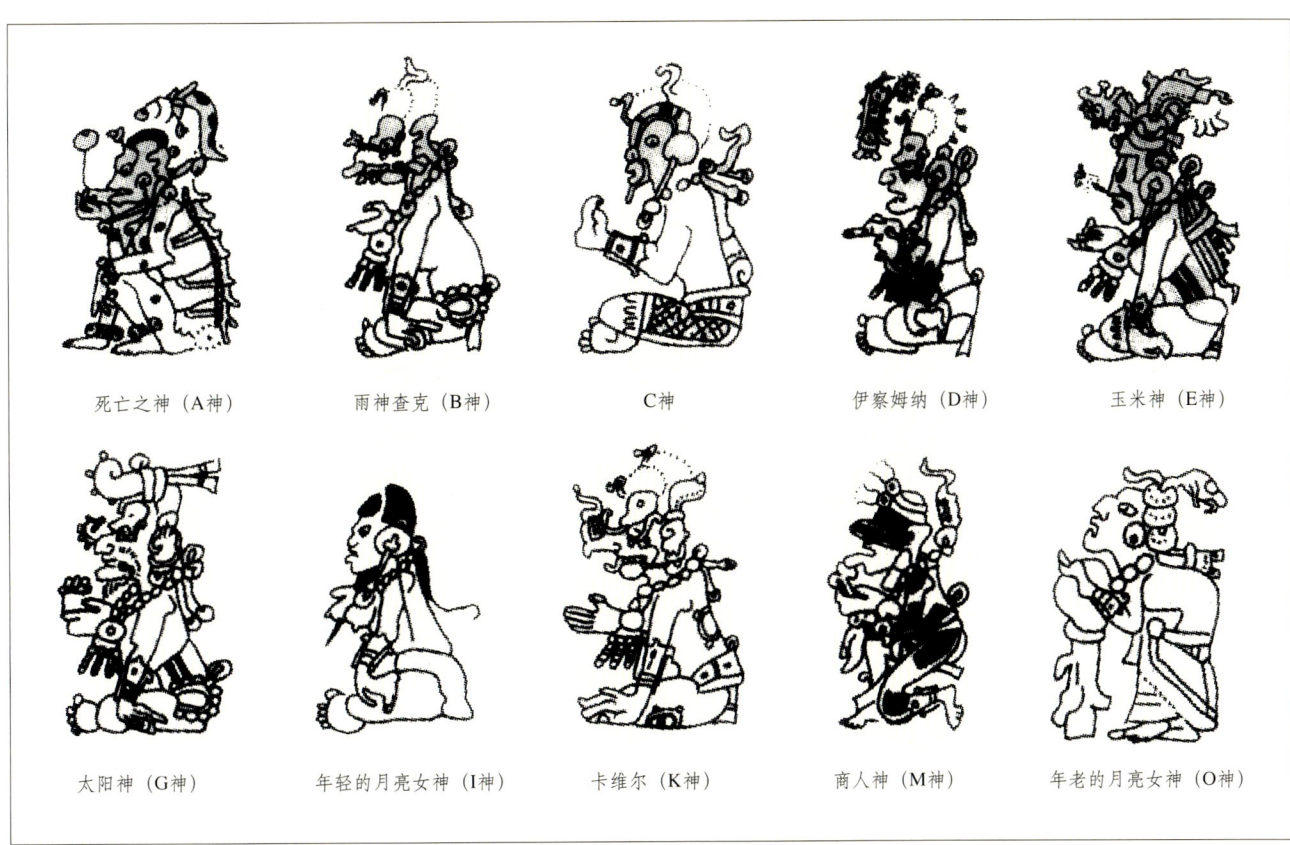

斯尔赫斯神表

自然的力量
FORCES OF NATURE

本件饰有伊扎姆·卡卡伊坐像。伊扎姆·卡卡伊是创世之神,尤卡坦的玛雅人称其为伊察姆纳,在斯尔赫斯神表中称之为D神。伊扎姆·卡卡伊被描绘为一个老人形象,高鼻深目,双眉下垂,面颊深陷。他是白昼、夜晚和天空的主宰,正是他安放了创造宇宙的三块石头中的最后一块。他也是书籍和文字的发明者,是宗教历法的守护神,因此常常被描绘为书吏的形象。

2.1 伊扎姆·卡卡伊纹陶罐

出自伯利兹、危地马拉或墨西哥,玛雅文明

公元600-900年

釉陶

22.4 × 10.9厘米

2.1 Cylinder Vessel with Itzam Kokaaj and Vulture

Belize, Guatemala, or Mexico, Maya

600–900 CE

Slip-painted ceramic

22.4 × 10.9cm

洛杉矶郡艺术博物馆藏古代玛雅艺术品
ANCIENT MAYA ARTS FROM THE LOS ANGELES COUNTY MUSEUM OF ART

2.2 伊扎姆·卡卡伊、狗和双子英雄纹陶罐

出自伯利兹、危地马拉或墨西哥，玛雅文明

公元600—900年

釉陶

16.1×11.4厘米

2.2 Cylinder Vessel with Itzam Kokaaj, Dog, and Hero Twins

Belize, Guatemala, or Mexico, Maya

600–900 CE

Slip-painted ceramic

16.1 × 11.4cm

2.3 伊扎姆·卡卡伊纹陶罐

出自危地马拉佩滕,序顿或邻近地区,玛雅文明
公元650–800年
釉陶
15.2 × 10.7厘米

2.3 Cylinder Vessel with Offering of Many Rabbits to Itzam Kokaaj

Guatemala, Petén, Xultún or vicinity, Maya
650–800 CE
Slip-painted ceramic
15.2 × 10.7cm

本件描绘了英雄和矮人向伊扎姆·卡卡伊献祭鸟和兔子的场景。

洛杉矶郡艺术博物馆藏古代玛雅艺术品
ANCIENT MAYA ARTS FROM THE LOS ANGELES COUNTY MUSEUM OF ART

2.4 神鸟纹三足陶盘
出自墨西哥坎佩切或尤卡坦，玛雅文明
公元550—700年
釉陶
11.4×35.6厘米

2.4 Tripod Plate with Mythological Bird
Mexico, Campeche or Yucatán, Maya
550–700 CE
Slip-painted ceramic
11.4 × 35.6cm

神鸟认为是伊扎姆·卡卡伊的化身，因为他也被称为大鸟神。玛雅人将世界分为四个空间与一个中心。这个中心轴是一棵大树，树枝上栖息在神鸟伊查姆—耶（Itzam-Ye）。

2.5 N神石挂饰
出自伯利兹、危地马拉或墨西哥，玛雅
公元600—900年
彩绘翡翠
7.1×7.6×1.5厘米

2.5 Pendant with God N Emerging from Shell
Belize, Guatemala, or Mexico, Maya
600–900 CE
Jadeite with pigment
7.1 × 7.6 × 1.5cm

斯尔赫斯神表中的N神负有支撑天空的职责。他被描绘为一个老者，身背乌龟或贝壳，头上裹着网格状的布。

二、太阳神和月神

随着太阳从白昼到黑夜,从天空到地下的往复运动,玛雅人拥有多个太阳神。他们的脸常被涂成红色,代表着热量;瞳孔多为正方形或螺旋形,表明他们拥有特殊的视觉功能。白昼太阳神基尼什·阿哈瓦(K'inich Ajaw)是一位成熟的男子,长着方形瞳孔,大鼻子,T形门牙,内斜视,嘴里吐着鱼须,脸颊、眼睛或额头带有太阳印记。美洲虎神代表夜间的太阳,也是一位火神,他长着螺旋瞳孔和扇眉,眼睛之间有纹线,长着虎耳(展品2.7)。另一位太阳神是鲨鱼太阳神,他通过蜈蚣咽喉从地狱水域跃出,长着螺旋瞳孔,只有一颗三角形鲨鱼齿,嘴里常吐着鱼须(展品2.6)。

太阳神常被描绘成无身体的头像或端坐在宫殿中的坐像,与统治者类似(展品2.7)。许多统治者都将自己比作太阳神,吸取太阳热量,模拟太阳日复一日的运转,暗喻生死轮回。王室妇女以月亮自喻,死后会重生为月神。太阳神和月神也会出现在与其他神灵的冲突故事以及上天战胜地狱的场景中(展品2.9)。有些形象可能标志着季节的变化,比如被捆绑和燃烧的下界美洲虎神可能代表每年干湿季节的转变(展品2.8)。

梅根·奥尼尔

Solar and Lunar Deities

The multiple Maya solar deities followed the sun over the course of the day and night, from the sky to the underworld and back again. Their faces are often colored red, signifying heat, and their pupils are squares or spirals, indicating their special vision. K'inich Ajaw, a diurnal solar deity, is a mature male with squared and crossed pupils, large nose, T-shaped front tooth, catfish barbels emerging from his mouth, and k'in (sun) signs on his cheeks, eyes, or forehead. The Jaguar God of the Underworld, the nocturnal sun, and also a fire god, has spiral pupils, scalloped eyebrows, a twisted cord between his eyes, and jaguar ears (2.7). Another solar deity is the Shark Sun God that rises from the waters of the underworld through the centipede maw portal. This being is characterized by spiral pupils, a single triangular shark tooth, and, often, curled fish barbels in his mouth (2.6).

Solar deities are portrayed as disembodied heads or as seated figures in palace-like settings, as if they were rulers (2.7). Many rulers likened themselves to solar deities, drawing upon solar heat and emulating the sun's daily rebirth, a metaphor for resurrection after death. Royal women were affiliated with the moon and, following death, reborn as the lunar goddess. Solar and lunar deities also appear in narratives of conflict with other entities, in scenes recounting victories of celestial entities over underworld beings (2.9). Some may mark the change of seasons; for example, the bound and burning Jaguar God of the Underworld may personify the annual transition from the dry to the wet season (2.8).

—MEO

本件作鲨鱼太阳神形，长着螺旋瞳孔，张嘴漏出三角形鲨鱼齿。

洛杉矶郡艺术博物馆藏古代玛雅艺术品
ANCIENT MAYA ARTS FROM THE LOS ANGELES COUNTY MUSEUM OF ART

2.6 太阳神形陶香炉 | **2.6 Censer with Solar Deities**
出自危地马拉北部或墨西哥东南部，玛雅文明 | Northern Guatemala or Southeastern Mexico, Maya
公元300–600年 | 300–600 CE
陶器，烧后施彩绘 | Ceramic with post-fire pigment
41.4 × 60.5 × 31.8厘米 | 41.4 × 60.5 × 31.8cm

自然的力量
FORCES OF NATURE

本件绘有基尼什·阿哈瓦坐像。基尼什·阿哈瓦下巴上有胡须，脸颊上有蛇形的曲线，身体上饰有涡纹符号，这种符号代表着太阳和白昼。万物的生长都要依靠太阳的热量，因此太阳神也是火神，能够喷出火焰。

2.7 太阳神纹陶罐

出自伯利兹、危地马拉或墨西哥，玛雅文明

公元600–900年

釉陶

18.3×9.9厘米

2.7 Cylinder Vessel with Solar Deities

Belize, Guatemala, or Mexico, Maya

600–900 CE

Slip-painted ceramic

18.3 × 9.9cm

太阳神白天以基尼什·阿哈瓦的身份穿行于天上,晚上便以美洲虎的形象行走下界。本件描绘了美洲虎神被神蛇束缚的场景,由于太阳象征万物热量,这一场景可能象征着旱季和雨季的转换。

2.8 太阳神纹陶罐

出自危地马拉佩滕,纳兰霍或邻近地区,玛雅文明

公元650–850年

釉陶

16.9×8.2厘米

2.8 Cylinder Vessel with Solar Deities

Guatemala, Petén, Naranjo or vicinity, Maya

650–850 CE

Slip-painted ceramic

16.9 × 8.2cm

2.9 月亮女神纹陶罐
出自墨西哥或危地马拉，玛雅文明

2.9 Cylinder Vase with Moon Goddess and other
Mexico or Guatemala, Maya

三、水、雨、风暴和闪电

　　水的各种形态——雨、风暴、水池、云——以及雷、电等现象相互关联，对于平衡人类生活所需的水分与洪水、飓风和干旱等破坏力量非常关键。恰克（Chahk）作为雨、风暴、闪电和雷之神常出现在浮雕容器的纹饰上，他长着蛇纹脸，耳朵好似菊花贝，身上有代表神性的涡纹徽记。他挥动着斧头，吞烟吐火，象征着风暴和闪电。一条神蛇盘旋在他身旁，可能代表着闪电（展品2.11）。在一个带盖祭碗上，恰克的上半身连接着四只野猪脚，扁平的鼻子像天柱一样支撑着恰克（展品2.12）。另一件陶罐上，恰克和玉米神站在地下世界的水中，为玉米神的重生作准备（展品2.10）。

　　闪电神卡维尔（K'awiil）长着人的身体，右腿却是一条蛇。他的脸也常布满蛇纹，一个燃烧着的火把从额头上的镜子伸出。作为闪电，卡维尔在天地间驰骋，纵横各界，为玉米生长劈开土地。他还体现了变化过程，比如出生、加入统治者之列和召唤祖先。有些陶器只描绘了卡维尔的半身像（展品2.17、2.15、2.16、2.18）；他喷出燃烧着的火炬同时也是身体四周的涡纹装饰，暗示这是另一界的卡维尔，或者他是来自一个超脱尘世的地方。

　　在卡密拉胡尤（Kaminaljuyú），雨和风暴神是jaguarian（展品2.14）。墨西哥中部地区的这些雨、风暴和闪电神是指特奥蒂瓦坎风暴神，其蒙面形态起源于特奥蒂瓦坎（Teotihuacan），后传入玛雅地区（展品2.13）。阿兹特克人后来将其称为特拉洛克（Tlaloc）。

梅根·奥尼尔

Water, Rain, Storms, and Lightning

　　Entities of water in various forms—rain, storms, pools, and clouds—and associated phenomena like thunder and lightning were interrelated and critical in balancing the nourishing moisture needed for human life and the destructive forces of floods, hurricanes, and drought. Chahk, deity of rain, storms, lightning, and thunder, appears on a carved vessel, identified by his characteristic serpentine face, Spondylus-shell ear flare, and mirror signs on his body. He wields an axe and breathes fire; these are features relating to his role in storms and lightning. A coiled supernatural serpent, perhaps visualizing lightning, appears next to him (2.11). A lidded offering bowl renders Chahk's upper body set on four peccary-head feet, while flattened snouts support Chahk and symbolize sky-bearers (2.12). Another vessel portrays Chahk and the Maize God in the watery underworld, preparing for the Maize God's rebirth (2.10).

　　The lightning god K'awiil has a human body, but his right leg is a serpent. His face, also often serpentine, is characterized by a fiery torch emerging from a mirror in the forehead. As lightning, K'awiil travels from sky to earth, across cosmic levels, breaking open the earth for maize growth. He also embodied transformative processes such as birth, accession to rulership, and ancestor conjuring. Some vessels show only K'awiil's bust (2.17, 2.15, 2.16, 2.18); his fiery torch also can double as a cartouche that surrounds his body, suggesting this is a glimpse of K'awiil in another realm, or that he has surfaced from an otherworldly location.

　　At Kaminaljuyú, the deity of rain and storms is jaguarian (2.14). The Central Mexican cognate of these rain, storm, and lightning deities was the Teotihuacan Storm God, whose characteristic masked form originated at Teotihuacan and was adopted in the Maya area (2.13). This being was later called Tlaloc by the Aztecs.

—MEO

自然的力量
FORCES OF NATURE

2.10 玉米神和恰克纹陶碗

出自危地马拉佩滕，玛雅文明

公元250-550年

泥彩釉陶

14×15.2厘米

2.10 Bowl with Maize God and Chahk in Watery Locale

Guatemala, Petén, Maya

250–550 CE

Slip-painted ceramic with post-fire pigment

14×15.2cm

本件描绘了恰克站在水中的场景。恰克有着尖嘴和鲶鱼的鳃须。玛雅人认为雨神恰克住在岩洞之中，而岩洞是孕育云、雨、雷电之地。

洛杉矶郡艺术博物馆藏古代玛雅艺术品
ANCIENT MAYA ARTS FROM THE LOS ANGELES COUNTY MUSEUM OF ART

2.11 恰克和神蛇纹陶罐
出自危地马拉佩滕北部，玛雅文明
公元650–800年
釉陶
10.9 × 12.2厘米

2.11 Cylinder Vessel with Chahk and Serpent
Guatemala, Northern Petén, Maya
650–800 CE
Slip-painted ceramic
10.9 × 12.2cm

本件中恰克仰面倚靠在地上，身旁是神蛇，蛇象征着闪电。玛雅人认为恰克能控制闪电，当他用闪电将岩石劈开时，玉米就从中生长出来。

自然的力量
FORCES OF NATURE

2.12 恰克和野猪纹四足陶罐
出自危地马拉佩滕或墨西哥坎佩切,玛雅文明
公元250–450年
釉陶
27.4 × 17.3 × 17.8厘米

2.12 Quadrupod Vessel with Chahk and Peccaries
Guatemala or Mexico, Petén or Campeche, Maya
250–450 CE
Slip-painted ceramic
27.4 × 17.3 × 17.8cm

2.13 风暴神形三足陶罐 | 2.13 Tripod Vessel with Storm God

出自危地马拉或墨西哥太平洋海岸，玛雅文明
公元900–1200年
釉陶
19.1 × 15.7 × 16.5厘米

Guatemala or Mexico, Pacific Coast, Maya
900–1200 CE
Slip-painted ceramic
19.1 × 15.7 × 16.5cm

自然的力量
FORCES OF NATURE

2.14 雨神石雕
出自危地马拉卡密拉胡尤,玛雅文明
公元100–200年
彩绘玄武岩
114.3 × 40.6 × 5.1厘米

2.14 Sculpture with Rain Deity
Guatemala, Kaminaljuyú, Maya
100–200 CE
Basalt with pigment
114.3 × 40.6 × 5.1cm

洛杉矶郡艺术博物馆藏古代玛雅艺术品
ANCIENT MAYA ARTS FROM THE LOS ANGELES COUNTY MUSEUM OF ART

2.15 卡维尔纹陶罐
出自危地马拉佩滕北部或墨西哥坎佩切南部，玛雅文明
公元650–800年
釉陶
14.5 × 10.9厘米

2.15 Codex-style Cylinder Vessel with K'awiil
Guatemala or Mexico, Northern Petén or Southern Campeche, Maya
650–800 CE
Slip-painted ceramic
14.5 × 10.9cm

卡维尔是一位长着蛇脚和长嘴的神灵，他的特点是前额插着一个类似火炬的东西，象征闪电。他手中有时握着权杖。因此玛雅君主通过手拿刻着卡维尔神的权杖显示王权。

2.16 卡维尔纹陶盘
出自危地马拉佩滕北部或墨西哥坎佩切南部，玛雅文明
公元650–800年
釉陶
4.6 × 21.1厘米

2.16 Codex-style Plate with K'awiil
Guatemala or Mexico, Northern Petén or Southern Campeche, Maya
650–800 CE
Slip-painted ceramic
4.6 × 21.1cm

自然的力量
FORCES OF NATURE

卡维尔双脚为蛇，可劈开土地，令玉米生长，因此他可能具有玉米神的特征，带着高高的羽毛头饰。因为他具有在宇宙各个层级创造联系的能力，他也与出生、统治者就位和召唤祖先等转换过程相联系。

2.17 卡维尔纹陶罐

出自危地马拉佩滕西北部，玛雅文明

公元600—900年

釉陶

18.7×16.5厘米

2.17 Cylinder Vessel with K'awiil

Guatemala, Northwestern Petén, Maya

600–900 CE

Slip-painted ceramic

18.7 × 16.5cm

洛杉矶郡艺术博物馆藏古代玛雅艺术品
ANCIENT MAYA ARTS FROM THE LOS ANGELES COUNTY MUSEUM OF ART

2.18 卡维尔纹陶罐

出自危地马拉或墨西哥，玛雅文明

公元600–900年

釉陶，烧后施灰泥和彩绘

17.8 × 11.4厘米

2.18 Footed Vessel with K'awiil

Guatemala or Mexico, Maya

600–900 CE

Slip-painted ceramic with post-fire stucco and pigment

17.8 × 11.4cm

四、大地的果实：玉米和巧克力

玉米是一种主食，而以年轻男子形象出现的玉米神也是一个主神，他倾斜的前额好似一穗玉米。他的生命周期就像田里的玉米，其形象代表着活力、死亡和重生的不断轮回。这种轮回很让统治者着迷，他们常以玉米神的形象自居，多是双臂伸开，优雅地跳着舞，好像玉米秆在风中摇曳（展品2.23、2.24）。复活之后，他会得到玉米女神的帮助。玉米女神通常为局部或全部赤裸，年纪很轻但腹部皱巴巴，表明她们已生过孩子，具有传播生命的能力（展品2.19）。以羽毛为装饰的玉米神也会与小矮人跳舞，庆祝世界重生（展品2.20、2.21）。在某些场景中他会像鸟儿一样跃离地面，在另一些场景中他会以鸟的形象出现（展品2.25、2.26）。

在中美洲，可可树产出的巧克力是一种奢侈品。展品中的一件陶罐上画着第一棵可可树和闪电神卡维尔的诞生，他劈开了大地，让可可树生长（展品2.27）。巧克力与玉米等混合在一起，再以香料和鲜花调味，便可当作食物酱汁来食用。在前古典晚期（约公元前200年－公元250年），玛雅人常使用带流容器来盛放可可（展品2.23）。在古典早期（公元250－550年），他们制作出了带盖容器来存放可可。在古典晚期（公元550－900年），他们使用的是筒形（展品2.20）和葫芦形容器（展品2.28），这些形制应源于易腐烂的葫芦碗。

梅根·奥尼尔

Fruits of the Earth: Maize and Chocolate

Maize was a staple food, and the Maize God, a youthful male figure with a sloping forehead evoking an ear of corn, was a principal deity. His life cycle is like that of corn in the fields, and portrayals of him convey that cycle of vitality, death, and rebirth. Promises of such resurrection were appealing to human rulers, who frequently represented themselves in the Maize God's image, often with outstretched arms and dancing gracefully, comparable to cornstalks swaying in the wind (2.23, 2.24). Following his resurrection, he is assisted by maize goddesses, who are generally depicted partially or fully nude and are shown to be youthful but with wrinkled bellies—to indicate they have borne children and to accentuate their life-giving qualities (2.19). The feather-bedecked Maize God also may dance with supernatural dwarfs in a world-renewal dance (2.20, 2.21). In some scenes, he leaps off the earth as if a bird; in others, he is visualized in avian form (2.25, 2.26).

Chocolate, which comes from the Theobroma cacao tree, was a luxury item that was traded across Mesoamerica. One vessel pictures the birth of the first cacao tree along with the lightning god K'awiil, who breaks open the earth so the tree can emerge (2.27). Mixed with substances such as corn and flavored with spices and flowers, chocolate was both drunk and consumed as sauces on foods. In the Late Preclassic period (circa 200 BCE–250 CE), the Maya used spouted vessels for cacao (2.23). In the Early Classic (250–550 CE), they made lidded vessels to store cacao. And in the Late Classic (550–900 CE), they drank from cylindrical (2.20) and gourd-shaped vessels, the form of which was derived from perishable drinking bowls made from gourds (2.28).

—MEO

洛杉矶郡艺术博物馆藏古代玛雅艺术品
ANCIENT MAYA ARTS FROM THE LOS ANGELES COUNTY MUSEUM OF ART

本件为玉米女神像，全身赤裸，双臂高举，腹部的皱纹象征其生育能力。

2.19 玉米女神陶像

出自危地马拉北部或墨西哥东南部，玛雅文明

公元600—900年
陶，烧后施彩绘
22.4 × 9.7 × 7.1厘米

2.19 Figurine of a Maize Goddess

Northern Guatemala or Southeastern Mexico, Maya

600–900 CE
Ceramic with post-fire pigment
22.4 × 9.7 × 7.1cm

自然的力量
FORCES OF NATURE

玉米神在斯尔赫斯神表中被称为E神，他通常被描绘为年轻的男性，头上戴着玉米穗状的冠。玉米神背负巨大的羽状后背架，装有无数作物及不同的超自然动物。

2.20 玉米神纹陶罐

出自危地马拉佩滕，霍尔姆尔或邻近地区，玛雅文明

公元650–850年

釉陶

23.9 × 9.7厘米

2.20 Cylinder Vessel with Maize God Dancers and Dwarfs

Guatemala, Petén, Holmul or vicinity, Maya

650–850 CE

Slip-painted ceramic

23.9 × 9.7cm

自然的力量
FORCES OF NATURE

本件绘有起舞的玉米神和矮人。玉米是中美洲最重要的农作物。玛雅人认为神首先用泥土造人,随后用木头造人,但两次都没有成功。最后以玉米和鲜血混合的面团成功创造了人类。

2.21 玉米神纹陶罐
出自危地马拉佩滕,序顿或邻近地区,玛雅文明
公元650—850年
釉陶
16.3×7.6厘米

2.21 Cylinder Vessel with Maize God Dancers and Dwarf
Guatemala, Petén, Xultún or vicinity, Maya
650–850 CE
Slip-painted ceramic
16.3 × 7.6 cm

2.22 小矮人形陶哨 | **2.22 Figurine Whistle of a Dwarf**
出自危地马拉北部或墨西哥东南部,玛雅文明 | Northern Guatemala or Southeastern Mexico, Maya
公元600–800年 | 600–800 CE
彩陶 | Ceramic with post-fire pigment
10.2 × 5.1 × 5.1厘米 | 10.2 × 5.1 × 5.1 cm

洛杉矶郡艺术博物馆藏古代玛雅艺术品
ANCIENT MAYA ARTS FROM THE LOS ANGELES COUNTY MUSEUM OF ART

2.23 玉米神纹陶盘 | **2.23 Tripod Plate with Maize God Dancer**

出自危地马拉佩滕北部，玛雅文明 | Guatemala, Northern Petén, Maya

公元550—700年 | 550–700 CE

釉陶 | Slip-painted ceramic

9 × 34.1厘米 | 9 × 34.1cm

自然的力量
FORCES OF NATURE

2.24 玉米神纹方形陶盘 | 2.24 Squared Plate with Maize God

出自危地马拉佩滕，贝戴克斯巴顿地区，玛雅文明 | Guatemala, Petén, Petexbatún region, Maya
公元700–850年 | 700–850 CE
釉陶 | Slip-painted ceramic
12.7 × 30.5 × 33厘米 | 12.7 × 30.5 × 33cm

2.25 鸟形玉米神纹陶碗 | 2.25 Codex-style Bowl with Avian Maize God
危地马拉佩滕北部或墨西哥坎佩切南部，玛雅文明 | Guatemala or Mexico, Northern Petén or Southern Campeche, Maya
公元650–800年 | 650–800 CE
釉陶 | Slip-painted ceramic

自然的力量
FORCES OF NATURE

本件为抄本风格陶器，绘有匍匐在地上作鸟状的玉米神。玛雅人在耕种时要举行宗教仪式来祭祀玉米神，土地需要经过丈量，确定基本方位，之后再在中心处种下第一株玉米，象征玉米神对世界的统治。

2.26 鸟形玉米神纹陶罐
出自危地马拉佩滕北部或墨西哥坎佩切南部，玛雅文明
公元650–800年
釉陶
14×9.4厘米

2.26 Codex-style Cylinder Vessel with Avian Maize God
Guatemala or Mexico, Northern Petén or Southern Campeche, Maya
650–800 CE
Slip-painted ceramic
14 × 9.4cm

自然的力量
FORCES OF NATURE

本件上绘有卡维尔在类似神殿的场所中劈开大地，第一个可可树生长的场景。可可最早由奥尔梅克人种植，但玛雅地区气候炎热、土地肥沃，所产可可质量最佳。可可是玛雅主要的经济作物，通常被用来制作供上层社会饮用的巧克力饮料。

2.27 神殿纹三足陶罐

出自危地马拉佩滕，圣何塞的摩特或邻近地区，玛雅文明

公元750–850年

釉陶

30.5×16厘米

2.27 Tripod Vessel with Supernatural Palace Scene and Cacao Tree

Guatemala, Petén, Motul de San José or vicinity, Maya

750–850 CE

Slip-painted ceramic

30.5 × 16cm

自然的力量
FORCES OF NATURE

2.28 涡纹球形陶碗 | 2.28 Globular Bowl with Cartouches

出自危地马拉佩滕，纳兰霍或邻近地区，玛雅文明

公元6世纪末
釉陶
18.3 × 19.1厘米

Guatemala, Petén, Naranjo or vicinity, Maya
late 6th century
Slip-painted ceramic
18.3 × 19.1cm

本件为可可豆外形。一株可可树可以产1000至2500颗可可豆，可可豆也能够用作货币。

2.29 可可果形陶罐
出自危地马拉太平洋海岸，埃斯昆特拉
公元300–600年
釉陶
8.1 × 13.5 × 7.6厘米

2.29 Cacao Pod Vessel
Guatemala, Pacific Coast, Escuintla
300–600 CE
Slip-painted ceramic
8.1 × 13.5 × 7.6cm

2.30 带流盛可可陶容器
出自伯利兹或危地马拉，玛雅文明
公元前100年–公元250年
釉陶
12.2 × 16.5 × 15.2厘米

2.30 Spouted Vessel for Cacao
Belize or Guatemala, Maya
100 BCE–250 CE
Slip-painted ceramic
12.2 × 16.5 × 15.2cm

五、中美洲的玉米、雨和收获

玉米、雨水和农业生产是中美洲人的生存基础。公元前1200至公元前400年，墨西哥湾沿岸和特万特佩克地峡生活着玛雅人的祖先奥尔梅克人。展品中的一件牌饰上刻画着蹲伏着的奥尔梅克雨神，他长着杏仁眼，扁鼻，猫嘴下翻（展品2.32），头上的裂缝便是玉米生长的地面裂口。这些神以人形呈现出来，要么是一种艺术表达手法，要么暗示着与超自然存在关系。翡翠和蛇纹石等绿宝石的翠绿之色与玉米植株和水相似。砍凿工具（凿子或斧头）的形状类似于用于播种玉米的农具；这些工具常由贵重材料制成，常被用于礼仪活动（展品2.37、2.36）。其中一个工具酷似玉米粒（展品2.35）。

墨西哥瓦哈卡州萨巴特克人的雨和闪电神科奇乔（Cocijo）有类似于奥尔梅克雨神的狰狞面目（展品2.40、2.42）。然而，墨西哥中部阿兹特克人的水和玉米女神却是年轻女子，每年都会被祭拜以祈求农业丰收（展品2.39）。阿兹特克人还会为风暴神特拉洛克（Tlaloc）和春神西佩·图泰克（Xipe Totec）一起举行祭拜仪式，春神常身披晒干的俘虏的皮（展品2.38）。晒干的皮被祭司披四十天，好似干燥了的玉米皮，暗示着春天的重生。萨巴特克人、阿兹特克人和玛雅人认为这些雕塑充满了灵性（分别是pée、teotl和k'uh），是它们所代表的自然元素的化身。

安东尼·迈耶

Maize, Rain, and Harvest in Greater Mesoamerica

Maize, rain, and the agricultural cycle were fundamental to Mesoamerican livelihoods. The Olmec, predecessors to the Maya, occupied the Gulf Coast and Isthmus of Tehuantepec from 1200 to 400 BCE. A rectangular plaque shows the crouching Olmec rain deity with characteristic almond-shaped eyes, flat nose, and down-turned, snarling feline mouth (2.32); the cleft on his head is the terrestrial opening from which maize emerges. Human representations assume aspects of these deities, either as aesthetic choices or to suggest relationships with the supernatural. The verdant colors of greenstones, such as jadeite and serpentine, resemble those of maize plants and water. The celt (chisel or axe) shape recalls agricultural tools used to sow maize seeds; as cached offerings in precious materials, they are ceremonial versions of those implements (2.37, 2.36). One is incised to resemble a maize kernel (2.35).

Images of Cocijo, the rain and lightning deity among the Zapotec of Oaxaca, Mexico, resemble the ferocious features of the Olmec rain god (2.40, 2.42). Yet the Aztecs of Central Mexico depicted water and maize goddesses in the forms of young women, whom they celebrated in annual festivals to ensure agricultural prosperity (2.39). The Aztecs also held festivals for the storm god Tlaloc in conjunction with the springtime deity Xipe Totec, who bears the flayed skin of captives (2.38). Worn by priests for forty days, the dried skin mimicked the desiccation of maize husks and alluded to vernal rebirth. The Zapotec, Aztec, and Maya perceived these sculptures as imbued with animistic forces—pée, teotl, and k'uh, respectively—and embodiments of the natural elements they represented.

—AJM

2.31 雨神石吊坠
出自墨西哥格雷罗、塔巴斯科或韦拉克鲁斯，奥尔梅克文明
公元前900–公元前400年
蛇纹石
8.9×7.6×2.5厘米

2.31 Pendant with Rain Deity
Mexico, Guerrero, Tabasco, or Veracruz, Olmec
900–400 BCE
Serpentine
8.9×7.6×2.5cm

2.32 雨神或玉米神石牌饰
出自墨西哥格雷罗、塔巴斯科或韦拉克鲁斯，奥尔梅克文明
公元前900–公元前400年
蛇纹石
6.9×8.1×3.8厘米

2.32 Plaque with Rain or Maize Deity
Mexico, Guerrero, Tabasco, or Veracruz, Olmec
900–400 BCE
Serpentine
6.9×8.1×3.8cm

自然的力量
FORCES OF NATURE

2.33 人面石吊坠
出自墨西哥格雷罗、塔巴斯科或韦拉克鲁斯,奥尔梅克文明

公元前900–公元前400年

蛇纹石

10.2 × 7.6 × 4.6厘米

2.33 Pendant with Human Face

Mexico, Guerrero, Tabasco, or Veracruz, Olmec

900–400 BCE

Serpentine

10.2 × 7.6 × 4.6cm

2.34 人面石吊坠
出自墨西哥格雷罗、塔巴斯科或韦拉克鲁斯,奥尔梅克文明

公元前900–400年

翡翠

5.1 × 3.2 × 1.6厘米

2.34 Pendant with Human Face

Mexico, Guerrero, Tabasco, or Veracruz, Olmec

900–400 BCE

Jadeite

5.1 × 3.2 × 1.6cm

2.35 加工玉米的石凿
出自墨西哥格雷罗、塔巴斯科或韦拉克鲁斯，奥尔梅克文明
公元前900–400年
蛇纹石
22.2×7×3.8厘米

2.35 Maize Kernel Celt
Mexico, Guerrero, Tabasco, or Veracruz, Olmec
900–400 BCE
Serpentine
22.2×7×3.8cm

2.36 石凿
出自墨西哥格雷罗、塔巴斯科或韦拉克鲁斯，奥尔梅克文明
公元前900–400年
翡翠
23.5×9.8×3.8厘米

2.36 Celt
Mexico, Guerrero, Tabasco, or Veracruz, Olmec
900–400 BCE
Jadeite
23.5×9.8×3.8cm

2.37 石凿
出自墨西哥格雷罗、塔巴斯科或韦拉克鲁斯，奥尔梅克文明
公元前900–400年
翡翠
13.7×5.7×1.9厘米

2.37 Celt
Mexico, Guerrero, Tabasco, or Veracruz, Olmec
900–400 BCE
Jadeite
13.7×5.7×1.9cm

洛杉矶郡艺术博物馆藏古代玛雅艺术品
ANCIENT MAYA ARTS FROM THE LOS ANGELES COUNTY MUSEUM OF ART

2.38 西佩·图泰克旗手石像

出自墨西哥，墨西哥谷，阿兹特克文明

公元1325–1521年

玄武岩

85.1 × 32.4 × 20.3厘米，63.5 × 25.4 × 17.8厘米

2.38 Xipe Totec Standard Bearer

Mexico, Valley of Mexico, Aztec

1325–1521 CE

Basalt

85.1 × 32.4 × 20.3cm, 63.5 × 25.4 × 17.8cm

自然的力量
FORCES OF NATURE

2.39 神庙头饰女神石像

出自墨西哥，墨西哥谷，阿兹特克文明

公元1325–1521年

玄武岩

58.4 × 22.9 × 14.6厘米

2.39 Goddess with Temple Headdress

Mexico, Valley of Mexico, Aztec

1325–1521 CE

Basalt

58.4 × 22.9 × 14.6cm

科奇乔的形象是人、美洲虎和蛇的综合体,叉状舌头代表闪电。

2.40 C形头饰科奇乔(雨神)陶像
出自墨西哥瓦哈卡、蒙特阿尔班或邻近地区,萨巴特克文明
公元500–600年
陶,烧后施彩绘
22.9 × 17.8 × 16.5厘米

2.40 Cocijo (Rain Deity) with Glyph C Headdress
Mexico, Oaxaca, Monte Albán or vicinity, Zapotec
500–600 CE
Ceramic with post-fire pigment
22.9 × 17.8 × 16.5cm

自然的力量
FORCES OF NATURE

2.41 C形头饰男子陶像 | **2.41 Seated Male Figure with Glyph C Headdress**

出自墨西哥瓦哈卡、蒙特阿尔班或邻近地区，萨巴特克文明

公元500–600年
陶，烧后施彩绘
49.5 × 30.5 × 26.7厘米

Mexico, Oaxaca, Monte Albán or vicinity, Zapotec
500–600 CE
Ceramic with post-fire pigment
49.5 × 30.5 × 26.7cm

洛杉矶郡艺术博物馆藏古代玛雅艺术品
ANCIENT MAYA ARTS FROM THE LOS ANGELES COUNTY MUSEUM OF ART

2.42 科奇乔形陶瓶

出自墨西哥瓦哈卡、蒙特阿尔班或邻近地区，萨巴特克文明

公元前200年–公元100年

釉陶

17.8 × 10.5厘米

2.42 Bottle with Cocijo (Rain Deity) Mask

Mexico, Oaxaca, Monte Albán or vicinity, Zapotec

200 BCE–100 CE

Slip-painted ceramic

17.8 × 10.5cm

六、超自然的蛇

蛇在玛雅艺术中呈现多种形式，常是天地之间发挥门户作用的超自然神灵。它们也常与战争有关。特奥蒂瓦坎战蛇长着又大又圆的眼睛，蝴蝶状的鼻子，有着扇形头饰，4世纪玛雅文化与特奥蒂瓦坎接触时被首次融入玛雅服饰，后被用来象征过去和战争。作为一种常见的士兵头饰，它也会出现在危地马拉北部联盟王国权贵用于喝巧克力的抄本风格陶杯上（展品2.44、2.43）。在一个盘子上它衬托着白色和黑色背景渲染了两次，也许是描绘其在光明和黑暗中的身影（展品2.45）。

睡莲蛇的脸或丰满或消瘦，头顶为睡莲或花朵（展品2.46、2.47）。它一般出现在水生环境中，坐在水塘之上，呈对角线构图（如同浮动一般）；或位于代表原始水域的黑色背景之中（展品1.25、1.23）。展品中的一件陶罐上画着水下世界的场景，骷髅形睡莲蛇的卷须间出现了拟人化的神（展品2.49）。另一件陶罐上面画着一个小矮人躺在睡莲蛇头上的莲叶内，吹着海螺壳召唤另一个世界的神灵（展品2.50）。睡莲位于大地与地下世界的交汇处，因为其花开在陆地上水的表面，因此这种神物与转化相关，玛雅贵族常以它自居。其在转化中的作用也可能与睡莲秆的致幻作用有关，它可能有助于模仿和转化仪式。

梅根·奥尼尔

Supernatural Serpents

Serpents appear in a variety of forms in Maya art, frequently as supernatural entities serving as portals between cosmic realms. They also are often associated with warfare. The Teotihuacan War Serpent, with characteristically large round eyes, butterfly proboscis, and fanned headdress, was first incorporated into Maya costuming during fourth-century contacts with Teotihuacan and was later used as a symbol related to the past and to warfare. A common warrior headdress, it was also rendered on codex-style vessels (for drinking chocolate) whose owners bore titles used by allied kingdoms in northern Guatemala (2.44, 2.43). On one plate, it is rendered twice, on white and black backgrounds, perhaps to visualize the creature in light and darkness (2.45).

The Water Lily Serpent has a fleshed or skeletal serpentine face, with a water lily pad or flower on its head (2.46, 2.47). It appears in aquatic contexts—situated above stacked water bands, positioned diagonally (as if floating), or set within a black background representing the primordial waters of creation (1.25, 1.23). One carved vessel portrays an aquatic underworld scene, in which anthropomorphic deities emerge from tendrils radiating from skeletal water lily serpents (2.49). Another features a dwarf lying on a lily pad on the Water Lily Serpent head and blowing a conch shell to conjure an entity from another realm (2.50). Water lilies flower at the surface of terrestrial waters, liminal loci at the intersection of earth and underworld. This entity is thus associated with transformation, and Maya nobles often impersonated it. Its role in transformation also may relate to the psychoactive qualities of the water lily stalk, whose hallucinogenic effects may have aided in rituals of impersonation and transformation.

—MEO

洛杉矶郡艺术博物馆藏古代玛雅艺术品
ANCIENT MAYA ARTS FROM THE LOS ANGELES COUNTY MUSEUM OF ART

2.43 神蛇纹陶杯
出自危地马拉佩滕北部或墨西哥坎佩切南部，玛雅文明
公元650–800年
釉陶
13.2 × 11.4厘米

2.43 Codex-style Cylinder Vessel with Teotihuacan-style Serpent
Guatemala or Mexico, Northern Petén or Southern Campeche, Maya
650–800 CE
Slip-painted ceramic
13.2 × 11.4cm

本件为抄本风格陶器。蛇在玛雅艺术中被认为是沟通天地等不同世界的神灵。

2.44 神蛇纹陶杯
出自危地马拉佩滕北部或墨西哥坎佩切南部，玛雅文明
公元650–800年
釉陶
14 × 10.9厘米

2.44 Codex-style Gadrooned Vessel with Teotihuacan-style Serpent
Guatemala or Mexico, Northern Petén or Southern Campeche, Maya
500–600 CE
Slip-painted ceramic
14 × 10.9cm

本件为抄本风格陶器，杯身上的蛇头戴翎羽冠冕，可能象征和武士的形象有关。

自然的力量
FORCES OF NATURE

本件陶盘分为两个区域，分别以黑、白作为背景色，绘有两条头戴冠冕的神蛇，可能象征着它光明和黑暗中的身影。

2.45 战蛇纹陶盘

出自危地马拉佩滕北部或墨西哥坎佩切南部，玛雅文明

公元650–800年

釉陶

7.6 × 40.4厘米

2.45 Plate with Teotihuacan War Serpent on White and Black Backgrounds

Guatemala or Mexico, Northern Petén or Southern Campeche, Maya

650–800 CE

Slip-painted ceramic

7.6 × 40.4cm

洛杉矶郡艺术博物馆藏古代玛雅艺术品
ANCIENT MAYA ARTS FROM THE LOS ANGELES COUNTY MUSEUM OF ART

本件绘有头戴睡莲的蛇，蛇头作骷髅状。玛雅人认为宇宙空间具有多个层面，岩洞、深井、水塘等具有蓄水功能的地方就是沟通各个空间的通道，睡莲生长于水面，因此具有在宇宙中穿行的功能。

2.46 骷髅睡莲蛇纹陶盘
出自危地马拉佩滕北部或墨西哥坎佩切南部，玛雅文明
公元650–800年
釉陶
5.1×30厘米

2.46 Plate with Skeletal Water Lily Serpent
Guatemala or Mexico, Northern Petén or Southern Campeche, Maya
650–800 CE
Slip-painted ceramic
5.1×30cm

自然的力量
FORCES OF NATURE

2.47 睡莲蛇纹陶罐
出自危地马拉佩滕北部或墨西哥坎佩切南部，玛雅文明
公元650–800年
釉陶
16.5 × 12.2厘米

2.47 Codex-style Cylinder Vessel with Water Lily Serpent
Guatemala or Mexico, Northern Petén or Southern Campeche, Maya
650–800 CE
Slip-painted ceramic
16.5 × 12.2cm

本件上浮雕了神蛇，但已经有抽象化的意味。

洛杉矶郡艺术博物馆藏古代玛雅艺术品
ANCIENT MAYA ARTS FROM THE LOS ANGELES COUNTY MUSEUM OF ART

2.48 神蛇纹陶碗 | **2.48 Bowl with Supernatural Serpent**

出自危地马拉或墨西哥，玛雅文明 | Guatemala or Mexico, Maya
公元600–900年 | 600–900 CE
釉陶 | Slip-painted ceramic
12.7 × 19.1厘米 | 12.7 × 19.1cm

2.49 睡莲蛇纹陶罐
出自危地马拉,上维拉帕斯,玛雅文明

公元600-900年

釉陶

20 × 24.5厘米

2.49 Vessel with Water Lily Serpent and Underworld Imagery
Guatemala or Mexico, Maya
600–900 CE
Slip-painted ceramic
20 × 24.5cm

本件描绘了睡莲蛇与地下世界的场景。画面中除了能看到蛇外,还有鱼和海龟。玛雅人认为下界是孕育着生命的潮湿之地,流淌着两条河流。海龟凸凹不平的龟壳象征着大地的山峦起伏的地貌。

洛杉矶郡艺术博物馆藏古代玛雅艺术品
ANCIENT MAYA ARTS FROM THE LOS ANGELES COUNTY MUSEUM OF ART

本件描绘了一个小矮人躺在睡莲蛇头上的莲叶内，吹着海螺壳召唤另一个世界的场景。

2.50 睡莲蛇与矮人纹陶罐 | **2.50 Vessel with Water Lily Serpent and Dwarf**

出自墨西哥尤卡坦，查查拉或邻近地区，玛雅文明

公元700–900年

釉陶，烧后施彩绘

13.5 × 13.5厘米

Mexico, Yucatán, Chocholá or vicinity, Maya

700–900 CE

Slip-painted ceramic with post-fire pigment

13.5 × 13.5cm

自然的力量
FORCES OF NATURE

蛇在玛雅文明中被用来象征转化，因为蛇会蜕皮，而这一过程常与重生和更新联系在一起。而且它们在地上、地下、树上和水中等不同的环境中活动，类似于跨越宇宙之境的仪式。

2.51 男子和睡莲蛇纹陶碗 | **2.51 Bowl with Male Figure and Water Lily Serpent**

出自墨西哥尤卡坦，查查拉或邻近地区，玛雅文明

公元700–900年

釉陶

11.9 × 10.9厘米

Mexico, Yucatán, Chocholá or vicinity, Maya

700–900 CE

Slip-painted ceramic

11.9 × 10.9cm

七、黑暗与梦境的神灵

地下的神灵常出现在地下宫殿，有时是与年轻贵族或神灵对立。这种对立的构图代表着光明战胜了黑暗，或是与夜空中星星的移动和季节的变化有关。在查马风格的容器上，年轻领主将斧头对准了N神或地狱入口中的猴子（展品2.55）。一些场景描述了地下年迈的贸易和烟草神 L神和闪电神卡维尔（展品2.52），这可能与闪电从天空到地下的移动有关。其他作品描绘了喧闹的地下宫殿景象：一个陶器描绘了地下神庙中的凸目夫妇，地下年老的神灵戴着围兜饮酒作乐，死亡和醉酒神A神握着灌肠注射器，同时呕吐不止（展品2.54）。

其他与黑暗和冲突相关的生物是梦境（Wahy）之神，有些被视为统治者的另一个自我。彩绘陶器将梦境之神形象描绘为扮演人类或者动作滑稽的复合动物，比如手持灌肠注射器的睡莲虎、猴子和自己抓痒的虎爪狗（展品2.59、2.60）。展品中的另一画面则更可怕：各种奇异生物中有一些身穿藤条的年轻男子，周围满是头骨和头颅；面对他们的是人形骨架，其中一个提着血淋漓的头颅，附近的男子手握着用眼球和骨头装饰的遮阳伞（展品2.58）。事实上，梦境之神有着阴暗面，他通过梦境中的冲突传播疾病。一些人手持灌肠器或在吸烟的场景，可能与摄入致幻剂以诱发迷幻状态和梦境有关。

梅根·奥尼尔

Entities of Darkness and Dreaming

Underworld entities are portrayed in subterranean palaces, sometimes in confrontation with young lords or celestial beings. These narratives of confrontation relate to the victory of light over darkness, to the movement of stars in the night sky, or to the changing seasons. On Chamá-style vessels, young lords level axes toward God N or a monkey in the maws of the underworld (2.55). Some scenes show God L, aged underworld deity of trade and tobacco, with K'awiil (2.52, M.2010.115.794); these encounters may relate to the movement of lightning traveling from sky to the underworld. Other objects picture lively underworld palaces: one vessel depicts a couple in an underworld temple marked by extruded eyeballs, aged underworld deities drinking and wearing vomit bibs, and God A Prime, deity of death and drunkenness, holding an enema syringe while vomiting (2.54).

Other creatures of darkness and conflict are wahy entities, some named as alter egos of rulers. Painted vessels visualize wahy creatures as hybrid animals performing human or humorous actions, such as a Water Lily Jaguar holding an enema syringe, and a monkey and jaguar-pawed dog scratching themselves (2.59, 2.60). Another painting is more macabre: amid multiple fantastic creatures are youthful males in arbors marked with skulls and decapitated heads; facing them are skeletal figures, one holding a bleeding head, and nearby men grip parasols decorated with eyeballs and bones (2.58). Indeed, there is a dark side to wahy entities, who may spread illness during hostile interactions in dreams. The fact that some hold enema implements or smoke tobacco may relate to the practice of ingesting hallucinogens to incite altered states and dreams.

—MEO

2.52 Bottle with Molded Design of K'awiil and God L

本组陶瓶上浮雕了卡维尔和L神对坐的场景。L神是一位年老的神灵，长着方形的眼睛，身着斗篷，戴着宽沿大帽，帽子上落着乌鸦。L神既是冥神，也是商人的保护神和烟草之神。

2.52 卡维尔和L神纹陶瓶
出自危地马拉或洪都拉斯，玛雅文明
公元600–900年
釉陶，烧后施彩绘
8.8×7.9×3.5厘米，8.6×7.6×3.5厘米

2.52 Bottle with Molded Design of K'awiil and God L
Guatemala or Honduras, Maya
600–900 CE
Slip-painted ceramic with post-fire pigment
8.8×7.9×3.5cm, 8.6×7.6×3.5cm

本件浮雕了L神抽雪茄的场景。

2.53 L神纹梨形陶罐

出自伯利兹、危地马拉、洪都拉斯或墨西哥，玛雅文明

公元800–950年

釉陶

16.5×8.4厘米

2.53 Pear-shaped Vessel with God L

Belize, Guatemala, Honduras, or Mexico, Maya

800–950 CE

Slip-painted ceramic

16.5×8.4cm

自然的力量
FORCES OF NATURE

本件描绘了冥界的场景。一对夫妻坐在建筑内，面前的人在饮酒狂欢。A神手持灌肠器，在他们背后狂吐不止。A神是玛雅神话中的死神，样子丑陋，身体浮肿。

2.54 神话饮酒场景纹陶罐

出自危地马拉佩滕，玛雅文明

公元600–900年

釉陶

24.1 × 19.1厘米

2.54 Cylinder Vessel with Mythological Drinking Scene

Guatemala, Petén, Maya

600–900 CE

Slip-painted ceramic

24.1 × 19.1cm

本件描绘了手持灌肠注射器的睡莲虎。Wahy一词在玛雅语言中意思是"睡眠",但它表示在梦境中人转化为动物,或者动物之间的转化,这一转化往往是为了危害人间。

2.59 梦境神纹陶罐 | **2.59 Vessel with Wahy Entities**
出自危地马拉佩滕北部,玛雅文明 | Guatemala, Northern Petén, Maya
公元700–850年 | 700–850 CE
釉陶 | Slip-painted ceramic
14.7 × 13.5厘米 | 14.7 × 13.5cm

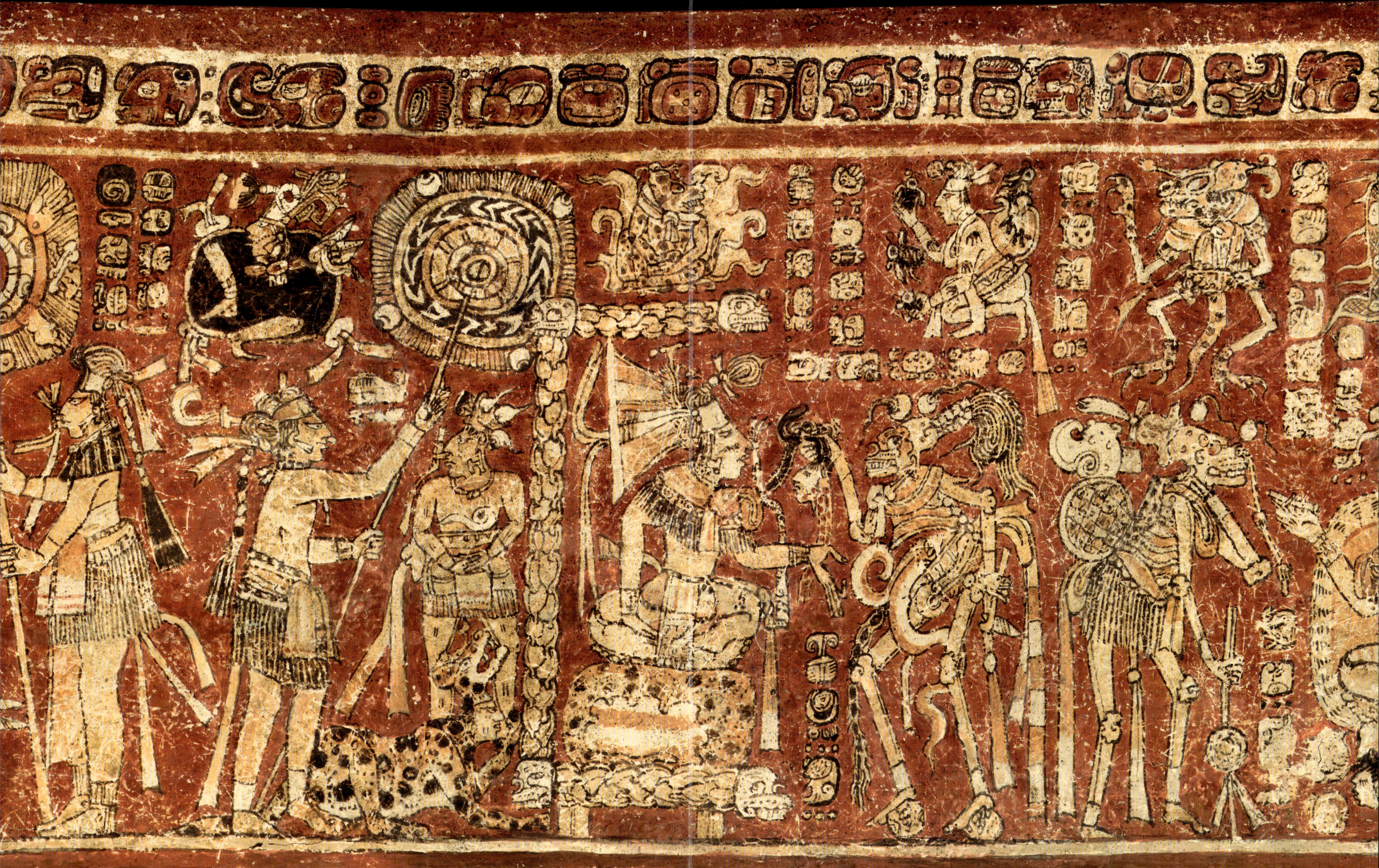

本件描绘了正在给自己搔痒的猴子和手持灌肠器的狗。

洛杉矶郡艺术博物馆藏古代玛雅艺术品
ANCIENT MAYA ARTS FROM THE LOS ANGELES COUNTY MUSEUM OF ART

2.60 梦境神纹陶罐
出自危地马拉佩滕北部，玛雅文明
公元700–850年
釉陶
11.4 × 12.2厘米

2.60 Bowl with Wahy Entities
Guatemala, Northern Petén, Maya
700–850 CE
Slip-painted ceramic
11.4 × 12.2cm

Zaculeu遗址

143

第三部分　玛雅艺术和宗教中的动物

PART III　Animals in Maya Art and Religion

一、空中的生灵

无论是在世俗世界还是在超自然世界，人类和动物总是交织在一起。从金刚鹦鹉、秃鹫和水生鸬鹚等热带鸟类到穴居蝙蝠，玛雅艺术和社会到处可见飞禽。统治者常会采用鸟类的名字，比如洪都拉斯科潘的一位统治者叫做K'inich Yax K'uk' Mo'（光芒四射的第一只绿金刚鹦鹉）。统治者也会以被视为珍贵商品的羽毛为衣，或在舞会和仪式上装扮成鸟类。

秃鹫与统治者密切相关，蒂卡尔的古典早期地窖中就发现了四只帝王秃鹰，揭示出它们具有重要的仪式意义。展品中的两件陶罐上，扮演祭司角色的秃鹫各举起一只翅膀，似乎是在演讲（展品3.4）。

但是，鸟类也可能具有负面意义。16世纪创作的《波波尔·乌》被奉为基切玛雅文明的圣书，记载了神话和历史时期的创世故事以及神灵和人类的行为，其中讲到双子英雄弄瞎并击败了自负的七金刚鹦鹉，寓意为过分骄傲或专横便会自取灭亡。古典时期的七金刚鹦鹉类比于鸟神之首亚克斯·卡卡伊·穆特，他形似猛禽，长着螺旋瞳孔，戴有羽毛头饰（展品3.1、3.2）。

蝙蝠是夜间才会飞上天空的地下生灵，它们被认为是黑暗生物，有时甚至预示着死亡，因为在《波波尔·乌》中它们斩首了西瓦尔巴的乌纳普。不过，蝙蝠也是重要的热带传粉昆虫，得到了玛雅人的青睐，科潘的统治者还会使用蝙蝠头作为他们的象征。上维拉帕斯的一件陶器上画了很多长着叶形鼻的蝙蝠头，或许描绘的是每天日落时分成千上万只蝙蝠飞出洞穴的情景。

安东尼·迈耶和梅根·奥尼尔

Creatures of the Sky

The worlds of humans and animals were intertwined, both in quotidian life and in the supernatural realm. Creatures of the sky, from tropical birds like macaws, vultures, and aquatic cormorants to cave-dwelling bats, appear throughout Maya art and society. Rulers often took the names of birds, such as K'inich Yax K'uk' Mo' (Radiant First Quetzal Macaw) from Copán, Honduras. Rulers also dressed in feathers, which were valued as precious commodities, or costumed as birds in dances and rituals.

Vultures are closely tied with rulers, and four king vultures were found in an Early Classic cache at Tikal, revealing their ceremonial importance. On two vessels, priest-like vultures each raise a wing, as if engaged in animate speech (3.4, M.2010.115.672).

However, birds also could have negative connotations. In the Popol Vuh, a significant collection of K'iche' Maya narratives recorded in the sixteenth century that recount the creation of the world and actions of deities and humans in mythical and historic time, the Hero Twins blind and defeat the conceited Seven Macaw, forewarning the downfall of overly prideful or despotic individuals. The Classic-period analogue of Seven Macaw was the Principal Bird Deity, Yax Kokaaj Muut, who has raptorial features, spiraled pupils, and a feathered headdress (3.1, 3.2).

Bats, residents of the underworld who fly into the sky at night, are considered beings of darkness and sometimes harbingers of death, for in the Popol Vuh they decapitate Hunahpu in Xibalba. Yet bats also were important tropical pollinators and valued by the Maya, and the kings of Copán used the bat head as their emblem glyph. The repetition of leaf-nosed bat heads on a vessel from Alta Verapaz perhaps mimics the daily sunset egress of thousands of bats from caves (M.90.168.18).

—AJM and MEO

洛杉矶郡艺术博物馆藏古代玛雅艺术品
ANCIENT MAYA ARTS FROM THE LOS ANGELES COUNTY MUSEUM OF ART

本件内底有两只大鸟。玛雅人的天神伊察姆纳的化身是大神鸟，栖息在世界之树上，即玛雅创世传说中神圣的木棉树上。

3.1 神鸟纹三足陶盘

出自墨西哥坎佩切或尤卡坦，玛雅文明

公元550–700年

釉陶

9.7×35.6厘米

3.1 Tripod Plate with Supernatural Birds

Mexico, Campeche or Yucatán, Maya

550–700 CE

Slip-painted ceramic

9.7 × 35.6cm

自然的力量
FORCES OF NATURE

本件内底饰有神鸟纹,边缘饰有藤状之物

3.2 神鸟纹三足陶盘

出自墨西哥坎佩切或尤卡坦,玛雅文明

公元550–700年

釉陶

7.6 × 28.9厘米

3.2 Tripod Plate with Supernatural Bird

Mexico, Campeche or Yucatán, Maya

550–700 CE

Slip-painted ceramic

7.6 × 28.9cm

3.3 神鸟纹灰泥陶罐

危地马拉佩滕北部或墨西哥坎佩切南部,
玛雅文明

公元600–900年
陶,烧后灰泥和彩绘
19.1 × 9.5厘米

3.3 Stucco-painted Vessel with Supernatural Birds

Guatemala or Mexico, Northern Petén or Southern Campeche,
Maya
600–900 CE
Ceramic with post-fire stucco and pigment
19.1 × 9.5cm

自然的力量
FORCES OF NATURE

本件外壁饰有拟人化的秃鹫，头戴头巾，向前匍匐，手臂前伸，似乎扮作祭司的形象。

3.4 人形秃鹫纹陶碗 | **3.4 Bowl with Anthropomorphic Vultures**

出自危地马拉或墨西哥，玛雅文明
公元600–900年
釉陶
7.6×11.4厘米，11.4×15.2厘米

Guatemala or Mexico, Maya
600–900 CE
Slip-painted ceramic
7.6×11.4cm，11.4×15.2cm

本件外壁上满绘蝙蝠的头部，可能表现的是黄昏时蝙蝠飞出栖身的洞穴的场景。

3.5 蝙蝠头像纹陶罐

出自危地马拉上维拉帕斯，科班或邻近地区，玛雅文明

公元650—850年

釉陶

15.2 × 17.8厘米

3.5 Vessel with Bat Heads

Guatemala, Alta Verapaz, Cobán or vicinity, Maya

650–850 CE

Slip-painted ceramic

15.2 × 17.8cm

二、地上的生灵

玛雅艺术中，走兽常会以自然形态和拟人形态出现。夜间捕食者美洲虎与皇室密切相关，因肌体强健而受崇敬。统治者和其他贵族成员常会以"巴拉姆"（美洲虎）命名，活着时常穿虎皮短裙，死后也会以虎皮裹尸。一些图像表现着温顺的美洲虎（展品3.8），但大多数都强调这种动物的掠夺本性：一件陶盘上描绘着美洲虎抓着一颗头颅，可能象征着获得胜利的士兵（展品3.7）。

鹿是繁殖力的象征，既是祭品也是食物。祭祀的地窖中曾出土了鹿骨，许多场景也描绘以鹿作为祭品。展品中的一件陶器画着猎人正在将鹿做成祭品，旁边是美洲虎。狩猎本身是一种重要的活动，这从实际意义和仪式作用来说都是如此。另一件陶盘中的纹饰中描绘了猎人正在争夺鹿和鸟，中间则躺着一只垂死的鹿（展品3.9）。猎人和统治者也会佩戴鹿徽，也许是为了狩猎或举行球赛（展品4.1、4.38）。

吼猴和蜘蛛猴在热带森林非常多。根据《波波尔·乌》的记载，猴子被认为是早期的人类，并承担着书吏的职责。猴子也因幽默的本性而讨人喜欢，图案中常会描绘它们富有表情的面孔和因咆哮长大的嘴巴（展品3.14、3.13）。有时这些生物还会拿着它们喜欢的可可豆荚（展品3.12）。有时它们可能是在进行人类的活动：一个盘子画着一只跳舞的猴子，身上还穿着用于灌肠仪式的围兜（展品3.16）。

夜行性的犰狳常会穿戴盔甲，正如展品中一件被塑成长着神灵面孔的犰狳的陶罐一样（展品3.18）；一件陶罐上描绘着一只翻倒的犰狳，表示将犰狳壳用作碗来盛放犰狳肉（展品3.17）。

安东尼·迈耶和梅根·奥尼尔

Creatures of the Earth

Terrestrial animals take on naturalistic and anthropomorphic forms in Maya art. Jaguars, nocturnal predators that were closely associated with royalty, were revered for their powerful physicality. Rulers and other nobles took the name of the bahlam (jaguar), wore jaguar-pelt skirts, and wrapped deceased royal bodies in pelts. Some images show docile jaguars (3.8), but most emphasize the creatures' predatory nature: on one plate a jaguar holds a decapitated head, though this jaguar might be a stand-in for a triumphant warrior (3.7).

Deer were symbols of fertility and valued both as sacrificial offerings and as food. Their bones are present in offering caches, and many painted scenes portray deer offerings. One carved vessel depicts a hunter preparing a deer for sacrifice near a supernatural reptilian jaguar (M.2010.115.776). The hunt itself was an important activity, both for practical and ceremonial reasons. The dynamic circular composition of a plate that illustrates hunters vying for deer and birds features a dying deer at its center (3.9). Hunters and rulers also wear deer insignia, perhaps to help with the hunt or the ballgame (4.1, 4.38).

Howler and spider monkeys heavily populate the tropical forest. In the Popol Vuh, monkeys are identified as humans from an earlier era and perform scribal duties. Monkeys were also celebrated for their humorous nature, and depictions emphasize their expressive faces and howling mouths (3.14, 3.13). Sometimes these creatures are holding their favored cacao pods (3.12). Or they may engage in human activities; one plate features a dancing monkey wearing a bib used in enema rituals (3.16).

Nocturnal armadillos appear with their characteristic plated armor, as in the lidded vessel that is a supernatural armadillo with a deity face (3.18) and in another bowl that is an armadillo turned upside down, recalling the use of armadillo shells as bowls for their meat (3.17).

—AJM and MEO

洛杉矶郡艺术博物馆藏古代玛雅艺术品
ANCIENT MAYA ARTS FROM THE LOS ANGELES COUNTY MUSEUM OF ART

本件盖上的捉手被塑造成一只张嘴的美洲虎形象。玛雅人及阿兹特克人等都将美洲虎奉为天神的化身。美洲虎也是统治者的象征。

3.6 美洲虎形捉手陶罐 | **3.6 Lidded Vessel with Jaguar**

出自危地马拉佩滕或墨西哥坎佩切，玛雅文明 | Guatemala or Mexico, Petén or Campeche, Maya

公元250–500年 | 250–500 CE

釉陶 | Slip-painted ceramic

28×35.6厘米 | 28×35.6cm

153

自然的力量
FORCES OF NATURE

本件内底绘有一只抓着头颅的美洲虎，它抓着的可能是敌人或俘虏的头颅。因为美洲虎具有力量，因此也是统治者武力的标志。

3.7 美洲虎纹三足陶盘 | 3.7 Tripod Plate with Jaguar Holding Decapitated Head

出自危地马拉佩滕北部，玛雅文明　|　Guatemala, Northern Petén, Maya
公元700–850年　|　700–850 CE
釉陶　|　Slip-painted ceramic
12.7 × 33.5厘米　|　12.7 × 33.5 cm

本件外壁绘有匍匐的美洲虎,它的头上是睡莲。因为美洲虎是夜间活动的,因此与冥界相联系,和睡莲具有同样的能力,因此睡莲虎具有沟通不同世界的能力。本件口沿上的符号仅仅是模仿成文字的纹饰,而不是真正的文字。

3.8 睡莲美洲虎纹陶碗 | 3.8 Bowl with Water Lily Jaguars
出自危地马拉佩滕,玛雅文明 | Guatemala, Petén, Maya
公元600–900年 | 600–900 CE
釉陶 | Slip-painted ceramic
18.5 × 17.8厘米 | 18.5 × 17.8cm

自然的力量
FORCES OF NATURE

本件中描绘了猎人正在狩猎鹿和鸟,中间躺着一只垂死的鹿。

3.9 猎人、鹿和鸟纹陶盘
出自墨西哥坎佩切或金塔纳罗奥,玛雅文明
公元700–850年
釉陶
9.2×35.6厘米

3.9 Plate with Hunters, Deer, and Birds
Mexico, Campeche or Quintana Roo, Maya
700–850 CE
Slip-painted ceramic
9.2×35.6cm

3.10 公鹿纹陶罐

出自危地马拉太平洋海岸，埃斯昆特拉

公元600–900年

釉陶

3.10 Cylinder Vessel with Male Deer

Guatemala, Pacific Coast, Escuintla

600–900 CE

Slip-painted ceramic

19.5 × 15.7cm

自然的力量
FORCES OF NATURE

3.11 鳄鱼捕鹿纹陶罐

出自危地马拉太平洋海岸，埃斯昆特拉
公元600–900年
釉陶
21.1 × 14厘米

3.11 Cylinder Vessel with Supernatural Crocodile and Captured Deer

Guatemala, Pacific Coast, Escuintla
600–900 CE
Slip-painted ceramic
21.1 × 14cm

自然的力量
FORCES OF NATURE

3.12 猴形捉手三足陶罐
出自危地马拉佩滕，玛雅文明
公元450–550年
釉陶
25.4 × 16.5厘米

Guatemala, Petén, Maya
3.12 Tripod Vessel with Monkey and Cacao Pod
450–550 CE
Slip-painted ceramic
25.4 × 16.5cm

本件的捉手为手持可可的猴子造型。玛雅人认为猴子是舞蹈、歌唱等艺术的化身。

3.13 蜘蛛猿形陶罐
出自危地马拉或墨西哥，玛雅或特奥蒂瓦坎文明
公元450–650年
釉陶
17.3 × 19.1 × 12.2厘米

3.13 Whistling Vessel with Spider Monkey
Guatemala or Mexico, Maya or Teotihuacan
450–650 CE
Slip-painted ceramic
17.3 × 19.1 × 12.2cm

本件杯身前雕有一只猴子，憨态可掬。

洛杉矶郡艺术博物馆藏古代玛雅艺术品
ANCIENT MAYA ARTS FROM THE LOS ANGELES COUNTY MUSEUM OF ART

本件外壁饰有一只猴子，猴子的身体为彩绘，头部为堆塑，尾巴被描绘得较为夸张。

3.14 蜘蛛猿纹三足陶罐

出自萨尔瓦多西部，玛雅玛雅

公元650-750年

釉陶

21.6×30厘米

3.14 Tripod Vessel with Spider Monkeys

Guatemala, Petén, Maya

450–550 CE

Slip-painted ceramic

21.6 × 30cm

161

自然的力量
FORCES OF NATURE

3.15 吼猴形陶罐

出自危地马拉或墨西哥，玛雅文明

公元600–900年

釉陶，烧后施彩绘

19.8 × 13.5厘米

3.15 Vase with Howler Monkey and Offering Scenes

Guatemala or Mexico, Maya

600–900 CE

Slip-painted ceramic with post-fire pigment

19.8 × 13.5cm

自然的力量
FORCES OF NATURE

本件内底绘有一只跳舞的猴子，头戴羽毛，身上穿着用于灌肠仪式的围兜。

3.16 神猴纹陶盘

出自危地马拉佩滕，玛雅文明

公元600-900年

釉陶

5.8×30.5厘米

3.16 Plate with Supernatural Monkey

Guatemala, Petén, Maya

450–550 CE

Slip-painted ceramic

5.8 × 30.5cm

3.17 犰狳纹陶罐
出自危地马拉，上卡纳莱斯河谷，玛雅文明
公元700–850年
釉陶

3.17 Vessel in Form of an Armadillo
Guatemala, Upper Motagua River Valley, Maya
700–850 CE
Slip–painted ceramic

自然的力量
FORCES OF NATURE

3.18 犰狳形陶罐

出自危地马拉佩滕，玛雅文明

公元300–600年

釉陶

20.3 × 17.8 × 15.2厘米

3.18 Two-part Vessel in Form of an Armadillo

Guatemala, Petén, Maya

300–600 CE

Slip-painted ceramic

20.3 × 17.8 × 15.2cm

3.19 饰有负鼠和燃烧香炉的陶罐

出自危地马拉太平洋海岸,埃斯昆特拉

公元600–900年

釉陶,烧后施彩绘

19.1 × 10.9厘米

3.19 Cylinder Vessel with Opossums and Burning Censers

Guatemala, Pacific Coast, Escuintla

600–900 CE

Slip-painted ceramic with post-fire pigment

19.1 × 10.9cm

三、水中的生灵

由于水是转化之地,鱼、鳄鱼和其他水生物因此构成了玛雅神话的基础。水域(nahb)是自然和超自然之间的过渡境域,养育着水生生灵。风格化的超自然的鱼类具有水和天之灵性,因此能同时生活在两个空间(展品3.20、3.21)。据《波波尔·乌》记载,西瓦尔巴领主打败双子英雄之后,双子的骨灰被撒入河中,后转世为鲶鱼。这个神话被描绘在一件陶罐上,两条鲶鱼长着特有的触须,在红色背景中游泳(展品3.22)。此外,鲶鱼是栖息在水深处的觅食者,那里更接近地下世界。一只抄本风格杯子上画着水下的人头骨和鱼,代表着鱼与地下世界之间的密切联系(展品3.23)。

鳄鱼可以在水中和陆地上生存的能力,体现了这种过渡性或自然转化,它们高低不平的鳞甲和皮内成骨象征着中美洲的多山地貌(展品3.26)。在创世神话中,土地是从原始水体中升起的巨型鳄鱼或海龟的背。它被撕裂成了天空和大地,两者也都可被想象成鳄鱼。展品中的一件陶香炉上,一条鳄鱼爬在洞口,太阳神坐在它身上休息,这一场景描绘了创世故事的一段情节,象征着诞生和转化(展品4.80)。

安东尼·迈耶

Creatures of the Water

Because water is a place for transformation, fish, crocodiles, and other aquatic creatures were fundamental to Maya mythology. Bodies of water, nahb, are transitional spaces between the natural and supernatural, situating aquatic inhabitants in a liminal locale. Stylized supernatural fish have attributes of both water and sky that echo their ability to occupy both spaces (3.20, 3.21). In the Popol Vuh, after the Lords of Xibalba defeated the Hero Twins, the twins' bones were ground and sprinkled into the river, and the twins were then reborn as catfish. That myth may be represented on a cylinder vessel that portrays two catfish (with characteristic barbels) swimming on a red background (3.22). Moreover, catfish are bottom-feeders, inhabiting the depths of bodies of water, closer to the underworld. A codex-style cup painted with an underwater scene of animated human skulls and fish speaks to the close connection between fish and the underworld (3.23).

Crocodiles, with their ability to live both in water and on land, exemplify this transitional, or natural, fluidity, and their bumpy scutes and osteoderms evoke the mountainous surface of the Mesoamerican landscape (3.26). In creation mythology, the earth is the backside of an enormous crocodile or turtle that rises from primordial waters. This is the creature that was torn apart to create sky and earth, both of which can be envisioned as crocodilian. A censer with the Sun God perched on a crocodile at the entrance of a cave depicts an episode of the creation story and summons similar ideas of transition and emergence (4.80).

—AJM

3.20 神鱼纹陶罐

出自危地马拉佩滕北部或墨西哥坎佩切南部，玛雅文明

公元650–800年

釉陶

16.5 × 10.7厘米

3.20 Codex-style Vessel with Supernatural Fish

Guatemala or Mexico, Northern Petén or Southern Campeche, Maya

650–800 CE

Slip-painted ceramic

16.5 × 10.7cm

3.21 神鱼纹陶罐

出自危地马拉佩滕北部或墨西哥坎佩切南部，玛雅文明

公元650–800年

釉陶

14.7 × 12.7厘米

3.21 Codex-style Gadrooned Vessel with Supernatural Fish

Guatemala or Mexico, Northern Petén or Southern Campeche, Maya

650–800 CE

Slip-painted ceramic

14.7 × 12.7cm

洛杉矶郡艺术博物馆藏古代玛雅艺术品
ANCIENT MAYA ARTS FROM THE LOS ANGELES COUNTY MUSEUM OF ART

3.22 鲶鱼纹陶罐
出自危地马拉佩滕北部，玛雅文明
公元700–850年
釉陶
20.3 × 11.4厘米

3.22 Cylinder Vessel with Catfish
Guatemala, Northern Petén, Maya
700–850 CE
Slip-painted ceramic
20.3 × 11.4cm

本件描绘了《波波尔·乌》中的神话，两条鲶鱼代表了双子英雄。

3.23 头骨和鱼纹陶罐
出自危地马拉佩滕北部或墨西哥坎佩切南部，玛雅文明
公元650–800年
釉陶
10.2 × 10.4厘米

3.23 Codex-style Vessel with Animate Skull and Fish
Guatemala or Mexico, Northern Petén or Southern Campeche, Maya
650–800 CE
Slip-painted ceramic
10.2 × 10.4cm

本件抄本风格陶杯上画着水下的人头骨和鱼，代表着鱼与地下世界之间的密切联系。

自然的力量
FORCES OF NATURE

3.24 鸬鹚和鱼纹陶罐

出自危地马拉佩滕北部，玛雅文明

公元700–850年

釉陶

17 × 8.9厘米

3.24 Cylinder Vessel with Cormorants and Fish

Guatemala, Northern Petén, Maya

700–850 CE

Slip-painted ceramic

17 × 8.9cm

洛杉矶郡艺术博物馆藏古代玛雅艺术品
ANCIENT MAYA ARTS FROM THE LOS ANGELES COUNTY MUSEUM OF ART

3.25 水鸟纹陶碗

出自萨尔瓦多或洪都拉斯，玛雅文明

公元600–900年

釉陶

8.9×16.5厘米

3.25 Bowl with Waterbirds

El Salvador or Honduras, Maya

600–900 CE

Slip-painted ceramic

8.9 × 16.5cm

自然的力量
FORCES OF NATURE

3.26 鳄鱼形陶罐

出自伯利兹、危地马拉或墨西哥，玛雅文明

公元300–600年

釉陶，烧后施彩绘

17.3 × 43.2 × 15.2厘米

3.26 Vessel in Form of a Crocodile

Belize, Guatemala, or Mexico, Maya

300–600 CE

Slip-painted ceramic with post-fire pigment

17.3 × 43.2 × 15.2cm

四、奥尔梅克艺术中的动物

就某些文化和艺术特征而言，拉斯博卡斯（Las Bocas）和特拉蒂科（Tlatilco）等墨西哥中部地区与分散的奥尔梅克文明类似，奥尔梅克文明的中心地带位于墨西哥湾沿岸。这些地方和周边地区的陶器上常饰有蛇、鳄鱼和美洲虎的抽象图案。与喜欢描绘完整动物或其头部的玛雅人相比，奥尔梅克人常会选择动物身体的一部分指代整体，比如翅膀或爪子。一个陶瓶上画着风格化的美洲虎爪，三个长而突出的爪子与球状的身体水平（展品3.29）。它做工精细，瓶子呈现深灰色，是在低氧环境下烧制形成的。

与玛雅人一样，奥尔梅克人也喜欢描绘复合动物，通常是鸟类和爬行动物。将鸟类、走兽和水生动物的特性组合起来，便赋予了这些超自然生物穿越世界之轴和宇宙各界的能力。展品中的一件陶碗就是这样的组合，上面画着带有焰眉的蛇头，另一侧是爪子一样的翅膀（展品3.28）。背景的阴刻菱形图案，也许代表着爬虫类动物的鳞片。玛雅人后来将这种类型的图案修改成了睡莲蛇。另一个碗上描绘的是另一种抽象的两栖动物，眼睛里面布满了十字线，长着火焰状的眉毛，背上有很多突起（展品3.27）。这种生物可能是鳄鱼，与创世有关，代表着山地从原始海洋中隆起。

安东尼·迈耶

Animals in Olmec Art

Inhabitants of the Central Mexican sites of Las Bocas and Tlatilco shared some cultural and artistic characteristics with the dispersed Olmec civilization, whose heartland was on the Gulf Coast. Vessels from these places and surrounding regions feature abstracted images of serpents, crocodiles, and jaguars. In contrast to the Maya, who focused primarily on picturing a complete animal or its head, the Olmec chose a body part, such as a wing or paw, as a synecdoche for the creature it represented. For example, one tall bottle is marked with a stylized jaguar paw with three long, prominent claws carved horizontally along its spherical body (3.29). Finely burnished, the bottle's dark gray color was created by firing in a reduced-oxygen atmosphere.

Like the Maya, the Olmec rendered hybrid creatures, often combining birds and reptiles. The meshing of avian, terrestrial, and aquatic animal attributes enabled these supernatural creatures to travel the axis mundi, transcending various levels of the cosmos. One carved bowl exemplifies such a synthesis, showing profile serpent heads with flame eyebrows and wings that morph into paws on the vessel's other side (3.28). The background is recessed with an incised diamond pattern, perhaps to represent reptilian scales. The Maya would later modify this type of imagery to portray the Water Lily Serpent. A second bowl presents another abstract, amphibious being with crossed bands in its eyes, flame eyebrows, and projections on its back (3.27). This creature might be a crocodile, related in creation accounts as rising from the primal ocean to form the mountainous earth.

—AJM

自然的力量
FORCES OF NATURE

本件描绘的动物十分抽象,从背上的突起看,可能是鳄鱼,代表着大地从原始海洋中诞生。

3.27 兽形生物纹陶碗

出自墨西哥,墨西哥湾沿岸或墨西哥中部,奥尔梅克文明

公元前1200–公元前800年

釉陶,烧后施彩绘

10.2 × 23.2厘米

3.27 Bowl with Zoomorphic Creature

Mexico, Gulf Coast or Central Mexico, Olmec

1200–800 BCE

Slip-painted ceramic with post-fire pigment

10.2 × 23.2cm

3.28 蛇头纹陶碗

出自墨西哥,墨西哥湾沿岸或墨西哥中部,奥尔梅克文明

公元前1200–公元前800年

釉陶

11.4 × 10.2厘米

3.28 Bowl with Serpent Head

Mexico, Gulf Coast or Central Mexico, Olmec

1200–800 BCE

Slip-painted ceramic

11.4 × 10.2cm

本件陶碗上面画着带有焰眉的蛇头,另一侧是爪子一样的翅膀,这可能是睡莲蛇的原型。

3.29 美洲虎爪纹陶瓶

出自墨西哥,墨西哥湾沿岸或墨西哥中部,奥尔梅克文明

公元前1200–公元前800年

陶

27.4 × 15.2厘米

3.29 Bottle with Stylized Jaguar Paw

Mexico, Gulf Coast or Central Mexico, Olmec

1200–800 BCE

Ceramic

27.4 × 15.2cm

本件陶瓶上的美洲虎爪纹饰高度风格化,重点表现了三个长而突出的爪子。它做工精细,瓶子呈现深灰色,是在低氧环境下烧制形成的。

3.30 防染印花纹陶碗

出自墨西哥,墨西哥湾沿岸或墨西哥中部,奥尔梅克文明

公元前1200–公元前800年

釉陶

8.9 × 11.4厘米

3.30 Bowl with Resist-painted Designs

Mexico, Gulf Coast or Central Mexico, Olmec

400–100 BCE

Slip-painted ceramic

8.9 × 11.4cm

科潘大球场

第四部分　国王和王后的神圣仪式

PART IV Divine Rites of Kings and Queens

一、宫廷

玛雅绘画中经常出现王室宫廷的场景。统治者举办的封赏、音乐和舞蹈仪式等的宫殿场景中会出现柱子、楼梯和长凳等物品（展品4.1）。这些绘画中的建筑与真实的宫殿结构一致：梁柱建筑物设有宽敞的门，挂着帘子。玛雅的统治者常是男性，带有"圣主"（k'uhul Ajaw）的头衔。在古典时期的画作中，他们可单独出现，坐在美洲虎皮垫上（展品4.2、4.6），也可与访客、侍者和祭司同时出现。统治者也是人，但拥有通神之术，他们的形象经常与玉米神等神灵混合在一起，同样长着倾斜的前额和羽毛背架，戴着绿宝石首饰（展品4.28）。

容器和雕像上经常出现宫廷男女的形象（展品4.4、4.3），他们身穿彩色衣物，戴动物形的头饰，珍贵的耳坠、手镯和项链。小矮人的衣着也很华丽，他们是宫廷成员和玉米神的助手（展品4.5）。

衣物像大多数易腐物一样未能保存至今，不过翡翠和贝壳制成的服装饰品却经受住了时间的考验。"圣主"的王冠（hunal）是一块蛇形翡翠牌饰，头顶有着代表玉米的植物，与统治者的头巾缝在一起（展品4.7）。玛雅精英还会佩戴翡翠和贝壳耳饰，以耳钉固定或以串珠配重。有些耳饰是四瓣花形，将穿戴者置于假想的花香之中（展品4.8）。翡翠等绿宝石非常珍贵，象征着宝物、植物和水。

梅根·奥尼尔

Royal Courts

Maya royal courts were frequently portrayed in palace settings, with pillars, stairs, and benches framing such palatial activities as gift-giving, music, and dancing, often to honor the ruler (4.1). The architecture depicted on these objects aligns with actual palace structures, whose post-and-lintel buildings had wide, curtained doorways. Maya rulers, who were usually male, bore the title k'uhul ajaw (sacred lord). In Classic-period representations, they may be depicted alone, seated on a jaguar-pelt cushion (4.2, 4.6), or with visitors, attendants, and priests. Rulers were considered human but had special access to the divine, and their representations often overlap with such deities as the Maize God, sharing characteristics like a sloping forehead and wearing greenstone jewelry and a feathered backrack (4.28).

Vessels and figurines visualize men and women of the court (4.4, 4.3), and these individuals are frequently bedecked in painted textiles, animal headdresses, and precious ear flares, wristlets, and necklaces. Dwarfs, who were valued court members and mythological assistants to the Maize God, were also well dressed (4.5).

Textiles, like most other perishable materials, have not survived; however, examples of costume elements made from jadeite and shell have. The crown of the k'uhul ajaw, the hunal, a delicate jadeite plaque in the form of a serpentine entity with vegetation growing from its head and related to maize growth, was sewn onto a ruler's headband (4.7). Elite Maya also wore ear ornaments of jadeite and shell that were held in the ear with a plug or beaded counterweights. Some are four-petal flowers and place the wearer amid imagined floral fragrances (4.8). Jadeite and other greenstones were highly valued and symbolized preciousness, plants, and water.

—MEO

4.1 宫殿场景纹陶罐

出自危地马拉佩滕,圣何塞的摩特或邻近地区,玛雅文明
公元600–800年
釉陶
16.8 × 11.9厘米

4.1 Cylinder Vessel with Palace Scene

Guatemala, Petén, Motul de San José or vicinity, Maya
600–800 CE
Slip-painted ceramic
16.8 × 11.9cm

本件描绘了玛雅宫廷的场景。统治者坐于正中,侍从在两侧侍候,舞者在面前起舞,可以看到柱子和长凳等物品。

自然的力量
FORCES OF NATURE

本件绘有一位君主的形象,他坐在虎皮之上,头戴高冠,可能是模仿了玉米神,脖子和手臂上有珠宝串饰。

4.2 君王纹陶盘

出自危地马拉或墨西哥,可能是坎佩切,玛雅文明

公元650–850年

釉陶

5.1 × 25.4厘米

4.2 Plate with Enthroned Ruler Wearing Solar Headdress

Guatemala or Mexico, possibly Campeche, Maya

650–850 CE

Slip-painted ceramic

5.1 × 25.4cm

4.3 男子形陶哨
出自危地马拉北部或墨西哥东南部，玛雅文明
公元600–900年
陶器，烧后施彩绘
10.9 × 7.6 × 7.6厘米

4.3 Figurine Whistle of a Seated Male, Possibly a Ruler
Northern Guatemala or Southeastern Mexico, Maya
600–900 CE
Ceramic with post-fire pigment
10.9 × 7.6 × 7.6cm

本件为君主坐像。君主头戴头巾，脖子上有巨大的项链，耳朵上有厚重的耳塞。

4.4 肥胖男子陶像
出自危地马拉北部或墨西哥东南部，玛雅文明
公元600–900年
陶器，烧后施彩绘
15.2 × 11.4 × 9.7厘米

4.4 Figurine of a Portly Man
Northern Guatemala or Southeastern Mexico, Maya
600–900 CE
Ceramic with post-fire pigment
15.2 × 11.4 × 9.7cm

自然的力量
FORCES OF NATURE

4.5 小矮人形陶哨

出自危地马拉北部或墨西哥东南部，玛雅文明

公元600–900年

陶

12.2×6.4×5.8厘米

4.5 Figurine Whistle of a Seated Dwarf

Northern Guatemala or Southeastern Mexico, Maya

600–900 CE

Ceramic

12.2×6.4×5.8cm

4.6 君王纹陶瓶

出自危地马拉或洪都拉斯，玛雅文明

公元600–900年

釉陶

6.2×6×3厘米

4.6 Bottle in Form of a Building with Enthroned Ruler

Guatemala or Honduras, Maya

600–900 CE

Slip-painted ceramic

6.2x6x3cm

本件陶瓶正面浮雕一位君主的形象，整个陶瓶又模拟了宫殿建筑的造型。

4.7 王冠石牌饰
出自危地马拉佩滕北部，玛雅文明
公元450–750年
翡翠
6.7 × 5.4 × 7厘米

4.7 Hunal Plaque
Guatemala, Northern Petén, Maya
450–750 CE
Jadeite
6.7 × 5.4 × 7cm

本件为是一块蛇形翡翠牌饰，与统治者的头巾缝在一起，象征玉米。

4.8 花形石耳环
出自伯利兹或危地马拉、洪都拉斯、墨西哥，玛雅文明
公元300–900年
翡翠
3.3 × 3.3 × 3.3厘米

4.8 Floral Ear Spools
Belize, Guatemala, Honduras, or Mexico, Maya
300–900 CE
Jadeite
3.3 × 3.3 × 3.3cm

君主的耳环常用翡翠等宝石制成，这种耳环一般十分厚重。

4.9 侧面人脸纹贝壳耳坠
出自危地马拉或墨西哥，玛雅文明
公元300–900年
彩绘贝壳
6.4 × 6.4 × 2.5厘米

4.9 Ear Flares with Incised Faces
Guatemala or Mexico, Maya
300–900 CE
Shell with pigment
6.4 × 6.4 × 2.5cm

二、妇女、婚姻和抚养儿童

彩绘陶、石碑和灰泥壁画经常刻画女王和勤劳的市井妇女，陶像常描绘各个年龄段和从事各种活动的女子。雕像经常展示婚姻仪式和子女养育方面的女性生活，超自然的神灵与人类偶尔共同出现，有时难以区分。比如，一件彩绘陶器展示了一个神话场景，一些年轻女子被带到一位老年神灵（可能是L神）面前，可能是结婚的仪式（展品4.12）。一个模制陶像也出现了这种年龄搭配，一个年长男性（不是神灵）任性地坐在一位年轻女子（可能是月亮女神）的腿上（展品4.14）。

与彩绘陶器相比，雕像突出了暗示性别角色或社会地位的职业或活动，比如一位年轻织女（展品4.15）或一位年老男性背着一个头戴宽边帽的女子（展品4.13）。坐着的母亲怀抱婴儿也是经常出现的主题，但怀抱稍年长的幼儿就很少见。这些妇女有的地位高贵，身穿传统的惠毕尔（上衣），佩戴着珠宝（展品4.16）；有的是赤裸着上身的中年妇女，露出松垂的乳房（展品4.17）。这种母性主题也出现于拟人化的猴子雕像中（展品4.18），它应是一个响铃，与哨子一样，可能是孩童的玩具或乐器。

米歇尔·里奇

Women, Marriage, and Child Rearing

Ruling queens and industrious market women appear in complex narratives on polychrome vessels, carved stone monuments, and stucco murals, but ceramic figurines portray the widest range of women, at various ages and engaged in diverse activities. Figurines provide intimate glimpses of aspects of female life such as marriage rites and child rearing, and supernatural deities and humans are occasionally shown as coexisting or indistinguishable from one another. For example, one polychrome cylinder vessel illustrates an ostensibly mythological scene in which young women are carried and presented—perhaps in marriage—to an aged deity, possibly God L (4.12). This juxtaposition of age and youth is echoed in a mold-made figurine featuring an older male (in this case, not clearly a deity), mischievously sitting in the lap of a youthful, voluptuous woman (who may represent the moon goddess) (4.14).

Comparable to the narratives on polychrome vessels, figurines highlight occupations or activities alluding to gendered labor roles or social status, such as a young female weaver (4.15) or an aged male porter carrying a woman sporting a broad-brimmed traveling hat (4.13). Seated motherly women cradling babies is a repeated theme, yet infants and children are otherwise infrequently portrayed. These women can be clothed in the traditional handwoven huipil (blouse) and adorned with jewelry suggesting high status (4.16), or illustrated shirtless, revealing sagging breasts characterizing an elderly midwife (4.17). This maternal theme is mimicked in the anthropomorphized monkey figurine (4.18), which is a rattle and, like the other figurines that are whistles, may have functioned as a child's toy or musical instrument.

—MER

洛杉矶郡艺术博物馆藏古代玛雅艺术品
ANCIENT MAYA ARTS FROM THE LOS ANGELES COUNTY MUSEUM OF ART

4.10 模制妇女陶像

出自危地马拉北部或墨西哥东南部,可能是坎佩切,
玛雅文明

公元600–900年

陶

20.3 × 9.5 × 5.7厘米

4.10 Mold-made Figurine of a Standing Woman

Northern Guatemala or Southeastern Mexico, possibly Campeche, Maya

600–900 CE

Ceramic

20.3 × 9.5 × 5.7cm

自然的力量
FORCES OF NATURE

4.11 模制妇女陶像
出自危地马拉北部或墨西哥东南部，
可能是坎佩切，玛雅文明
公元600–900年
陶
22.5 × 10.2 × 5.7厘米

4.11 Mold-made Figurine of a Standing Woman
Northern Guatemala or Southeastern Mexico,
possibly Campeche, Maya
600–900 CE
Ceramic
22.5 × 10.2 × 5.7cm

4.12 婚礼场景纹陶罐

出自危地马拉佩滕,玛雅文明
公元600—900年
釉陶
24.9 × 14厘米

4.12 Cylinder Vessel with Scene of Supernatural Marriage Rituals

Guatemala, Petén, Maya
600–900 CE
Slip-painted ceramic
24.9 × 14cm

本件描绘了婚礼的场景。玛雅人的婚姻不能由自己决定,双方不能来自同一宗族。一旦配偶确定下来,祭司会被请来主持婚礼。婚礼一般在女方家进行,新郎和新娘将保留各自的姓氏。

自然的力量
FORCES OF NATURE

4.13 夫妇形陶哨
出自危地马拉北部或墨西哥东南部，可能是坎佩切，
玛雅文明
公元600–900年
陶，烧后施彩绘
20.3 × 8.4 × 8.4厘米

4.13 Figurine Whistle of a Couple
Northern Guatemala or Southeastern Mexico, possibly Campeche, Maya
600–900 CE
Ceramic with post-fire pigment
20.3 × 8.4 × 8.4cm

4.14 老人和女子形陶哨 | 4.14 Figurine Whistle of an Old Man and a Young Woman

出自危地马拉北部或墨西哥东南部，可能是坎佩切，玛雅文明
公元600–900年
陶，烧后施彩绘
15.2 × 11.4 × 8.9厘米

Northern Guatemala or Southeastern Mexico, possibly Campeche, Maya
600–900 CE
Ceramic with post-fire pigment
15.2 × 11.4 × 8.9cm

自然的力量
FORCES OF NATURE

本件为一位使用纺织的妇女形象。玛雅人的织机是背带纺织机,这一技术今天仍在中美洲使用。他们能够织出1米宽的布条,如果需要更宽的布,就将几块布条缝在一起使用。

4.15 妇女形陶哨
出自危地马拉北部或墨西哥东南部,可能是坎佩切,
玛雅文明
公元600–900年
陶,烧后施彩绘
18.4 × 9.2 × 14.3厘米

4.15 Figurine Whistle of a Woman with a Backstrap Loom
Northern Guatemala or Southeastern Mexico, possibly Campeche, Maya
600–900 CE
Ceramic with post-fire pigment
18.4 × 9.2 × 14.3cm

4.16 抱婴女子形陶哨

出自危地马拉北部或墨西哥东南部，玛雅文明
公元600-900年
陶，烧后施彩绘
17.8×8.3×7.6厘米

4.16 Figurine Whistle of a Young Woman and a Baby

Northern Guatemala or Southeastern Mexico, Maya
600–900 CE
Ceramic with post-fire pigment
17.8 × 8.3 × 7.6cm

本件为一位怀抱婴儿的贵族妇女，身穿传统的惠毕尔，佩戴着项链。玛雅人一结婚很快就生育孩子，生育年龄在20岁左右，他们希望自己的子女众多。妇女通常向女神伊尔祈祷并献祭，以求多产和顺利生产。婴儿受到长时期的照顾，尽管财产的继承只局限于家庭中的男性，但是子女都继承父母双方的姓氏。

4.17 抱婴老妇形陶哨

出自危地马拉北部或墨西哥东南部，玛雅文明
公元600-900年
陶，烧后施彩绘
14×7.6×7.6厘米

4.17 Figurine Whistle of an Old Woman and a Baby

Northern Guatemala or Southeastern Mexico, Maya
600–900 CE
Ceramic with post-fire pigment
14 × 7.6 × 7.6cm

4.18 怀抱幼猴猴形陶响铃

出自危地马拉北部或墨西哥东南部，玛雅文明

公元600-900年

陶，烧后施彩绘

12.7 × 8.4 × 7.6厘米

4.18 Figurine Rattle of a Monkey and a Baby

Northern Guatemala or Southeastern Mexico, Maya
600–900 CE
Ceramic with post-fire pigment
12.7 × 8.4 × 7.6cm

4.19 老妇形陶哨

出自危地马拉北部或墨西哥东南部，玛雅文明

公元600-900年

陶，烧后施彩绘

13.7 × 8.4 × 7.6厘米

4.19 Figurine Whistle of an Old Woman

Northern Guatemala or Southeastern
Mexico, Maya
600–900 CE
Ceramic with post-fire pigment
13.7 × 8.4 × 7.6cm

洛杉矶郡艺术博物馆藏古代玛雅艺术品
ANCIENT MAYA ARTS FROM THE LOS ANGELES COUNTY MUSEUM OF ART

4.20 带女子和小矮人的寺庙模型
出自危地马拉北部或墨西哥东南部,可能是坎佩切,
玛雅文明
公元600–900年
陶
20.6×15.2×5.1厘米

4.20 Temple Model with a Female Figure and Dwarfs
Northern Guatemala or Southeastern Mexico, possibly Campeche, Maya
600–900 CE
Ceramic
20.6×15.2×5.1cm

三、音乐

音乐是古代玛雅生活和仪式中不可或缺的部分,常会在舞蹈和仪式表演中演奏。歌曲被认为是对祖先和其他超自然神灵的祈祷或祭品,乐器也会放在坟墓中陪葬。波南帕克的彩绘壁画和玛雅地区的彩绘陶器都描绘有乐师在宫殿内打鼓、击打响铃、龟壳、吹奏木制号角和海螺壳的场景。一件陶器上,两位乐师正在为一位边唱边跳的舞者伴奏:一位在用刮条和葫芦演奏,另一位可能在摩擦鼓(展品4.21)。另一个陶罐上,一位身穿鸟服的统治者端坐于宝座上,面前是一位扮作卡维尔的蒙面舞者和一些使用响铃、号角和大鼓演奏的乐师(展品4.23)。另一个陶器上绘有七位头戴面具的舞者和乐师,其中包括演奏响铃的狗,一只敲鼓的犰狳和一只敲着龟甲的囊地鼠(展品4.22)。

虽然由木头或葫芦制成的乐器未能保存至今,但许多地方都发现了贝壳喇叭和陶鼓,并从墓中出土了龟壳。更常见的是人形陶笛和哨子,这些物品在耆那岛等地的墓葬中出土得尤其多。一些哨子被塑成乐师形象(展品4.24),但更多刻画了人们参与各种与音乐无关的活动。玛雅人还将响铃放在陶罐的底座和脚部,将这些简单的陶罐变成乐器(展品4.25)。还有些容器能在装液体时发出哨声并前后摇摆(展品3.13)。

梅根·奥尼尔

Music

Music, which was played during dances and ritual processions, was integral to ancient Maya life and ritual. Songs were considered prayers or offerings to ancestors and other supernatural entities, and musical instruments were deposited in graves. The painted murals of Bonampak and polychrome vessels from the Maya region depict musicians playing drums, rattles, turtle shells, and wooden and conch-shell trumpets within palace settings. On one vessel, two musicians—one playing a gourd with a rasp, the other playing what may be a friction drum—accompany a royal dancer who is also singing (4.21). Another cylinder vessel shows a masked K'awiil dancer and musicians playing rattles, trumpets, and a large drum before an enthroned ruler wearing a bird costume (4.23). Seven costumed dancers and musicians, including a canine with rattles, an armadillo playing a tall drum, and a gopher playing a tortoise shell, decorate another cylinder vessel (4.22).

Although musical instruments made of wood or gourds have not survived, shell trumpets and ceramic hand drums have been found at multiple sites, and turtle shells have been unearthed in tombs. More common are figural ocarinas and whistles, particularly those found in abundance in graves on Jaina Island and elsewhere. Some whistles portray musicians (4.24), but often they render people participating in a variety of activities unrelated to music. The Maya also placed rattle balls inside vessels' pedestals and feet, turning these simple containers into musical instruments (4.25). Other vessels were constructed so that they whistled when filled with liquid and rocked back and forth (3.13).

—MEO

4.21 乐舞纹陶罐

出自危地马拉北部或墨西哥东南部，玛雅文明
公元600–900年
釉陶
23.2 × 13.7厘米

4.21 Cylinder Vessel with Musicians and Dancer

Northern Guatemala or Southeastern Mexico, Maya
600–900 CE
Slip-painted ceramic
23.2 × 13.7cm

本件描绘了两位乐师正在为一位边唱边跳的舞者伴奏的场景：一位在用刮条和葫芦演奏，另一位可能用的是摩擦鼓。鼓是最常见的玛雅乐器，包括有海龟壳做成的鼓和木鼓等各种类型

自然的力量
FORCES OF NATURE

本件陶罐上绘有七位头戴面具的舞者和乐师，面具都是动物造型：演奏响铃的狗，一只敲鼓的犰狳和一只敲着龟甲的囊地鼠。陶响铃也是一种常见乐器，摇动响铃时，内部的小球会发出响声。

4.22 乐舞纹陶罐

出自危地马拉上维拉帕斯、查马或邻近地区，玛雅文明

公元600–800年

釉陶

19.1 × 17.8厘米

4.22 Cylinder Vessel with Procession of Masked Dancers and Musicians

Guatemala, Alta Verapaz, Chamá or vicinity, Maya

600–800 CE

Slip-painted ceramic

19.1 × 17.8cm

洛杉矶郡艺术博物馆藏古代玛雅艺术品
ANCIENT MAYA ARTS FROM THE LOS ANGELES COUNTY MUSEUM OF ART

本件绘有一位身穿鸟服的统治者，扮作卡维尔的蒙面舞者，和使用响铃、号角和大鼓演奏的乐师在为其表演。对于玛雅人来说，身着各种不同服装的表演者扮演了不同的神灵，再现了玛雅创世的故事。国王身着鸟的服饰，可能他在扮演伊察姆纳的化身大鸟神，这一形象常常和国王联系在一起。

4.23 乐舞纹陶罐
出自危地马拉佩滕，圣何塞的摩特或邻近地区，玛雅文明
公元700–850年
釉陶
21.1×12.7厘米

4.23 Cylinder Vessel with Musicians and Dancers in a Palace Scene
Guatemala, Petén, Motul de San José or vicinity, Maya
700–850 CE
Slip-painted ceramic
21.1×12.7cm

4.24 号手形陶哨
出自危地马拉北部或墨西哥东南部，玛雅文明
公元600–900年
陶，烧后施彩绘
16.5 × 7.1 × 5.8厘米

4.24 Figurine Whistle of a Man with Trumpet
Northern Guatemala or Southeastern Mexico, Maya
600–900 CE
Ceramic with post-fire pigment
16.5 × 7.1 × 5.8cm

号在玛雅也很常见，有些号用木头制成，在末端装有葫芦，此外还有海螺制成的号。人形的陶哨被称为奥克瑞纳（Ocarinas），常在葬礼上使用，目的是希望用哨声引起众神对死者的注意

4.25 响铃和蛇纹陶碗
出自危地马拉北部或墨西哥东南部，玛雅文明
公元250–550年
釉陶，烧后施彩绘
14 × 15.2厘米

4.25 Bowl with Rattles and Serpent Design
Northern Guatemala or Southeastern Mexico, Maya
250–550 CE
Slip-painted ceramic with post-fire pigment
14 × 15.2cm

本件陶碗底部装有响铃，外表饰有神蛇

四、舞蹈和模仿

玛雅贵族喜欢在娱乐、政治和宗教活动中跳舞,这样既能结识其他贵族,又能接近超自然力量。舞蹈和模仿表演有时融合在一起。一些图案清晰刻画着有人身穿礼服,头戴面具(展品4.26、4.23),而另一些图像则融合了舞者和模仿神灵的行为,表明舞者已发生转变。贵族常会装扮成动物和神灵,比如美洲虎、狐狸、猴子和鸟类(展品4.27)。展品中的一件三足陶盘将一位年轻的统治者描绘成了玉米神,他身穿羽毛背架,虽为坐姿但手臂伸了出来,手掌向下,与玉米神舞者相差无几(展品4.28)。

有些舞者单独出现(展品2.23),有些进行集体表演。一件陶器上描绘了一个精美的鸭嘴的风神和一个猴子舞者(展品4.31),另一件陶器上刻画了多个舞者(展品4.30)。容器上还展示过为登基者(统治者或神灵)表演的盛装舞者(展品4.32、4.23)。鸟形舞者在玛雅等地区也很常见,扮演的是鸟形玉米神和鸟神之首等超自然鸟类。佩滕的一个陶器上画有蜂鸟舞者,他们似乎是戴着面具和翅膀的人类,但身体上的标志却暗示他们是神灵(展品4.33)。受特奥蒂瓦坎的影响,埃斯昆特拉地区的浮雕陶罐描绘了风格化的鸟形舞者,将舞者和鸟类融为一体,表明他们是正在跳舞的鸟类。陶罐外壁的舞蹈纹饰似乎表明了玛雅古代和现在常见的圆形舞蹈形态。

梅根·奥尼尔

Dance and Impersonation

Maya nobles engaged in dance for entertainment, politics, and religion both to forge alliances with other nobles and to tap into supernatural forces. There is some overlap of dance and impersonation rites. Some images show a person clearly in costume, wearing a mask or a suit (4.26, 4.23), whereas others fuse the identity of the dancer and the impersonated entity, suggesting transformation has taken place. Nobles dressed as animals, including jaguars, foxes, monkeys, and birds (4.27), and as deities. A tripod plate depicts a youthful enthroned ruler as the Maize God; he wears a feathered backrack, and although he is seated, his outstretched arm, with the palm extended down, is comparable to that of the Maize God dancer (4.28).

Some dancers appear alone (2.23); others are in groups. One vessel pictures an elaborately costumed duck-billed wind-god figure and a monkey dancer, among other figures (4.31), and another vessel portrays multiple repeating figures (4.30). Also illustrated on vessels are costumed dancers performing for enthroned figures, whether rulers or deities (4.32, 4.23). Avian dancers, common across the Maya region and beyond, perform as supernatural birds, including the avian Maize God and Principal Bird Deity. One vessel from the Petén presents hummingbird dancers who seem to be humans wearing masks and wings, yet mirror signs on their bodies intimate that they are deities (4.33). Carved vessels from the Escuintla area, which feature influences from Teotihuacan, render stylized avian dancers that merge dancer and bird, suggesting they are dancing birds (M.2010.115.851). Images of dances wrapping around cylindrical vessels seem to indicate circular dance formations common to the Maya, past and present.

—MEO

4.26 鸟装男子陶像

出自危地马拉北部或墨西哥东南部，玛雅文明
公元600–900年
釉陶
19.7×9.5×5.7厘米

4.26 Figurine of a Man in Avian Costume

Northern Guatemala or Southeastern Mexico, Maya
600–900 CE
Slip-painted ceramic
19.7×9.5×5.7cm

本件为身着鸟羽服饰的男子形象。对于玛雅人来说，舞蹈不仅是一种娱乐方式，更是表达宗教信仰的途径。他们通过舞蹈与祖先及神灵沟通，自己也可以转变为神灵。国王、贵族、祭司都是舞者。

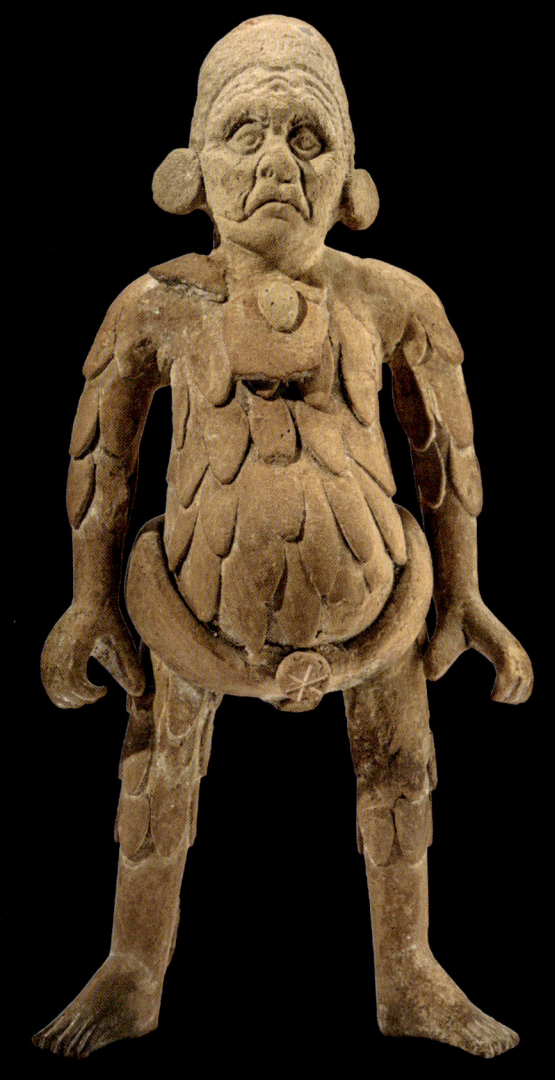

4.27 男子形陶哨

出自危地马拉北部或墨西哥东南部，玛雅文明
公元600–900年
陶，烧后施彩绘
8.9×5.1×5.7厘米

4.27 Figurine Whistle of a Man in a Fox Mask

Northern Guatemala or Southeastern Mexico, Maya
600–900 CE
Ceramic with post-fire pigment
8.9×5.1×5.7cm

本件为头戴面具的男子坐像。从面具的长嘴来看，此人扮演的可能是卡维尔神。

洛杉矶郡艺术博物馆藏古代玛雅艺术品
ANCIENT MAYA ARTS FROM THE LOS ANGELES COUNTY MUSEUM OF ART

本件陶盘描绘了扮成玉米神的统治者。他身穿羽毛背架，手掌向下。

4.28 君主（或玉米神）纹陶盘

出自危地马拉佩滕东北部，玛雅文明

公元650–850年

釉陶

15.2 × 36.3厘米

4.28 Plate with Seated Ruler as Maize God

Guatemala, Northeastern Petén, Maya

650–850 CE

Slip-painted ceramic

15.2 × 36.3cm

203

自然的力量
FORCES OF NATURE

4.29 卡维尔模仿者纹陶罐
出自危地马拉或墨西哥，玛雅文明
公元600—900年
釉陶，烧后施灰泥和彩绘
21.1×14厘米

4.29 Cylinder Vessel with K'awiil Impersonators
Guatemala or Mexico, Maya
600–900 CE
Slip-painted ceramic with post-fire stucco and pigment
21.1×14cm

洛杉矶郡艺术博物馆藏古代玛雅艺术品
ANCIENT MAYA ARTS FROM THE LOS ANGELES COUNTY MUSEUM OF ART

本件描绘列队的舞者，他们为登基者（统治者或神灵）表演而身着盛装。

4.30 舞蹈纹陶碗 | **4.30 Bowl with Procession of Dancers**

出自洪都拉斯乌鲁阿谷，玛雅文明 | Honduras, Ulúa Valley, Maya

公元600—650年 | 600–650 CE

釉陶，烧后施灰泥和彩绘 | Slip-painted ceramic with post-fire stucco and pigment

205

4.31 球手和舞蹈纹陶罐 | 4.31 Vessel with Ballplayer and Dancers
出自危地马拉或墨西哥，玛雅文明 | Guatemala or Mexico, Maya
公元300–600年 | 300–600 CE
釉陶 | Slip-painted ceramic

本件描绘了为庆祝统治者登基而起舞的场景。

洛杉矶郡艺术博物馆藏古代玛雅艺术品
ANCIENT MAYA ARTS FROM THE LOS ANGELES COUNTY MUSEUM OF ART

4.32 舞蹈纹陶碗
出自洪都拉斯乌鲁阿谷,玛雅文明
公元650–750年
釉陶
20.3 × 19.8厘米

4.32 Bowl with Masked Dancers Performing for Figure in a Temple
Honduras, Ulúa Valley, Maya
650–750 CE
Slip-painted ceramic
20.3 × 19.8cm

4.33 舞蹈纹陶罐

出自危地马拉佩滕，玛雅文明
公元550–700年
釉陶
19.8 × 14厘米

4.33 Vessel with Avian Dancers

Guatemala, Petén, Maya
550–700 CE
Slip-painted ceramic
19.8 × 14 cm

本件上的舞者扮作蜂鸟，他们似乎是戴着面具和翅膀的人类，但身体上绘有的涡纹饰却暗示他们具有神性

洛杉矶郡艺术博物馆藏古代玛雅艺术品
ANCIENT MAYA ARTS FROM THE LOS ANGELES COUNTY MUSEUM OF ART

本件陶罐外壁上浮雕了鸟形的舞者，但已经高度风格化，将舞者和鸟类融为一体。

4.34 浮雕舞蹈纹陶罐

出自危地马拉太平洋海岸，埃斯昆特拉

公元300–600年

釉陶

25.4×23.6厘米

4.34 Carved Vessel with Avian Dancers

Guatemala, Pacific Coast, Escuintla

300–600 CE

Slip-painted ceramic

25.4×23.6cm

自然的力量
FORCES OF NATURE

4.35 舞蹈纹陶罐
出自洪都拉斯乌鲁阿谷，玛雅文明
公元650–750年
釉陶
23.9 × 15.2厘米

4.35 Cylinder Vessel with Avian Dancers
Honduras, Ulúa Valley, Maya
650–750 CE
Slip-painted ceramic
23.9 × 15.2cm

4.36 舞蹈纹陶罐
出自洪都拉斯乌鲁阿谷,玛雅文明
公元650–750年
釉陶
20.3 × 11.9厘米

4.36 Cylinder Vessel with Avian Dancers
Honduras, Ulúa Valley, Maya
650–750 CE
Slip-painted ceramic
20.3 × 11.9cm

五、玛雅和中美洲的球赛

球赛是玛雅和其他中美洲文化的一项重要游戏。早在公元前1200年，人们就用两面平行的墙围成球场。运动员在臀部、胳膊和膝盖绑上衬垫，以便在将球传向球场侧壁上的石环或标记时保护自己不受伤。这种器材在中美洲随处可见，尤其是韦拉克鲁斯，其中包括系在臀部的轭（展品4.43、4.44、4.45）以及斧形的"哈恰"（展品4.46、4.48）和棕榈枝形的"帕尔马"（展品4.47、4.49）。由于过于沉重，这些石头物品可能只具有礼仪意义，作为奖品或陪葬品。

对于玛雅人来说，球赛也是一场生死攸关的战役，会重演《波波尔·乌》中双子英雄与西瓦尔巴领主的博弈。球赛仪式是为了确保神灵和玉米生长的持续性，球场被设想为大地的一个开口。一件陶碗以阶梯式剖面描绘了玉米神从球场出现，描绘了他重生的场景（展品4.42）。一件陶哨描绘了三个人抬着一顶轿子，上面是身穿球赛徽章的统治者，旁边为双头蛇，坐在另一个象征着球场的阶梯式壁龛内，下面是一场正在进行的比赛（展品4.41）。"球手"（piztil）是授予玛雅精英的一种头衔，与双子英雄的胜利联系在一起。球场是自然与超自然、死亡与重生之间的一个过渡地带。

安东尼·迈耶

Ballgame among the Maya and across Mesoamerica

The Mesoamerican ballgame was an important ritual game for the Maya and other Mesoamerican cultures. As early as 1200 BCE, it was played on a court formed by two long, parallel structures. Players wore padding on the hips, arms, and knees to protect themselves from injury when directing the ball toward stone hoops or markers attached to the side walls of the courts. This equipment, found throughout Mesoamerica, but especially in Veracruz, included yokes worn on the hips (4.43, 4.44, 4.45), as well as hachas (4.46, 4.48) and palmas (4.47, 4.49), which are named, respectively, for their axe-like and palm-branch shapes. Too heavy for actual use, versions made in stone were probably ceremonial, given as trophies or grave goods.

For the Maya, the ballgame represented a battle of life-and-death, reenacting the Hero Twins' mythical match against the Lords of Xibalba, as related in the Popol Vuh. The ballgame ritual was performed to ensure the continued cycles of heavenly bodies and maize growth, and the court was envisioned as an opening in the earth. On one carved bowl, the Maize God emerges from a ballcourt, rendered as a stepped profile, in a scene of his rebirth (4.42). A whistle depicts three figures raising a palanquin holding a ruler who, dressed in ballgame regalia and flanked by a two-headed serpent, sits within another stepped niche symbolizing the ballcourt; underneath, a supernatural game is under way (4.41). Piztil, "ballplayer," was a title awarded to elite Maya men, associating them with the triumphant nature of the Hero Twins. Ultimately, the court is a place of transition between the natural and supernatural, and between death and rebirth.

—AJM

4.37 球手形陶哨

出自危地马拉北部或墨西哥东南部，玛雅文明
公元600–900年
陶，烧后施彩绘
20.3 × 8.3 × 7.3厘米

4.37 Figurine Whistle of a Ballplayer

Northern Guatemala or Southeastern Mexico, Maya
600–900 CE
Ceramic with post-fire pigment
20.3 × 8.3 × 7.3cm

4.38 球手形陶哨

出自危地马拉北部或墨西哥东南部，玛雅文明
公元600–900年
陶
18.5 × 8.9 × 5.1厘米

4.38 Figurine Whistle of a Ballplayer

Northern Guatemala or Southeastern Mexico, Maya
600–900 CE
Ceramic
18.5 × 8.9 × 5.1cm

自然的力量
FORCES OF NATURE

本件描绘了球赛的场景。球手头戴华丽的头饰,上面插着珍贵的克沙尔鸟的羽毛。

4.39 球赛纹陶罐 | **4.39 Cylinder Vessel with Ballgame Scene**

出自危地马拉或墨西哥,玛雅文明 | Guatemala or Mexico, Maya
公元600–900年 | 600–900 CE
釉陶,烧后施彩绘 | Slip-painted ceramic with post-fire pigment
22.9 × 11.4厘米 | 22.9 × 11.4cm

本件陶瓶上绘有球手和一只囊地鼠。球手头戴动物形头饰，身带轭以保护自己。

4.40 球手和囊地鼠纹陶瓶

出自危地马拉或洪都拉斯，玛雅文明

公元600–900年

釉陶，烧后施彩绘

15.2 × 7.6 × 4.6厘米

4.40 Bottle in Form of a House with Ballplayer and Gopher

Guatemala or Honduras, Maya

600–900 CE

Slip-painted ceramic with post-fire pigment

15.2 × 7.6 × 4.6cm

自然的力量
FORCES OF NATURE

球赛在玛雅世界中有重要的宗教意义。虽然球赛具体的规则已不清楚，但由于球运动的方式与天体运动的方式相似，因此有球赛有宇宙论的含义。

4.41 统治者、双头蛇和球手形陶哨

出自危地马拉佩滕，玛雅文明

公元600-900年

陶，烧后施彩绘

17.3×7.6×10.2厘米

4.41 Whistle with Ruler, Bicephalic Serpent, and Ballplayers

Guatemala, Petén, Maya

600–900 CE

Ceramic with post-fire pigment

17.3 × 7.6 × 10.2cm

4.42 复活玉米神纹陶碗

出自危地马拉北部或墨西哥东南部,玛雅文明
公元600–900年
釉陶
16.5 × 17.8厘米

4.42 Bowl with Resurrection of the Maize God in a Ballcourt

Northern Guatemala or Southeastern Mexico, Maya
600–900 CE
Slip-painted ceramic
16.5 × 17.8cm

本件描绘了玉米神重生的场景。这一故事见于《波波尔·乌》。双子英雄通过在下界中与死神进行的球赛中获胜,使玉米神得到重生。球场本身也被视为大地的裂缝,球场边界由倾斜的墙壁构成。在神话中,玉米神是从大地的裂缝中复活的,因此球场被认为是一个与下界交流的场所。

轭一般用皮或柳条制成,以保护肋骨和臀部。这种石质的轭不用于球赛之中,可能是一种奖品

4.43 蟾蜍形石轭
出自墨西哥韦拉克鲁斯市中心,韦拉克鲁斯文明
公元300—600年
石
12.7×43.2×40.3厘米

4.43 Yoke in Form of a Toad
Mexico, Central Veracruz, Veracruz
300–600 CE
Stone
12.7 × 43.2 × 40.3cm

洛杉矶郡艺术博物馆藏古代玛雅艺术品
ANCIENT MAYA ARTS FROM THE LOS ANGELES COUNTY MUSEUM OF ART

4.44 蟾蜍形石轭
出自墨西哥，韦拉克鲁斯市中心，韦拉克鲁斯文明
公元300–600年
石
12 × 37.5 × 40厘米

4.44 Yoke in Form of a Toad
Mexico, Central Veracruz, Veracruz
300–600 CE
Stone
12 × 37.5 × 40cm

自然的力量
FORCES OF NATURE

4.45 美洲虎形石轭	4.45 Yoke in Form of a Jaguar
出自墨西哥韦拉克鲁斯市中心，韦拉克鲁斯文明	Mexico, Central Veracruz, Veracruz
公元600–900年	600–900 CE
流纹岩	Rhyolite
43.2 × 37.5 × 11.8厘米	43.2 × 37.5 × 11.8cm

4.46 蛇形石"哈恰"

出自萨尔瓦多或墨西哥，玛雅文明或韦拉克鲁斯文明
公元600–900年
玄武岩
19.1 × 10.2 × 13.5厘米，22.9 × 10.2 × 16厘米

4.46 Hacha in Form of a Serpent

\El Salvador or Mexico, Maya or Veracruz
600–900 CE
Basalt
19.1 × 10.2 × 13.5cm, 22.9 × 10.2 × 16cm

哈恰是一种类似斧子的石质工具，制成动物或人头的形状，系挂在球手的腰带上。人形的哈恰可能象征战俘的头颅

4.47 猫头鹰头形石"帕尔马"

出自墨西哥韦拉克鲁斯，韦拉克鲁斯文明
公元600–1000年
玄武岩
18.4 × 14.6 × 11.8厘米

4.47 Palma in Form of an Owl's Head

Mexico, Veracruz, Veracruz
600–1000 CE
Basalt
18.4 × 14.6 × 11.8cm

一些球员戴着被称为帕尔马的护胸，它可以被插入到轭中，立于胸前

4.48 兔形石"哈恰"

出自墨西哥韦拉克鲁斯南部，帕洛阿潘或邻近地区，韦拉克鲁斯文明

公元600–900年
玄武岩
21.9 × 18.4 × 8.3厘米

4.48 Hacha in Form of a Rabbit

Mexico, Southern Veracruz, Papaloapan or vicinity, Veracruz
600–900 CE
Basalt
21.9 × 18.4 × 8.3cm

4.49 箭袋形石"帕尔马"

出自墨西哥拉克鲁斯市中心，韦拉克鲁斯文明

公元600–1000年
玄武岩
65.4 × 20.3 × 11.4厘米

4.49 Palma in Form of a Quiver with Arrows

Mexico, Veracruz, Veracruz
600–1000 CE
Basalt
65.4 × 20.3 × 11.4cm

六、迷幻状态：烟草和致幻剂

借助于烈性烟草、发酵或致幻液体，玛雅人常制造迷幻状态来接近神灵。烟草会以雪茄、鼻烟或液体等方式被单独食用或与致幻剂混合起来吸入，产生一种迷幻和恍惚感。一件现藏美国国会图书馆的古典时期陶瓶内就曾发现尼古丁。还有些瓶子可能是烟草容器，但没有经过科学检测确认。展品中一对有鬼脸陶瓶内着黑色残渣，可能是烟草残留物，鬼脸似乎表明近期吸食了鼻烟；他们年纪较大，代表了常被描绘为雪茄吸食者的烟草神L神（展品4.52）。另外一些玛雅艺术品描绘了吸食雪茄的男子：一幅乐师队列图案中有两位吸烟的男子（展品4.51），一个宫廷场景描绘了手拿雪茄的统治者和访客（展品4.50）。

玛雅人还常饮用发酵的龙舌兰酒（龙舌兰的汁液）、蜂蜜和"巴尔切"（由树皮制成），以及睡莲和曼陀罗花等致幻剂，从而产生狂喜以及净化的体验（包括呕吐）。除了饮用这些液体，他们还会使用注射器将它们注入肛门以便快速吸收。注射器可能是将骨管插入由橡胶或动物肠道制成的可挤压球状物来制成。含有这种液体的壶在灌肠仪式中有所表现，其中的人物要么是自己注射，要么是侍者帮忙。有时这些场景还会带有超自然色彩（展品2.54）。一件球状陶碗上，三个坐着的人形和兽形神灵高举着注射器，也许是灌肠的致幻性让他们变成了复合动物。

安东尼·迈耶和梅根·奥尼尔

Altered States: Tobacco and Hallucinogens

With the aid of potent tobacco and fermented and hallucinogenic liquids, the Maya induced altered states to tap into the supernatural. Smoked in cigars, inhaled as powdered snuff, or imbibed as liquid, tobacco was consumed alone or mixed with hallucinogens for healing and to produce hallucinogenic trances. Nicotine has been found in one Classic-period bottle (now in the collection of the United States Library of Congress); other bottles likely were tobacco containers too, but they have not been tested. The interiors of two matching bottles with grimacing heads contain dark stains, possibly tobacco residue, and the figures' grimaces seem to convey recent inhalation of snuff; their aged features also evoke God L, deity of tobacco who is portrayed as a cigar smoker (4.52). Other Maya representations show men with cigars: one painting of a procession of musicians includes two men smoking (4.51), and a palace scene portrays a ruler and visitor holding cigars (4.50).

The Maya also ingested fermented pulque (maguey sap), honey, and balché (made from tree bark), as well as hallucinogens like water lilies and datura flowers, to induce ecstatic and purifying experiences that involved vomiting. In addition to drinking these liquids, they used syringes to inject them into the anus for quick absorption. Syringes may have consisted of a bone tube inserted into a squeezable bulb made of rubber or animal intestine. Bound jugs containing such fluids appear in depictions of enema rituals; in those scenes, figures either self-administer or attendants carry out the act (M.2010.115.243). Sometimes these scenes take on a supernatural quality (2.54). On one globular bowl, three seated deities with anthropomorphic and zoomorphic features raise syringes in the air; perhaps the enema's hallucinogenic properties induced their transformation into hybrid creatures (M.2010.115.860).

—AJM and MEO

自然的力量
FORCES OF NATURE

本件描绘了统治者抽雪茄的场景。玛雅人吸烟时将烟草卷起来或者放在陶土制成的烟斗中。烟草在宗教典礼中也可以作为迷幻剂来使用,被认为是奉献给神的祭品。

4.50 宫殿纹陶罐
出自墨西哥坎佩切或金塔纳罗奥,玛雅文明
公元800-950年
釉陶
16.2×13厘米

4.50 Cylinder Vessel with Palace Scene
Mexico, Campeche or Quintana Roo, Maya
800–950 CE
Slip-painted ceramic
16.2 × 13cm

洛杉矶郡艺术博物馆藏古代玛雅艺术品
ANCIENT MAYA ARTS FROM THE LOS ANGELES COUNTY MUSEUM OF ART

本件描绘了正在抽烟的乐师。

4.51 乐师纹陶罐	4.51 Cylinder Vessel with Procession of Musicians
出自危地马拉佩滕，玛雅文明	Guatemala, Petén, Maya
公元600–900年	600–900 CE
釉陶	Slip-painted ceramic
25.4 × 10.9厘米	25.4 × 10.9cm

225

本组鬼脸陶瓶内着黑色残渣,可能是烟草残留物。鬼脸皱纹密布,显得上了年纪,可能代表了雪茄吸食者的烟草神L神。

4.52 鬼脸神形陶瓶
出自危地马拉或洪都拉斯,玛雅文明
公元600–900年
釉陶
5.1×3.3×3.1厘米,5.1×3.3×3.3厘米

4.52 Bottle with Grimacing Aged Deity
Guatemala or Honduras, Maya
600–900 CE
Slip-painted ceramic
5.1×3.3×3.1cm, 5.1×3.3×3.3cm

4.53 供奉铭文及编织垫纹陶瓶
出自危地马拉或洪都拉斯,玛雅文明
公元600–900年
釉陶,烧后施彩绘
10.4×4.4×3.5厘米

4.53 Bottle with Dedicatory Inscription and Design of Woven Mat
Guatemala or Honduras, Maya
600–900 CE
Slip-painted ceramic with post-fire pigment
10.4×4.4×3.5cm

洛杉矶郡艺术博物馆藏古代玛雅艺术品
ANCIENT MAYA ARTS FROM THE LOS ANGELES COUNTY MUSEUM OF ART

4.54 灌肠男子纹陶碗	4.54 Bowl with Males Using Enemas
出自危地马拉或洪都拉斯，玛雅文明	Guatemala or Honduras, Maya
公元600–900年	600–900 CE
釉陶	Slip-painted ceramic
8.4×21.1厘米	8.4×21.1cm

玛雅文明等很多中南美洲的宗教仪式中使用灌肠。灌肠液体可含酒精、烟草、仙人掌等致幻剂，以达到宗教致幻目的。

4.55 表演灌肠仪式陶像 | 4.55 Figurine of a Man Performing an Enema Ritual
出自危地马拉，玛雅文明 | Guatemala, Maya
公元600–900年 | 600–900 CE
陶，烧后施彩绘 | Ceramic with post-fire pigment
10.2×17.3×7.1厘米 | 10.2×17.3×7.1cm

自然的力量
FORCES OF NATURE

4.56 灌肠仪式纹陶碗 | **4.56 Bowl with Enema Ritual**

出自危地马拉或洪都拉斯,玛雅文明 | Guatemala or Honduras, Maya

公元300–600年 | 300–600 CE

釉陶 | Slip-painted ceramic

10.9 × 37.6厘米 | 10.9 × 37.6cm

4.57 灌肠仪式纹球形陶碗

出自伯利兹或危地马拉,玛雅文明

公元550–700年

釉陶,烧后施灰泥和彩绘

17.8 × 14.7厘米

4.57 Globular Bowl with Supernatural Enema Ritual

Belize or Guatemala, Maya,

550–700 CE

Slip-painted ceramic with post-fire stucco and pigment

17.8 × 14.7cm

本件描绘了一种超自然的灌肠仪式。各种奇异的动物手持灌肠器。玛雅人认为通过迷幻剂的灌肠,能够使人进入超自然的状态,使得灵魂离开自己的身体,转化为其他形式,从而与祖先、神灵直接沟通

七、转化：出生、死亡、重生、祖先和神灵召唤

出生、死亡、重生、祖先和神灵召唤等转化过程被想象为通过超自然通道（蛇、鳄鱼或蜈蚣的咽喉）的一种过程。有些场景中只出现了神灵。一件抄本风格陶器描绘了一位被蛇缠着的年轻女子，这条蛇应是卡维尔的腿（展品4.60）。蛇头吐出了一位年长的神，他将手伸向女子裸露的乳房。旁边的文字叙述了神的诞生，表明这是一个超自然诞生的场景。

还有画面描述了人类召唤神灵和祖先，以举行出生、指定继承人、加入王室或转化为祖先或其他神灵等仪式。一个陶器上描绘着握着双头蛇的统治者（展品4.60），其他雕像展示了带有同样王室神圣徽记的女子（展品4.62）。另一个陶器上画着一位坐着的男子手握权杖，正在召唤一位年长的神（展品4.59），一块翡翠挂件刻画着一位统治者和从头顶蛇形中出现的祖先（展品4.68）。更加模糊的是一块浮雕海牛肋骨，描绘了一个人从鳄鱼咽喉出来，这可能是原始起源或来自地下世界的祖先（展品4.64）。还有一些图案描绘了对统治者死后的崇拜：一块牌饰显示了一个地方长官在向一位彼德拉斯内格拉斯统治者献祭，但文字（记载了统治者的死亡悼念和纪念仪式）显示这是回溯的情景，是在事情发生多年、统治者已成祖先之后的记录（展品4.67）。

玛雅人也常描绘尸体，比如一个雕像形似俘虏骨架，手臂被绑在背后（展品4.66）。

梅根·奥尼尔

Transformation: Birth, Death, Rebirth, Ancestors, and Conjuring

Transformative events such as birth, death, rebirth, and ancestor and deity conjuring were envisioned as movement through supernatural portals in the form of serpent, crocodile, or centipede maws. Some scenes involve only deities. A codex-style vessel depicts a young woman wrapped in a serpent that is K'awiil's leg (4.60). The serpent's head disgorges an aged deity who reaches back toward the woman's bare breasts. The adjacent text recounts a deity's birth, suggesting that this is a scene of supernatural birth.

Others illustrate humans conjuring deities and ancestors for rites relating to birth, heir designation, royal accession, or transformation into an ancestor or other entity. One vessel features a ruler holding a bicephalic serpent (4.60), and figurines show women with the same royal conjuring symbol (4.62). Another vessel pictures a seated male conjuring an aged deity through the ceremonial bar he holds (4.59), and a jadeite pendant exhibits a ruler with an ancestor emerging from a serpentine portal above his head (4.68). More ambiguous is a carved manatee rib portraying a figure coming out of a crocodile maw; this may be a primordial emergence or an ancestor rising from the underworld (4.64). Yet other images relate to the veneration of rulers after their deaths: a stone panel visualizes a regional governor making an offering to a Piedras Negras ruler, but the text, which commemorates that ruler's death and a ceremony performed in his memory, reveals that this is a retrospective scene, carved years following the event, after the honored ruler had already become an ancestor (4.67).

The Maya also depicted dead bodies; for example, one figurine features a captive skeleton, with arms tied behind its back (4.66).

—MEO

4.58 创世故事纹陶罐
出自危地马拉佩滕北部或墨西哥坎佩切南部，
玛雅文明
公元650–800年
釉陶
10.4 × 9.7厘米

4.58 Codex-style Vessel with Scene of Supernatural Birth
Guatemala or Mexico, Northern Petén or Southern Campeche, Maya
650–800 CE
Slip-painted ceramic
10.4 × 9.7cm

本件为抄本风格的陶器，描绘了一位被蛇缠着的年轻女子，这条蛇是卡维尔的腿。N神从旁边的龟壳中出现。这可能是创世神话的反映。

自然的力量
FORCES OF NATURE

本件为抄本风格陶器,描绘了一位坐着的男子手握权杖,召唤年长的神。玛雅的统治者是当地最高的萨满,他们可以与宇宙进行对话,保护其民众免受危害,还可以预测未来,因此国王具有神圣的转化能力。

4.59 人物和神蛇纹陶罐

出自危地马拉佩滕北部或墨西哥坎佩切南部,玛雅文明

公元650-800年

釉陶

12.2×12.7厘米

4.59 Codex-style Vessel with Seated Figure and Vision Serpent

Guatemala or Mexico, Northern Petén or Southern Campeche, Maya

650–800 CE

Slip-painted ceramic

12.2 × 12.7cm

洛杉矶郡艺术博物馆藏古代玛雅艺术品
ANCIENT MAYA ARTS FROM THE LOS ANGELES COUNTY MUSEUM OF ART

本件陶盖顶部饰有君主的形象。

4.60 君主形提手带盖陶罐 | **4.60 Lidded Vessel with Ruler Holding a Bicephalic Serpent**

出自危地马拉佩滕或墨西哥坎佩切，玛雅文明 | Guatemala or Mexico, Petén or Campeche, Maya

公元400–500年 | 400–500 CE

釉陶 | Slip-painted ceramic

34.3 × 12.2厘米 | 34.3 × 12.2cm

4.61 婴儿纹陶哨 | 4.61 Whistle with Infant Presentation Scene
出自危地马拉北部或墨西哥东南部,玛雅文明 | Northern Guatemala or Southeastern Mexico, Maya
公元600–900年 | 600–900 CE
陶 | Ceramic
12.7 × 12.7 × 5.1厘米 | 12.7 × 12.7 × 5.1cm

洛杉矶郡艺术博物馆藏古代玛雅艺术品
ANCIENT MAYA ARTS FROM THE LOS ANGELES COUNTY MUSEUM OF ART

4.62 王室女性形陶响铃
出自墨西哥，可能是坎佩切，玛雅文明
公元600–900年
陶
18.1×12.7×5.1厘米，
18.5×13.2×5.8厘米

4.62 Mold-made Rattle with Royal Woman and Bicephalic Serpent
Mexico, possibly Campeche, Maya
600–900 CE
Ceramic
18.1×12.7×5.1cm,
18.5×13.2×5.8cm

4.63 浮雕骨器

出自危地马拉，洪都拉斯，或墨西哥，玛雅文明
公元300–450年
彩绘骨器
2.7 × 14 × .8厘米

4.63 Carved Bone

Guatemala, Honduras, or Mexico, Maya
300–450 CE
Bone with pigment
2.7 × 14 × .8cm

4.64 浮雕海牛肋骨

出自墨西哥，可能是尤卡坦，玛雅文明
公元700–1000年
彩绘海牛骨
21.6 × 2.5 × 2.5厘米

4.64 Carved Manatee Rib with Figure Emerging from Crocodile

Mexico, possibly Yucatán, Maya
700–1000 CE
Manatee bone with pigment
21.6 × 2.5 × 2.5cm

本件描绘了一个人从鳄鱼咽喉出来，可能是来自地下的祖先或神灵。祖先对于玛雅人十分重要，所有的玛雅人都在祖先的荫庇下生活，少数强大的祖先会被神化。

4.65 头盖骨形陶罐

出自危地马拉，太平洋海岸，埃斯昆特拉

公元600–1100年

釉陶和云母

14.7 × 16.3 × 19.1厘米

4.65 Vessel in Form of a Human Skull with Fox Features

Guatemala, Pacific Coast, Escuintla

600–1100 CE

Slip-painted ceramic and mica

14.7 × 16.3 × 19.1cm

4.66 俘虏骨骼雕像

出自伯利兹或墨西哥，玛雅文明

公元600–900年

彩绘骨器

15.2 × 4.6 × 3.8厘米

4.66 Figurine of Skeletal Captive

Belize or Mexico, Maya

600–900 CE

Bone with pigment

15.2 × 4.6 × 3.8cm

4.67 殡葬用石牌饰

出自危地马拉佩滕或墨西哥恰帕斯，彼德拉斯内格拉斯邻近地区，玛雅文明

约公元687–800年

石灰岩

57.2 × 55.9 × 10.2厘米

4.67 Mortuary Panel

Guatemala or Mexico, Petén or Chiapas, vicinity of Piedras Negras, Maya

c. 687–800 CE

Limestone

57.2 × 55.9 × 10.2cm

本件牌饰显示了一个地方长官在向统治者献祭，但周边的文字说明这一场景是多年前的事，画面中的统治者已经去世而成为祖先。

4.68 饰有立像和祖先的石吊坠

出自危地马拉或洪都拉斯、墨西哥，玛雅文明

公元300–600年

彩绘翡翠

9.9 × 6.4 × 3.3厘米

4.68 Pendant with Standing Figure and Ancestor

Guatemala, Honduras, or Mexico, Maya

300–600 CE

Jadeite with pigment

9.9 × 6.4 × 3.3cm

八、日历和纪念日

古代玛雅人使用数字和日历系统来追溯和记载统治者及其他贵族的事迹,他们会将这些日期和事件记录在纪念性雕塑及其他材质上。他们还会计算和记录早期历史事件或神话事件的周年纪念活动,将自己与这些事件及相关人物(祖先或神灵)联系在一起。

本次展览中有一块由致密石灰岩制成的碑刻,它被精雕细琢,上有两列字迹精美的铭文浮雕以及Chak K'uh统治者的姓名Yax K'oj Ahk,Chak K'uh可能是在墨西哥恰帕斯坎卡拉(Chancalá)一带(展品4.69)。这块碑刻应为一块更大碑刻的一部分,上面的铭文更多,但其下落却不得而知。现存的这块应是历法循环日期(玛雅的日历周期,包括260天的圣历和365天的阳历,每52年重复一次)的第二部分(8 Zip),第一部分无疑是在丢失的那一部分上。接下来是后面的一个数字(虽然有误)连着一个新的日期:4 Ajaw 8 Kumk'u。这天的事件是"yilajiiy"(他看到了),见证者是Yax K'oj Ahk。他对这天的见证很有意义,因为这是几千年前创世(公元前3114年)的纪念日。伴随着这种见证的可能还有创世仪式。由于这部分文字片段的出处不明,因此所记录的政治、社会甚至物理环境也不得而知。尽管如此,这块石碑依然能够帮助我们深入了解坎卡拉(Chancalá)玛雅贵族的政治和宗教活动。

梅根·奥尼尔

Calendars and Anniversaries

The Classic Maya used numerical and calendrical systems to track and chronicle events in the lives of rulers and other nobles; they inscribed these dates and events on monumental sculptures and other media. They also calculated and recorded anniversaries of earlier events, whether historical or mythological, and connected themselves to those episodes and their actors, be they ancestors or deities.

One panel made of finely carved, dense limestone has two columns of inscriptions carved in relief in exquisite calligraphic form and names Yax K'oj Ahk, a ruler from a place called Chak K'uh, likely corresponding to the site of Chancalá, Chiapas, Mexico (4.69). This panel was cut from a larger panel with a longer inscription; the location of the rest of the panel is unknown. This fragment begins mid-phrase, with 8 Zip, the second part of a Calendar Round date (a Maya calendar cycle, which combines the 260-day sacred and 365-day solar calendars and repeats every fifty-two years); the first part undoubtedly is on the still-missing part of the panel. This is followed by a distance number that (although in error) connects to a new date, 4 Ajaw 8 Kumk'u. The event on that day is yilajiiy ("he saw it"), and the agent is Yax K'oj Ahk. His witnessing of this day was significant because it was the anniversary of the creation of the world thousands of years earlier, in 3114 BCE. World-renewal rituals likely accompanied this witnessing. Because this textual fragment was removed from its original location without documentation, the political, social, and even physical contexts of the carving are lost. Nonetheless, the panel provides insight into the political and religious activities of Maya nobles at Chancalá.

—MEO

自然的力量
FORCES OF NATURE

4.69 铭文石碑

出自墨西哥恰帕斯，乌苏马辛塔河谷，可能是坎卡拉，玛雅文明

公元9世纪

石灰岩

133.9 × 47.5 × 9.7厘米

4.69 Panel with Inscription

Mexico, Chiapas, Usumacinta River Valley, possibly Chancalá, Maya,

9th century

Limestone

133.9 × 47.5 × 9.7cm

玛雅人采用二十进制的记数体系。圆圈表示1，竖条表示5，两种符号合并使用，可表示20以内的数字。玛雅人还发现了"零"的概念，因此能够在空间记数体系中使用数字，这一体系用于历法和会计。玛雅的历法体系包括一个时长260天的卓尔金历和365天的阳历，二者每52年重复一次。

卓尔金历中20天的名称
Tzolk'in calendar: named days

1	Imix'		11	Chuwen	
2	Ik'		12	Eb'	
3	Ak'b'al		13	B'en	
4	K'an		14	Ix	
5	Chikchan		15	Men	
6	Kimi		16	Kib'	
7	Manik'		17	Kab'an	
8	Lamat		18	Etz'nab'	
9	Muluk		19	Kawak	
10	Ok		20	Ajaw	

九、献祭

为与超自然神灵和祖先进行交流,玛雅人举行一系列献祭活动。彩绘陶罐描绘了统治者和祭司手持捆扎的祭品和燃烧的柯巴脂,祭拜神和人(展品4.70、4.71、4.72)。墓穴、水和洞穴被认为是自然与超自然之间的贯通之地,是此类献祭的主要场所。一件陶碗的表面装饰着水鸟和珍贵的羽毛,里面是一种水生开花植物,由此意味着将祭品放在水中地下世界边缘的碗中(展品4.76)。底座装饰华丽的带盖大陶罐与古典时期早期墓穴和祭物地窖中发现的类似,可能储存过食物或熏香等祭品来"滋养"土地或逝者。盖子常被塑造为动物头部,由此赋予了整个容器一种灵气(展品4.73、4.74)。

香炉也被用来盛放燃烧的熏香和橡胶。烟、火和香气是与超自然世界交流的媒介。危地马拉的太平洋海岸曾出土过两个香炉,这个地区盛产可可,与特奥蒂瓦坎存在联系。因此,可可图案和特奥蒂瓦坎肖像便成了常见的主题,比如祖先头上的风暴神(展品4.79、4.77)。阿马蒂特兰湖(Lake Amatitlán)曾出土了几个埃斯昆特拉式香炉,它们自身便是祭物。另一个值得一提的香炉可能来自塔巴斯科(Tabasco)的特阿帕(Teapa),描绘着太阳神在一个洞口附近骑着鳄鱼,象征着太阳重生和创世(展品4.80)。

安东尼·迈耶

Offerings

To communicate with supernatural entities and ancestors, the Maya made a litany of offerings. Painted ceramic vessels portray deities, rulers, and priests making offerings of effigies, bundles, and burning rubber to both deities and people (4.70,4.71,4.72). Burials, bodies of water, and caves, considered permeable places between the natural and the supernatural, were prime locations to make such offerings. One bowl's exterior is adorned with waterbirds and precious feathers; painted inside is a flower in an aquatic locale, which thus situates offerings placed in the bowl at the boundary of a watery underworld (4.76). Large, ornately decorated basal-flange, scutate-lidded vessels are similar to ones found in Early Classic burials and offering caches and may have held offerings of food or incense to nourish the earth or interred individuals. Lids are often transformed into creature heads, animating the entire vessel (4.73, 4.74).

Censers were also used for offerings of burning incense and rubber. Smoke, fire, and aromas were agents of communication with the supernatural world. Two censers come from the Pacific Coast of Guatemala, a region with thriving cacao sources that had contact with Teotihuacan. Thus, pervasive themes are cacao imagery and Teotihuacan icons, such as that of the Storm God, which appears above an ancestor's head (4.79, 4.77). Several Escuintla-style censers were recovered from Lake Amatitlán, where they were deposited as offerings themselves. Another intriguing censer, likely from Teapa, Tabasco, depicts the Sun God riding a crocodile near a cave opening, relaying a narrative of solar rebirth and world creation (4.80).

—MEO

自然的力量
FORCES OF NATURE

4.70 献祭纹陶碗

出自伯利兹或危地马拉、墨西哥，玛雅文明

公元600–900年

釉陶

11.4 × 15.9厘米

4.70 Bowl with Men and Bundled Offerings

Belize, Guatemala, or Mexico, Maya

600–900 CE

Slip-painted ceramic

11.4 × 15.9cm

洛杉矶郡艺术博物馆藏古代玛雅艺术品
ANCIENT MAYA ARTS FROM THE LOS ANGELES COUNTY MUSEUM OF ART

4.71 献祭纹带盖陶罐	4.71 Lidded Vessel with Supernatural Offering Scenes
出自危地马拉佩滕或墨西哥坎佩切，玛雅文明	Guatemala or Mexico, Petén or Campeche, Maya
公元250–500年	250–500 CE
釉陶	Slip-painted ceramic
26.4 × 36.2厘米	26.4 × 36.2cm

自然的力量
FORCES OF NATURE

本件描绘了纳兰霍统治者Aj Wosal在战争后与祭司手持肖像、捆扎的祭品、燃烧的橡胶献祭的场景。玛雅人相信通过献祭，能确保农田肥沃，家族兴旺，在战争中所向披靡。

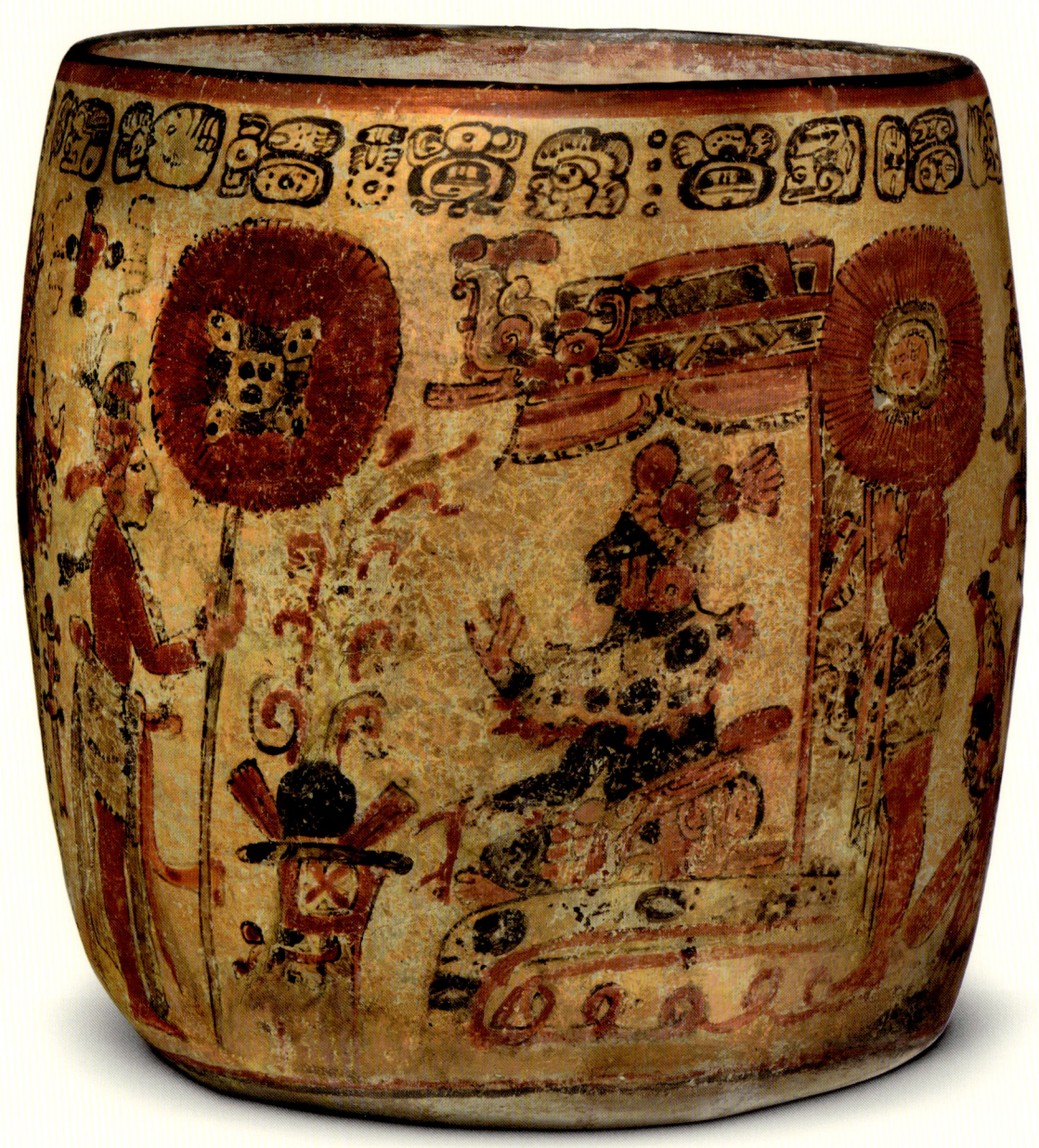

4.72 战争和献祭纹陶罐
出自危地马拉佩滕，纳兰霍或邻近地区，玛雅文明
约公元546–629年
釉陶
21.1×21.6厘米

4.72 Cylinder Vessel with Scenes of Warfare and Offerings
Guatemala, Petén, Naranjo or vicinity, Maya
c. 546–629 CE
Slip-painted ceramic
21.1 × 21.6cm

本件也是祭祀用陶罐，捉手为一只张嘴的美洲虎头部，四肢彩绘在器盖表面

4.74 美洲虎形提手带盖陶罐
出自危地马拉佩滕或墨西哥坎佩切，玛雅文明
公元250–500年
釉陶，烧后施彩绘
31.8×36.8厘米

4.74 Lidded Vessel with Supernatural Jaguar
Guatemala or Mexico, Petén or Campeche, Maya
250–500 CE
Slip-painted ceramic with post-fire pigment
31.8 × 36.8cm

自然的力量
FORCES OF NATURE

生火、燃烧树脂和树胶是献祭的基本程序。焚烧松树、柯巴脂和其它树脂产生的烟雾和香气是向神灵和祖先献祭的代表性食物，并且是与他们沟通的方式。

4.73 金刚鹦鹉形捉手带盖陶罐

出自危地马拉佩滕或墨西哥坎佩切，玛雅文明

公元250–500年

釉陶

45.7 × 48.3厘米

4.73 Lidded Vessel with Modeled Macaw

Guatemala or Mexico, Petén or Campeche, Maya

250–500 CE

Slip-painted ceramic

45.7 × 48.3cm

自然的力量
FORCES OF NATURE

4.75 猴子纹带盖四足陶罐
出自危地马拉北部或墨西哥东南部，玛雅文明
公元250–550年
釉陶
16.5 × 14.7厘米

4.75 Lidded Quadrupod Vessel with Monkeys
Northern Guatemala or Southeastern Mexico, Maya, 250–550 CE
Slip-painted ceramic
16.5 × 14.7cm

4.76 水鸟纹陶碗
出自危地马拉，佩滕东北部，玛雅文明
公元550–850年
釉陶
7.1 × 21.6厘米

4.76 Bowl with Water Birds and Feather Designs
Guatemala, Northeastern Petén, Maya
550–850 CE
Slip-painted ceramic
7.1 × 21.6cm

本件上的文字表明其所有者为Sihyaj Chan Chahk。本件陶碗的表面装饰着水鸟和珍贵的羽毛，里面是一种水生开花植物，由此意味着将祭品放在象征着水中地下世界边缘的碗中。

4.77 风暴神形特奥蒂瓦坎式陶香炉

出自危地马拉太平洋海岸，埃斯昆特拉文明

公元300–600年

陶，烧后施彩绘

27.9 × 22.9 × 23.6厘米

4.77 Teotihuacan-style Censer with Ancestor and Storm God

Guatemala, Pacific Coast, Escuintla

300–600 CE

Ceramic with post-fire pigment

27.9 × 22.9 × 23.6 cm

自然的力量
FORCES OF NATURE

4.78 玉米神形提手带盖三足陶罐

出自危地马拉埃尔基切，玛雅文明

公元650–850年

釉陶，烧后施彩绘

42.4 × 27.9厘米

4.78 Lidded Tripod Vessel with Maize Deity

Guatemala, El Quiché, Maya

650–850 CE

Slip-painted ceramic with post-fire pigment

42.4 × 27.9cm

洛杉矶郡艺术博物馆藏古代玛雅艺术品
ANCIENT MAYA ARTS FROM THE LOS ANGELES COUNTY MUSEUM OF ART

4.79 女子形陶香炉盖

出自危地马拉太平洋海岸，埃斯昆特拉、蒂基萨特或邻近地区

公元400–600年

陶

44.8×24.8×26.4厘米

4.79 Censer Lid with Female Holding Cacao Pod

Guatemala, Pacific Coast, Escuintla, Tiquisate or vicinity

400–600 CE

Ceramic

44.8 × 24.8 × 26.4cm

自然的力量
FORCES OF NATURE

本件陶香炉上，一条鳄鱼趴在洞口，太阳神坐在它身上休息，这一场景描绘了创世故事中的一段情节，象征着诞生和转化。

4.80 太阳神形陶香炉

出自墨西哥塔巴斯科，特阿帕或邻近地区，玛雅文明

公元600–900年

陶

50.8 × 35.6 × 30.5厘米

4.80 Censer with Sun God Riding a Crocodile

Mexico, Tabasco, Teapa or vicinity, Maya

600–900 CE

Ceramic

50.8 × 35.6 × 30.5cm

洛杉矶郡艺术博物馆藏古代玛雅艺术品
ANCIENT MAYA ARTS FROM THE LOS ANGELES COUNTY MUSEUM OF ART

展品目录 Exhibits List

编号 No.	名称 Name	藏品编号 Object No.	
1.1	浮雕陶盒 Carved Box with Deities	M.2008.59	Purchased with funds provided by Camilla Chandler Frost through the 2008 Collectors Committee
1.2	浮雕石球 Carved Sphere	M.2010.115.247	
1.3	口形燧石 Eccentric Flint in Form of an Open Mouth	M.2010.115.1023	
1.4	人形燧石 Anthropomorphic Eccentric Flint	M.2010.115.1000	
1.5	人形燧石 Anthropomorphic Eccentric Flint	M.2010.115.992	
1.6	人形燧石 Anthropomorphic Eccentric Flint	M.2010.115.993	
1.7	异形燧石 Eccentric Flint	M.2010.115.994	
1.8	人形燧石 Anthropomorphic Eccentric Flint	M.2010.115.995	
1.9	人形燧石 Anthropomorphic Eccentric Flint	M.2010.115.996	
1.10	人形燧石 Anthropomorphic Eccentric Flint	M.2010.115.997	Purchased with funds provided by Camilla Chandler Frost
1.11	异形燧石 Eccentric Flint	M.2010.115.998	
1.12	虫形燧石 Eccentric Flint in Form of an Insect	M.2010.115.999	
1.13	异形燧石 Eccentric Flint	M.2010.115.1001	
1.14	异形燧石 Eccentric Flint	M.2010.115.1002	
1.15	人形燧石 Anthropomorphic Eccentric Flint	M.2010.115.1003	
1.16	节肢动物形燧石 Eccentric Flint in Form of an Arthropod	M.2010.115.1004	
1.17	异形燧石 Eccentric Flint	M.2010.115.1005	
1.18	蝎形燧石 Eccentric Flint in Form of a Scorpion	M.2010.115.1006	
1.19	异形燧石 Eccentric Flint	M.2010.115.1007	
1.20	石镜 Mirror	M.85.233.11	Gift of Constance McCormick Fearing
1.21	书吏坐像纹陶罐 Codex-style Cylinder Vessel with Scribes	M.2010.115.562	Anonymous gift
1.22	书吏坐像纹陶瓶 Bottle with Seated Scribe	M.2010.115.779	
1.23	睡莲蛇纹陶罐 Cylinder Vessel with Water Lily Serpent	M.2010.115.844	
1.24	玛雅文字陶碗 Cylindrical Bowl with Dedication Text	M.2010.115.824	
1.25	睡莲蛇纹陶罐 Cylinder Vessel with Water Lily Serpent	M.2010.115.572	Purchased with funds provided by Camilla Chandler Frost
1.26	睡莲蛇纹陶罐 Cylinder Vessel with Water Lily Serpent	M.2010.115.713	
1.27	玛雅文字陶碗 Codex-style Bowl with Dedication Text	M.2010.115.570	
2.1	伊扎姆·卡卡伊纹陶罐 Cylinder Vessel with Itzam Kokaaj and Vulture	M.2010.115.659	
2.2	伊扎姆·卡卡伊、狗和双子英雄纹陶罐 Cylinder Vessel with Itzam Kokaaj, Dog, and Hero Twins	M.2010.115.676	Purchased with funds provided by Camilla Chandler Frost
2.3	伊扎姆·卡卡伊纹陶罐 Cylinder Vessel with Offering of Many Rabbits to Itzam Kokaaj	M.2010.115.660	
2.4	神鸟纹三足陶盘 Tripod Plate with Mythological Bird	M.90.168.13	Gift of the Art Museum Council in honor of the museum's 25th anniversary
2.5	N 神石挂饰 Pendant with God N Emerging from Shell	M.2010.115.484	
2.6	太阳神形陶香炉 Censer with Solar Deities	M.2010.115.526	
2.7	太阳神纹陶罐 Cylinder Vessel with Solar Deities	M.2010.115.634	
2.8	太阳神纹陶罐 Cylinder Vessel with Solar Deities	M.2010.115.755	
2.9	月亮女神纹陶罐 Cylinder Vase with Moon Goddess and other Celestial Beings	M.2010.115.628	
2.10	玉米神和恰克纹陶碗 Bowl with Maize God and Chahk in Watery Locale	M.2010.115.740	Purchased with funds provided by Camilla Chandler Frost
2.11	恰克和神蛇纹陶罐 Cylinder Vessel with Chahk and Serpent	M.2010.115.816	
2.12	恰克和野猪纹四足陶罐 Quadrupod Vessel with Chahk and Peccaries	M.2010.115.888a-b	
2.13	风暴神形三足陶罐 Tripod Vessel with Storm God	M.2010.115.608	
2.14	雨神石雕 Sculpture with Rain Deity	M.2010.115.813	
2.15	卡维尔纹陶罐 Codex-style Cylinder Vessel with K'awiil	M.2010.115.225	
2.16	卡维尔纹陶盘 Codex-style Plate with K'awiil	M.2010.115.396	
2.17	卡维尔纹陶罐 Cylinder Vessel with K'awiil	M.90.168.17	Gift of the Art Museum Council in honor of the museum's 25th anniversary
2.18	卡维尔纹陶罐 Footed Vessel with K'awiil	M.2010.115.553	
2.19	玉米女神陶像 Figurine of a Maize Goddess	M.2010.115.166	Purchased with funds provided by Camilla Chandler Frost
2.20	玉米神纹陶罐 Cylinder Vessel with Maize God Dancers and Dwarfs	M.2010.115.495	
2.21	玉米神纹陶罐 Cylinder Vessel with Maize God Dancers and Dwarf	M.2010.115.616	
2.22	小矮人形陶哨 Figurine Whistle of a Dwarf	AC1992.134.20	Gift of Constance McCormick Fearing
2.23	玉米神纹陶盘 Tripod Plate with Maize God Dancer	M.2010.115.82	
2.24	玉米纹方形陶盘 Squared Plate with Maize God	M.2010.115.535	
2.25	鸟形玉米神纹陶碗 Codex-style Bowl with Avian Maize God	M.2010.115.461	Purchased with funds provided by Camilla Chandler Frost
2.26	鸟形玉米神纹陶罐 Codex-style Cylinder Vessel with Avian Maize God	M.2010.115.462	
2.27	神殿纹三足陶罐 Tripod Vessel with Supernatural Palace Scene and Cacao Tree	M.2010.115.430	
2.28	涡纹球形陶碗 Globular Bowl with Cartouches	M.2010.115.756	Purchased with funds provided by Camilla Chandler Frost
2.29	可可果形陶罐 Cacao Pod Vessel	M.2010.115.739	
2.30	带流盛可可容器 Spouted Vessel for Cacao	M.2010.115.827	
2.31	雨神石吊坠 Pendant with Rain Deity	M.86.311.1	Gift of Constance McCormick Fearing
2.32	雨神或玉米神石牌饰 Plaque with Rain or Maize Deity	M.2010.115.336	Purchased with funds provided by Camilla Chandler Frost
2.33	人面石吊坠 Pendant with Human Face	M.2010.115.110	
2.34	人面石吊坠 Pendant with Human Face	M.83.217.1	Gift of Constance McCormick Fearing
2.35	加工玉米的石锛 Maize Kernel Celt	AC1998.209.56	
2.36	石凿 Celt	M.89.64	Gift of the Gerard Junior Foundation
2.37	石凿 Celt	AC1998.209.67	
2.38	西佩·图泰克旗手石像 Xipe Totec Standard Bearer	AC1998.209.43	Gift of Constance McCormick Fearing
		AC1996.146.57	
2.39	神庙头饰女神石像 Goddess with Temple Headdress	AC1998.209.45	

编 号 No.	名 称 Name	藏品编号 Object No.	
2.40	C 形头饰科奇乔（雨神）陶像 Cocijo (Rain Deity) with Glyph C Headdress	M.2010.115.306	Purchased with funds provided by Camilla Chandler Frost
2.41	C 形头饰男子陶像 Seated Male Figure with Glyph C Headdress	M.2010.115.471	
2.42	科奇乔形陶瓶 Bottle with Cocijo (Rain Deity) Mask	M.2010.115.528	
2.43	神蛇纹陶杯 Codex-style Cylinder Vessel with Teotihuacan-style Serpent	M.2010.115.516	Purchased with funds provided by Camilla Chandler Frost
2.44	神蛇纹陶杯 Codex-style Gadrooned Vessel with Teotihuacan-style Serpent	M.2010.115.213	
2.45	战蛇纹陶盘 Plate with Teotihuacan War Serpent on White and Black Backgrounds	M.2010.115.488	
2.46	骷髅睡莲蛇纹陶盘 Plate with Skeletal Water Lily Serpent	M.2010.115.235	
2.47	睡莲蛇纹陶罐 Codex-style Cylinder Vessel with Water Lily Serpent	M.2010.115.674	
2.48	神蛇纹陶碗 Bowl with Supernatural Serpent	M.2010.115.707	
2.49	睡莲纹陶罐 Vessel with Water Lily Serpent and Underworld Imagery	M.2009.93	
2.50	睡莲蛇与矮人纹陶罐 Vessel with Water Lily Serpent and Dwarf	M.2010.115.810	
2.51	男子和睡莲蛇纹陶碗 Bowl with Male Figure and Water Lily Serpent	M.2010.115.625	
2.52	卡维尔和 L 神纹陶瓶 Bottle with Molded Design of K'awiil and God L	M.2010.115.393	
		M.2010.115.794	
2.53	L 神纹梨形陶罐 Pear-shaped Vessel with God L	M.2010.115.762	
2.54	神话饮酒场景纹陶罐 Cylinder Vessel with Mythological Drinking Scene	M.2010.115.543	Anonymous gift
2.55	青年贵族和猴子纹陶器 Vessel with Young Lord and Monkey	M.2010.115.15	Purchased with funds provided by Camilla Chandler Frost
2.56	梦境神纹陶罐 Cylinder Vessel with Procession of Wahy Entities	M.2010.115.249	
2.57	地下世界场景纹陶罐 Cylinder Vessel with Underworld Scene	M.2010.115.724	
2.58	双子英雄和死神纹陶罐 Cylinder Vessel with Hero Twins and Lords of Death	M.2010.115.409	
2.59	梦境神纹陶罐 Vessel with Wahy Entities	M.2010.115.825	
2.60	梦境神纹陶罐 Bowl with Wahy Entities	M.2010.115.855	
3.1	神鸟纹三足陶盘 Tripod Plate with Supernatural Birds	M.2010.115.797	
3.2	神鸟纹三足陶盘 Tripod Plate with Supernatural Bird	AC1998.209.48	Gift of Constance McCormick Fearing
3.3	神鸟纹灰泥陶罐 Stucco-painted Vessel with Supernatural Birds	M.2010.115.23	
3.4	人形秃鹫纹陶碗 Bowl with Anthropomorphic Vultures	M.2010.115.666	Purchased with funds provided by Camilla Chandler Frost
		M.2010.115.672	
3.5	蝙蝠头像纹陶罐 Vessel with Bat Heads	M.90.168.18	Gift of the Art Museum Council in honor of the museum's 25th anniversary
3.6	美洲虎形捉手陶罐 Lidded Vessel with Jaguar	M.2010.115.950a-b	Purchased with funds provided by Camilla Chandler Frost
3.7	美洲虎形三足陶盘 Tripod Plate with Jaguar Holding Decapitated Head	M.2010.115.78	
3.8	睡莲美洲虎纹陶碗 Bowl with Water Lily Jaguars	M.2010.115.777	
3.9	猎人、鹿和鸟纹陶盘 Plate with Hunters, Deer, and Birds	M.2010.115.168	
3.10	公鹿纹陶罐 Cylinder Vessel with Male Deer	M.2010.115.665	
3.11	鳄鱼捕鹿纹陶罐 Cylinder Vessel with Supernatural Crocodile and Captured Deer	M.2010.115.776	
3.12	猴形捉手三足陶罐 Tripod Vessel with Monkey and Cacao Pod	M.2010.115.1017a-b	
3.13	蜘蛛猿形陶罐 Whistling Vessel with Spider Monkey	M.2010.115.800	
3.14	蜘蛛猿纹三足陶罐 Tripod Vessel with Spider Monkeys	M.2010.115.238	
3.15	吼猴形陶罐 Vase with Howler Monkey and Offering Scenes	M.2010.115.497	
3.16	神猴纹陶盘 Plate with Supernatural Monkey	M.2010.115.723	
3.17	犰狳纹陶罐 Vessel in Form of an Armadillo	M.2010.115.408	
3.18	犰狳形陶罐 Two-part Vessel in Form of an Armadillo	M.2010.115.953a-b	
3.19	饰有负鼠和燃烧香炉的陶罐 Cylinder Vessel with Opossums and Burning Censers	M.2010.115.881	
3.20	神鱼纹陶罐 Codex-style Vessel with Supernatural Fish	M.2010.115.545	
3.21	神鱼纹陶罐 Codex-style Gadrooned Vessel with Supernatural Fish	M.2010.115.63	
3.22	鲶鱼纹陶罐 Cylinder Vessel with Catfish	M.2010.115.854	
3.23	头骨和鱼纹陶罐 Codex-style Vessel with Animate Skull and Fish	M.2010.115.76	
3.24	鸬鹚和鱼纹陶罐 Cylinder Vessel with Cormorants and Fish	M.2010.115.653	
3.25	水鸟纹陶碗 Bowl with Waterbirds	M.2010.115.885	
3.26	鳄鱼形陶罐 Vessel in Form of a Crocodile	M.2010.115.584	
3.27	兽形生物纹陶碗 Bowl with Zoomorphic Creature	M.2002.13	
3.28	蛇头纹陶碗 Bowl with Serpent Head	M.2010.115.626	
3.29	美洲虎爪纹陶瓶 Bottle with Stylized Jaguar Paw	M.2010.115.594	
3.30	防染印花纹 Bowl with Resist-painted Designs	M.2010.115.673	
4.1	宫殿场景纹陶罐 Cylinder Vessel with Palace Scene	M.2010.115.330	
4.2	君王纹陶盘 Plate with Enthroned Ruler Wearing Solar Headdress	M.2010.115.227	
4.3	男子形陶哨 Figurine Whistle of a Seated Male, Possibly a Ruler	M.2010.115.696	
4.4	肥胖男子陶像 Figurine of a Portly Man	M.2010.115.251	
4.5	小矮人形陶哨 Figurine Whistle of a Seated Dwarf	M.2010.115.603	
4.6	君王纹陶瓶 Bottle in Form of a Building with Enthroned Ruler	M.2010.115.795	
4.7	王冠石牌饰 Hunal Plaque	M.2010.115.245	
4.8	花形石耳环 Floral Ear Spools	M.2010.115.920a-b	
4.9	侧面人脸纹贝壳耳坠 Ear Flares with Incised Faces	M.2010.115.963a-b	
4.10	模制妇女陶像 Mold-made Figurine of a Standing Woman	M.90.168.22	Gift of the Art Museum Council in honor of the museum's 25th anniversary
4.11	模制妇女陶像 Mold-made Figurine of a Standing Woman	M.86.311.5	Gift of Constance McCormick Fearing
4.12	婚礼场景纹陶罐 Cylinder Vessel with Scene of Supernatural Marriage Rituals	M.2010.115.585	
4.13	夫妇形陶哨 Figurine Whistle of a Couple	M.2010.115.571	Purchased with funds provided by Camilla Chandler Frost
4.14	老人和女子形陶哨 Figurine Whistle of an Old Man and a Young Woman	M.2010.115.437	
4.15	妇女形陶哨 Figurine Whistle of a Woman with a Backstrap Loom	M.2010.115.16	Anonymous gift
4.16	抱婴女子形陶哨 Figurine Whistle of a Young Woman and a Baby	M.2010.115.705	Purchased with funds provided by Camilla Chandler Frost
4.17	抱婴老妇陶哨 Figurine Whistle of an Old Woman and a Baby	M.2010.115.410	
4.18	怀抱幼猴猴形陶响铃 Figurine Rattle of a Monkey and a Baby	M.2010.115.704	Purchased with funds provided by Camilla Chandler Frost
4.19	老妇形陶哨 Figurine Whistle of an Old Woman	M.2010.115.804	

编号 No.	名 称 Name	藏品编号 Object No.	
4.20	带女子和小矮人的寺庙模型 Temple Model with a Female Figure and Dwarfs	AC1998.209.49	Gift of Constance McCormick Fearing
4.21	乐舞纹陶罐 Cylinder Vessel with Musicians and Dancer	M.2010.115.504	Purchased with funds provided by Camilla Chandler Frost
4.22	乐舞纹陶罐 Cylinder Vessel with Procession of Masked Dancers and Musicians	M.2010.115.444	
4.23	乐舞纹陶罐 Cylinder Vessel with Musicians and Dancers in a Palace Scene	M.2010.115.722	
4.24	号手形陶哨 Figurine Whistle of a Man with Trumpet	M.2010.115.401	Purchased with funds provided by Camilla Chandler Frost
4.25	响铃和蛇纹陶碗 Bowl with Rattles and Serpent Design	M.2010.115.721	
4.26	鸟装男子陶像 Figurine of a Man in Avian Costume	M.83.217.37	Gift of Constance McCormick Fearing
4.27	男子形陶哨 Figurine Whistle of a Man in a Fox Mask	M.85.233.8	
4.28	君主（或玉米神）纹陶盘 Plate with Seated Ruler as Maize God	M.2010.115.774	Anonymous gift
4.29	卡维尔模仿者纹陶罐 Cylinder Vessel with K'awiil Impersonators	M.2010.115.741	
4.30	舞蹈纹陶碗 Bowl with Procession of Dancers	M.2010.115.97	
4.31	球手和舞蹈纹陶罐 Vessel with Ballplayer and Dancers	M.2010.115.412	
4.32	舞蹈纹陶碗 Bowl with Masked Dancers Performing for Figure in a Temple	M.2010.115.207	
4.33	舞蹈纹陶罐 Vessel with Avian Dancers	M.2010.115.743	
4.34	浮雕舞蹈纹陶罐 Carved Vessel with Avian Dancers	M.2010.115.851	
4.35	舞蹈纹陶罐 Cylinder Vessel with Avian Dancers	M.2010.115.605	Purchased with funds provided by Camilla Chandler Frost
4.36	舞蹈纹陶罐 Cylinder Vessel with Avian Dancers	M.2010.115.211	
4.37	球手形陶哨 Figurine Whistle of a Ballplayer	M.2010.115.805	
4.38	球手形陶哨 Figurine Whistle of a Ballplayer	M.2010.115.472	
4.39	球赛纹陶罐 Cylinder Vessel with Ballgame Scene	M.2010.115.868	
4.40	球手和囊地鼠纹陶瓶 Bottle in Form of a House with Ballplayer and Gopher	M.2010.115.780	
4.41	统治者、双头蛇和球手形陶哨 Whistle with Ruler, Bicephalic Serpent, and Ballplayers	M.2010.115.857	
4.42	复活玉米神纹陶碗 Bowl with Resurrection of the Maize God in a Ballcourt	M.2010.115.480	
4.43	蟾蜍形石轭 Yoke in Form of a Toad	AC1993.217.21	Gift of Constance McCormick Fearing
4.44	蟾蜍形石轭 Yoke in Form of a Toad	M.2010.115.692	Purchased with funds provided by Camilla Chandler Frost
4.45	美洲虎形石轭 Yoke in Form of a Jaguar	AC1992.134.25	Gift of Constance McCormick Fearing
4.46	蛇形石"哈恰" Hacha in Form of a Serpent	M.2010.115.647, M.2010.115.646	Purchased with funds provided by Camilla Chandler Frost
4.47	猫头鹰头形石"帕尔马" Palma in Form of an Owl's Head	AC1993.217.19	Gift of Constance McCormick Fearing
4.48	兔形石"哈恰" Hacha in Form of a Rabbit	M.71.73.183	The Phil Berg Collection
4.49	箭袋形石"帕尔马" Palma in Form of a Quiver with Arrows	AC1993.217.20	Gift of Constance McCormick Fearing
4.50	宫殿纹陶罐 Cylinder Vessel with Palace Scene	M.2010.115.685	
4.51	乐师纹陶罐 Cylinder Vessel with Procession of Musicians	M.2010.115.193	
4.52	鬼脸神形陶瓶 Bottle with Grimacing Aged Deity	M.2010.115.749 M.2010.115.750	
4.53	供奉铭文及编织垫纹陶瓶 Bottle with Dedicatory Inscription and Design of Woven Mat	M.2010.115.642	Purchased with funds provided by Camilla Chandler Frost
4.54	灌肠男子纹陶碗 Bowl with Males Using Enemas	M.2010.115.241	
4.55	表演灌肠仪式陶像 Figurine of a Man Performing an Enema Ritual	M.2010.115.243	
4.56	灌肠仪式纹陶碗 Bowl with Enema Ritual	M.2010.115.775	
4.57	灌肠仪式纹球形陶碗 Globular Bowl with Supernatural Enema Ritual	M.2010.115.860	
4.58	创世故事陶罐 Codex-style Vessel with Scene of Supernatural Birth	M.2010.115.4	Anonymous gift
4.59	人物和神蛇纹陶罐 Codex-style Vessel with Seated Figure and Vision Serpent	M.2010.115.852	
4.60	君主形捉手带盖陶罐 Lidded Vessel with Ruler Holding a Bicephalic Serpent	M.2010.115.431a-b	Purchased with funds provided by Camilla Chandler Frost
4.61	婴儿纹陶哨 Whistle with Infant Presentation Scene	M.2010.115.691	
4.62	王室女性形陶响铃 Mold-made Rattle with Royal Woman and Bicephalic Serpent	M.2010.115.259 AC1996.146.45	
4.63	浮雕骨器 Carved Bone	M.2010.115.136	Anonymous gift
4.64	浮雕海牛肋骨 Carved Manatee Rib with Figure Emerging from Crocodile	M.2010.115.216	
4.65	头盖骨形陶罐 Vessel in Form of a Human Skull with Fox Features	M.2010.115.510	Purchased with funds provided by Camilla Chandler Frost
4.66	俘虏骨骼雕像 Figurine of Skeletal Captive	M.2010.115.113	
4.67	殡葬用石牌饰 Mortuary Panel	M.2010.115.1064	Anonymous gift
4.68	饰有立像和祖先的石吊坠 Pendant with Standing Figure and Ancestor	M.2010.115.870	Purchased with funds provided by Camilla Chandler Frost
4.69	铭文石碑 Panel with Inscription	M.2010.115.112	Anonymous gift
4.70	献祭纹陶碗 Bowl with Men and Bundled Offerings	M.90.168.10	Gift of the Art Museum Council in honor of the museum's 25th anniversary
4.71	献祭纹带盖陶罐 Lidded Vessel with Supernatural Offering Scenes	M.90.104a-b	Purchased with funds provided by the Forman Family Fund through the 1990 Collectors Committee
4.72	战争和献祭纹陶罐 Cylinder Vessel with Scenes of Warfare and Offerings	M.2010.115.871	Purchased with funds provided by Camilla Chandler Frost
4.73	金刚鹦鹉形捉手带盖陶罐 Lidded Vessel with Modeled Macaw	M.2010.115.942a-b	Anonymous gift
4.74	美洲虎形带盖陶罐 Lidded Vessel with Supernatural Jaguar	M.2010.115.1024a-b	Purchased with funds provided by Camilla Chandler Frost
4.75	猴子纹带盖四足陶罐 Lidded Quadruped Vessel with Monkeys	M.2010.115.962a-b	
4.76	水鸟纹陶碗 Bowl with Water Birds and Feather Designs	M.2010.115.843	
4.77	风暴神形特奥蒂蒂坎式陶香炉 Teotihuacan-style Censer with Ancestor and Storm God	M.2010.115.1019a-b	
4.78	玉米神形捉手带盖三足陶罐 Lidded Tripod Vessel with Maize Deity	M.2010.115.943a-b	
4.79	女子形陶香炉盖 Censer Lid with Female Holding Cacao Pod	M.2010.115.956a	
4.80	太阳神形陶香炉 Censer with Sun God Riding a Crocodile	M.2010.115.848	

参考文献
References

Coe, Michael D., and Justin Kerr. 1998. The Art of the Maya Scribe. New York: Harry N. Abrams.

Houston, Stephen D. 2000. "Into the Minds of the Ancients: Advances in Maya Glyph Studies." Journal of World Prehistory 14 (2):121–201.

Stuart, David. 2005. "Glyphs on Pots. Decoding Classic Maya Ceramics." In Sourcebook for the 29th Maya Meetings at Texas, 110–97. Austin: The University of Texas at Austin, Department of Art and Art History, Maya Workshop Foundation. Accessed online: https://decipherment.files.wordpress.com/2013/09/stuartceramictexts.pdf.

Looper, Matthew, and Yuriy Polyukhovych. 2016. A "Pile of Rabbits" at LACMA, LACMA Ancient Americas Blog, September 12. Accessed online: http://ancientamericas.org/blog/matthew-looper-and-yuriy-polyukhovych/pile-rabbits-lacma.

Martin, Simon. 2015. "The Old Man of the Maya Universe: A Unitary Dimension to Ancient Maya Religion." In Maya Archaeology 3, edited by Charles Golden, Stephen Houston, and Joel Skidmore, 186–227. San Francisco: Precolumbia Mesoweb Press.

Stuart, David. 2005. "Glyphs on Pots. Decoding Classic Maya Ceramics." In Sourcebook for the 29th Maya Meetings at Texas, 110–97. Austin: The University of Texas at Austin, Department of Art and Art History, Maya Workshop Foundation. Accessed online: https://decipherment.files.wordpress.com/2013/09/stuartceramictexts.pdf.

Finamore, Daniel, and Stephen D. Houston, eds. 2010. Fiery Pool: The Maya and the Mythic Sea. Salem, MA; New Haven, CT: Peabody Essex Museum in association with Yale University Press.

Martin, Simon. 2015. "The Old Man of the Maya Universe: A Unitary Dimension to Ancient Maya Religion." In Maya Archaeology 3, edited by Charles Golden, Stephen Houston, and Joel Skidmore, 186–227. San Francisco: Precolumbia Mesoweb Press.

Taube, Karl. 1992. The Major Gods of Ancient Yucatan. Studies in Pre-Columbian Art and Archaeology, No. 32. Washington, DC: Dumbarton Oaks Research Library and Collection.

Taube, Karl. 2003. "Maws of Heaven and Hell: The Symbolism of the Centipede and Serpent in Classic Maya Religion." In Antropología de la eternidad: La muerte en la cultura maya, edited by A. Ciudad Ruiz, M. Humberto Ruz Sosa, and M. Josefa Iglesias Ponce de León, 405–42. Publicaciones de la Sociedad Española de Estudios Mayas (7). Madrid; México, D.F.: Sociedad Española de Estudios Mayas; Centro de Estudios Mayas, Instituto de Investigaciones Filológicas, Universidad Nacional Autónoma de México.

Doyle, James A. 2016. "Creation Narratives on Ancient Maya Codex-style Ceramics in the Metropolitan Museum." Metropolitan Museum Journal 51:42–63.

Finamore, Daniel, and Stephen D. Houston, eds. 2010. Fiery Pool: The Maya and the Mythic Sea. Salem, MA; New Haven, CT: Peabody Essex Museum in association with Yale University Press.

Ana García Barrios.2009年."Chaahk, el dios de la lluvia, en el Periodo Clásico Maya: aspectos religiosos y político."Tesis, Universidad Complutense de Madrid, Facultad de Geografía e Historia, Departamento de Historia de América II (Antropología de América).

Henderson, Lucia R. 2018 (expected publication). Bodies in Stone: The Sculpture of Preclassic Kaminaljuyú, Guatemala. Cambridge, MA: Peabody Museum Press.

García Barrios, Ana. 2009. "Chaahk, el dios de la lluvia, en el Periodo Clásico Maya: aspectos religiosos y político." Tesis, Universidad Complutense de Madrid, Facultad de Geografía e Historia, Departamento de Historia de América II (Antropología de América).

Coe, Michael D., and Sophie D. Coe. 2013. The True History of Chocolate, 3rd ed. London: Thames & Hudson.

Hall, Grant D., Stanley M. Tarka Jr., W. Jeffrey Hurst, David Stuart, and Richard E. W. Adams. 1990. "Cacao Residues in Ancient Maya Vessels from Rio Azul, Guatemala." American Antiquity 55 (1):138–43.

Martin, Simon. 2006. "Cacao in Ancient Maya Religion: First Fruit of the Maize Tree and Other Tales from the Underworld." In Chocolate in Mesoamerica: A Cultural History of Cacao, edited by Cameron McNeil, 154–83. Gainesville: University Press of Florida.

McNeil, Cameron, ed. 2006. Chocolate in Mesoamerica: A Cultural History of Cacao. Gainesville: University Press of Florida.

Taube, Karl A. 1985. "The Classic Maya Maize God: A Reappraisal."

In Fifth Palenque Round Table, 1983, edited by Merle Greene Robertson, 171–81. San Francisco: Pre-Columbian Art Research Institute.

Marcus, Joyce, and Kent V. Flannery. 1996. Zapotec Civilization: How Urban Society Evolved in Mexico's Oaxaca Valley. New York: Thames & Hudson.

Pohl, John, MD, and Claire L. Lyons. 2010. The Aztec Pantheon and the Art of Empire. Los Angeles: The J. Paul Getty Museum.

Taube, Karl. 2000. "Lightning Celts and Corn Fetishes: The Formative Olmec and the Development of Maize Symbolism in Mesoamerica and the American Southwest." In Olmec Art and Archaeology in Mesoamerica, edited by John E. Clark and Mary E. Pye, 297–337. New Haven, CT: Yale University Press.

McAnany, Patricia. 1998. "Ancestors and the Classic Maya Built Environment." In Function and Meaning in Classic Maya Architecture, edited by Stephen D. Houston, 187–222. Washington, DC: Dumbarton Oaks Research Library and Collection.

McDonald, J. Andrew, and Brian Stross. 2012. "Water Lily and Cosmic Serpent: Equivalent Conduits of the Maya Spirit Realm." Journal of Ethnobiology 32 (1):74–107 (Spring/Summer).

Taube, Karl, Reiko Ishihara, and Jaime Awe. 2006. "The Water Lily Stucco Masks at Caracol, Belize." Research Reports in Belizean Archaeology 3, edited by John Morris, Sherliyne Jones, Jaime Awe, and Christopher Helmke, 213–23. Belmopan: Institute of Archaeology.

Grube, Nikolai, and Werner Nahm. 1994. "A Census of Xibalba: A Complete Inventory of WAY Characters on Maya Ceramics." The Maya Vase Book 4, edited by Barbara Kerr and Justin Kerr, 686–715. New York: Kerr Associates.

Helmke, Christophe, and Jesper Nielsen. 2009. "Hidden Identity and Power in Ancient Mesoamerica: Supernatural Alter Egos as Personified Diseases." Acta Americana 17 (2):49–98.

Houston, Stephen D., and David Stuart. 1989. "Way Glyph: Evidence for Co-essences among the Classic Maya." Research Reports on Ancient Maya Writing 30. Washington, DC: Center for Maya Research.

Martin, Simon. 2015. "The Old Man of the Maya Universe: A Unitary Dimension to Ancient Maya Religion." In Maya Archaeology 3, edited by Charles Golden, Stephen Houston, and Joel Skidmore, 186–227. San Francisco: Precolumbia Mesoweb Press.

Benson, Elizabeth. 1996. "The Vulture: The Sky and the Earth." In Eighth Palenque Round Table, 1993, edited by Martha J. Macri and Jan McHargue, 309–19. San Francisco: Pre-Columbian Art Research Institute.

Boot, Erik. 2009. "The Bat Sign in Maya Hieroglyphic Writing: Some Notes and Suggestions, Based on Examples on Late Classic Ceramics." Maya Vase Database (February 20). Accessed online: www.mayavase.com/boot_bat.pdf.

Pohl, Mary. 1983. "Maya Ritual Faunas: Vertebrate Remains from Burials, Caches, Caves, and Cenotes in the Maya Lowlands." In Civilization in the Ancient Americas: Essays in Honor of Gordon R. Willey, edited by Richard M. Leventhal and Alan L. Kolata, 55–104. Albuquerque: University of New Mexico Press.

Benson, Elizabeth. 1994. "The Multimedia Monkey, or, the Failed Man: The Monkey as Artist." In Seventh Palenque Round Table, 1989, edited by Merle Greene Robertson and Virginia M. Fields, 137–43. Austin: University of Texas Press.

Saunders, Nicholas J. 1994. "Predators of Culture: Jaguar Symbolism and Mesoamerican Elites." World Archaeology 26 (1):104–17 (June).

Finamore, Daniel, and Stephen D. Houston, eds. 2010. Fiery Pool: The Maya and the Mythic Sea. New Haven, CT: Yale University Press.

Kettunen, Harri, and Christophe Helmke. 2013. "Water in Maya Imagery and Writing." Contributions in New World Archaeology 5:17–38.

Pool, Christopher A. 2007. Olmec Archaeology and Early Mesoamerica. Cambridge: Cambridge University Press.

Reilly, F. Kent. 1995. "Art, Ritual, and Rulership in the Olmec World." In The Olmec World: Ritual and Rulership, edited by Michael D. Coe, 27–45. New York: Harry N. Abrams.

Fields, Virginia M., and Dorie Reents-Budet, eds. 2005. Lords of Creation: The Origins of Sacred Maya Kingship. Los Angeles: Los Angeles County Museum of Art in association with Scala Publishers Ltd.

Houston, Stephen, and David Stuart. 1996. "Of Gods, Glyphs, and Kings: Divinity and Rulership among the Classic Maya." Antiquity 70:289–312.

Miller, Mary Ellen, and Simon Martin. 2004. Courtly Art of the Ancient Maya. New York: Thames & Hudson.

Taube, Karl A. 2005. "The Symbolism of Jade in Classic Maya Religion." Ancient Mesoamerica 16:23–50.

Ardren, Traci, ed. 2002. Ancient Maya Women. Walnut Creek, CA: Alta Mira Press.

Halperin, Christina T. 2014. Maya Figurines: Intersections between State and Household. Austin: University of Texas Press.

Houston, Stephen, David Stuart, and Karl Taube. 2006. The Memory of Bones: Body, Being, and Experience among the Classic Maya. Austin: University of Texas Press.

Donahue, John A. 2000. "Applying Experimental Archaeology to Ethnomusicology: Recreating an Ancient Maya Friction Drum through Various Lines of Evidence." FAMSI Research Material.

Accessed online: http://www.mayavase.com/frictiondrum.html.

Houston, Stephen, and Karl A. Taube. 2000. "An Archaeology of the Senses: Perception and Cultural Expression in Ancient Mesoamerica." Cambridge Archaeological Journal 10 (2):261–94 (October).

Miller. Mary E. 1998. "The Boys in the Bonampak Band." In Maya Iconography, edited by Elizabeth P. Benson and Gillett G. Griffin, 318–30. Princeton, NJ: Princeton University Press.

Grube, Nikolai. 1992. "Classic Maya Dance: Evidence from Hieroglyphs and Iconography." Ancient Mesoamerica 3:206–18.

Houston, Stephen, David Stuart, and Karl Taube. 2006. The Memory of Bones: Body, Being, and Experience among the Classic Maya. Austin: University of Texas Press.

Looper, Matthew. 2009. To Be Like Gods: Dance in Ancient Maya Civilization. Austin: University of Texas Press.

Stone, Andrea. 1991. "Aspects of Impersonation in Classic Maya Art." In Sixth Palenque Round Table, 1986, edited by Virginia M. Fields, 194–202. Norman, OK: University of Oklahoma Press.

Taube, Karl. 2009. "The Maya Maize God and the Mythic Origins of Dance." In The Maya and Their Sacred Narratives: Text and Context in Maya Mythologies (Acta Mesoamericana 20), edited by Geneviève Le Fort et al., 41–52.

Koontz, Rex. 2008. "Ballcourt Rites, Paradise, and the Origins of Power in Classic Veracruz." In Pre-Columbian Landscapes of Creation and Origin, edited by John E. Staller, 11–29. New York: Springer.

Schele, Linda, and David A. Freidel. 1991. "The Courts of Creation: Ballcourts, Ballgames, and Portals to the Maya Otherworld." In The Mesoamerican Ballgame, edited by Vernon L. Scarborough and David R. Wilcox, 289–316. Tucson: The University of Arizona Press.

Scott, John F. 2001. "Dressed to Kill: Stone Regalia of the Mesoamerican Ballgame." In The Sport of Life and Death: The Mesoamerican Ballgame, edited by Michael C. Whittington, 51–63. New York: Thames & Hudson.

Whittington, E. Michael, ed. 2001. The Sport of Life and Death: The Mesoamerican Ballgame. New York: Thames & Hudson.

De Smet, Peter A.G.M. 1985. Ritual Enemas and Snuffs in the Americas. Dordrecht: Foris Publications.

Hellmuth, Nicholas. 1978. Principal Diagnostic Accessories of Maya Enema Scenes. St. Louis, MO: Foundation for Latin American Anthropological Research.

Henderson, Lucia. 2008. "Blood, Water, Vomit, and Wine." Mesoamerican Voices 3.

Loughmiller-Cardinal, Jennifer A., and Dmitri Zagorevski. 2016. "Maya Flasks: The 'Home' of Tobacco and Godly Substances." Ancient Mesoamerica 27:1–11.

McAnany, Patricia A. 1998. "Ancestors and the Classic Maya Built Environment." In Function and Meaning in Classic Maya Architecture, 187–222. Washington, DC: Dumbarton Oaks Research Library and Collection.

Taube, Karl A. 2004. "Flower Mountain: Concepts of Life, Beauty, and Paradise among the Classic Maya." RES: Anthropology and Aesthetics 45:69–98 (Spring).

Stuart, David. 2011. "Reinterpreting a 'Creation' Text from Chancalá, Mexico." Maya Decipherment weblog, March 29. Accessed online: https://decipherment.wordpress.com/2011/03/29/reinterpreting-a-creation-text-from-chancala-mexico/.

Chinchilla Mazariegos, Oswaldo. 2016. "Human Sacrifice and Divine Nourishment in Mesoamerica: The Iconography of Cacao on the Pacific Coast of Guatemala." Ancient Mesoamerica 27:361–75.

Gallegos Gómora, Judith, and Ricardo Armijo Torres. 2007. "La Cerámica de Tabasco Durante el Clásico." In La Producción Alfarera en el México Antiguo 2, edited by Beatriz Leonor Merino Carrión and Ángel García Cook, 505–60. Mexico: Instituto Nacional de Antropología e Historia.

Houston, Stephen, Sarah Newman, Edwin Román, and Thomas Garrison. 2015. Temple of the Night Sun: A Royal Tomb at El Diablo, Guatemala. San Francisco: Precolumbia Mesoweb Press.

Andrieu, Chloé. 2014. "Maya Lithic Production." In Encyclopedia of the History of Science, Technology, and Medicine in Non-Western Cultures, edited by H. Selins, 1–13. Netherlands: Springer.

Staller, John E., and Brian Stross. 2013. Lightning in the Andes and Mesoamerica. New York: Oxford University Press.

Taube, Karl. 1992. "The Iconography of Mirrors at Teotihuacan." In Art, Polity, and the City of Teotihuacan, edited by Janet C. Berlo, 169–204. Washington, DC: Dumbarton Oaks Research Library and Collection.

致　谢

洛杉矶郡艺术博物馆（LACMA）能有机会将永久收藏的艺术作品展示给中国观众，我们深感荣幸。我馆许多工作人员都为本次展览和目录编排做出了贡献。展览策划部副总监佐伊·卡尔和高级展览协调员塞布丽娜·洛维特与湖北省博物馆共同组织了这次中国之行。中国和韩国艺术部的曹万钢为展览标题的翻译提供了咨询。我在洛杉矶郡艺术博物馆"古代美洲艺术项目"的同事提供了实践与智力支持，其中包括副总监兼项目主任黛安娜·马格罗尼-可贝尔。研究助理安东尼·迈耶编辑了目录、研究了参展文物，策展助理艾米·克鲁姆提供了必要的行政协助，梅隆博士后策展研究员朱莉娅·伯滕肖和米歇尔·里奇帮助评估了展品。梅隆本科策展研究员莉莉娅·塔沃阿达和劳伦·丘奇威尔整理了策展笔记和照片并协助编制了最终目录。

洛杉矶郡艺术博物馆保护中心、图片服务部和藏品管理部的工作人员对这些作品进行了仔细处理，为展览和目录编辑做好准备。高级物品保护员约翰·赫尔克斯认真审查了每件文物，对陶器制作提出了自己的见解；高级保护摄影师约西·波泽洛夫拍摄了清晰、精美的照片。大卫·阿门多利斯亲自监督文物装箱，卡里恩·克拉里斯菲尔德参与了一些文物的保护工作。摄影师彼得·布雷内、乔纳森·厄本和史帝夫·奥利弗为劳拉·谢里制作的图录拍摄了新照片。阿莉莎·莫拉索、苏珊·森哥兹、乔·洛佩斯帮助抽检了展品，参与了包装。他们对艺术品倍加呵护，工作耐心细致，我们在此特表感谢。我还要感谢洛杉矶郡艺术博物馆编辑出版部（包括丽莎·马克和派珀·塞弗伦斯）以及编辑玛杰里·施瓦兹在制作图录方面给予的帮助。

衷心感谢对于许多协助研究洛杉矶郡艺术博物馆展品文献的外界人士。耶鲁大学的玛丽·艾伦·米勒名誉教授迈克尔·科是我中美洲艺术和考古学方面的启蒙老师，他们讲解了有关展品的专业知识。数位碑铭研究家欣然解答了铭文方面的问题，其中包括布朗大学的斯蒂芬·休斯顿、德克萨斯大学奥斯汀分校的戴维·斯图尔特、宾夕法尼亚大学考古与人类博物馆的西蒙·马丁、阿拉巴马大学塔斯卡卢萨分校的亚历山大·托维维宁、墨西哥国立自治大学的埃里克·威拉斯克斯·加西亚、加利福尼亚州立大学奇可分校的马修·卢珀尤里·波里唔科瓦奇。加州大学河滨分校的卡尔·陶伯对图像提出了宝贵见解，斯基德莫尔学院的希瑟·赫斯特对玛雅绘画发表了真知灼见，波士顿美术博物馆的多莉·里恩斯—布德特分享了玛雅陶器方面的知识。此外，危地马拉弗朗西斯科·马罗金大学的芭芭拉·阿罗约、耶鲁大学的奥斯瓦尔多·钦奇拉·马扎里戈斯和敦巴顿橡树园的卢西亚·亨德森也针对卡密拉胡尤和危地马拉太平洋海岸贡献了自己的智慧。另外，加州大学河滨分校的安吉尔·冈萨雷斯·洛佩兹还提供了有关阿兹特克雕塑的重要信息，休斯敦大学的雷克斯·孔茨为我们提供了有关韦拉克鲁斯球赛设备的最新研究。大卫·斯基尔准许我们在图录中使用琳达·斯基尔的绘画，贾斯廷·克尔向我们提供了他的照片。图形遗产技术研究所的凯文·凯恩不仅对展品提出了见解，整理了目录插图，而且还给了我们莫大鼓励，对此我表示由衷感谢。

梅根·奥尼尔博士
洛杉矶郡艺术博物馆古代美洲艺术部副主任

Acknowledgements

It is an immense pleasure to present this exhibition of artworks from the permanent collection of the Los Angeles County Museum of Art (LACMA) to museum visitors in China. Many people at LACMA contributed to bringing this exhibition and catalogue to fruition. Zoe Kahr, Deputy Director for Exhibitions and Planning, and Sabrina Lovett, Senior Exhibition Coordinator, organized the tour to China, along with the Hubei Provincial Museum. Wan Kong, Tsao Fellow in the Chinese and Korean Art Department, consulted on the translation of the exhibition title. My colleagues in LACMA's Program for the Art of the Ancient Americas, including Diana Magaloni-Kerpel, Deputy Director and Director of the Program, offered practical and intellectual support. Research Assistant Anthony J. Meyer wrote for the catalogue and researched objects, Curatorial Assistant Amy Crum provided essential administrative assistance, and Mellon Postdoctoral Curatorial fellows Julia Burtenshaw and Michelle Rich helped evaluate pieces for the exhibition. Mellon Undergraduate Curatorial fellows Lilia Taboada and Lauren Churchwell organized curatorial notes and photos and assisted with final details of catalogue preparation.

LACMA staff members in the Conservation Center, Photo Services Department, and Collections Management carefully handled the artworks and prepared them for both the exhibition and the catalogue. Senior Objects Conservator John Hirx examined every piece and offered perceptive observations about ceramics manufacture, and Senior Conservation Photographer Yosi Pozeilov produced clear and beautiful rollout photographs. David Armendariz made the object mounts, and Carinne Klaristenfeld undertook conservation on several pieces. Photographers Peter Brenner, Jonathan Urban, and Steve Oliver produced new photography for the catalogue that was orchestrated by Laura Cherry. Alyssa Morasco, Suzan Sengoz, Joe Lopez, Emory Marshall, Kristin Strid, and Ben Balken pulled objects for curatorial examination and packed them for their global journey. We are grateful for their vigilant stewardship of the art and for their patience during our viewing sessions. I thank LACMA's Publications Department, including Lisa Mark and Piper Severance, as well as editor Margery L. Schwartz, for their assistance in the production of the catalogue manuscript.

I also am indebted to the many people outside of LACMA who assisted with research on pieces in the LACMA collection. Mary Ellen Miller of Yale University and Michael Coe, Professor Emeritus of Yale University, my first teachers of Mesoamerican art and archaeology, shared their expertise on several aspects of the collection. Multiple epigraphers, including Stephen Houston of Brown University, David Stuart of the University of Texas at Austin, Simon Martin of the University of Pennsylvania Museum of Archaeology and Anthropology, Alexandre Tokovinine of the University of Alabama Tuscaloosa, Érik Velásquez García of the National Autonomous University of Mexico, and Matthew Looper and Yuriy Polyukhovych of California State University, Chico, were generous in answering questions about inscriptions. Karl Taube of the University of California, Riverside, offered keen observations about iconography, Heather Hurst of Skidmore College provided valuable insights about Maya painting, and Dorie Reents-Budet of the Museum of Fine Arts, Boston, gratefully shared her knowledge about Maya ceramics. In addition, Barbara Arroyo of the Francisco Marroquín University in Guatemala, Oswaldo Chinchilla Mazariegos of Yale University, and Lucia Henderson of Dumbarton Oaks contributed their wisdom about Kaminaljuyú and the Pacific Coast of Guatemala. Also, Angel Gonzalez Lopez of the University of California, Riverside, provided important information about Aztec sculptures, and Rex Koontz of the University of Houston directed us to the latest research on Veracruz ballgame equipment. David Schele granted permission to use Linda Schele's drawings in the catalogue, and Justin Kerr gave access to his photographic archive. I am most indebted to Kevin Cain of INSIGHT (Institute for the Study of Graphical Heritage Techniques) for his observations about objects, assistance with catalogue illustration, and steadfast encouragement.

Megan E. O'Neil, PhD
Associate Curator, Art of the Ancient Americas, LACMA

后 记
Postscript

  本次"自然的力量：洛杉矶郡艺术博物馆藏古代玛雅艺术品展"通过以陶器为主的200余件玛雅文物，向中国观众介绍了古代玛雅文明的宇宙观、自然观和神话，展品不仅具有丰富的文化内涵，也是精美的艺术品。

  这次展览是中国博物馆与洛杉矶郡艺术博物馆（LACMA）继"印度的世界"展览之后的第二次合作。2015年2月，湖北省博物馆工作人员在洛杉矶工作期间，参观了LACMA的玛雅艺术藏品并确定了此次展览项目。经过3年的努力，展览终于成功举办。

  展览在筹备过程中，得到了湖北、广东、四川各省文物局及海关的支持。深圳博物馆、成都金沙遗址博物馆的同仁以及中译语通科技股份有限公司、汉森珍品（北京）国际货运代理有限公司等机构都为展览的成功举办付出了艰辛努力，在此我们一并致谢！

编者

2018年4月于武昌东湖